Working the Diaspora

Working
the Diaspora

*The Impact of African Labor
on the Anglo-American
World, 1650–1850*

Frederick C. Knight

NEW YORK UNIVERSITY PRESS
New York and London

NEW YORK UNIVERSITY PRESS
New York and London
www.nyupress.org

First published in paperback in 2012.

Library of Congress Cataloging-in-Publication Data

Knight, Frederick C.
Working the diaspora : the impact of African labor on the Anglo-
American world, 1650–1850 / Frederick C. Knight.
p. cm.
Includes bibliographical references and index.
ISBN-13: 978-0-8147-4818-3 (cl : alk. paper)
ISBN-13: 978-0-8147-6369-8 (pb : alk. paper)
ISBN-10: 0-8147-4818-x (cl : alk. paper)
1. Slave labor—America—History. 2. Agricultural laborers—
America—History. 3. Africans—America—History.
4. Blacks—America—History. 5. Agriculture—America—History.
6. African diaspora. I. Title.
HD4865.A45K65   2009
331.11'7340970903—dc22   2009026860

Manufactured in the United States of America
10 9 8 7 6 5 4 3 2 1

For Herman and Frances Knight

Contents

Acknowledgments

As I wrote this book, a myriad of friends, family members, colleagues, and mentors walked beside me. First, the Knight family gave me the encouragement and space that I needed to complete this project. Throughout my years on the road and in the academic world, my kin have kept me grounded. I send them all of my love. Sages at Morehouse College, particularly Marcellus Barksdale, Alton Hornsby Jr., William Parker, and Jacquelyn Rouse, set the foundation for my graduate training.

This project began in earnest while I was pursuing graduate studies in the history department at the University of California (UC) Riverside. Fellow graduate students Darnetta Bell, Carol Henderson, Ron Schneck, and Irene Vasquez created an oasis during my years in the desert, and Maurice Webb offered me invaluable friendship while I stood at a personal crossroad. Brian Lloyd, Robert Patch, Roger Ransom, Irwin Wall, and Devra Weber lived as model scholars and deepened my thinking about economic and labor history. I am particularly grateful to the always good-humored Sharon Salinger, whose expertise in early American history and comments on an earlier draft of the book challenged me to rethink the project in significant ways. Without Ray Kea's guidance on African history, this project would not have taken form. His scholarly excellence and basic human decency have inspired me to become a better person.

UC Riverside's history department funded my participation in the University of California's Education Abroad program at the University of Ghana, where I took courses and conducted research in African studies. Graduate seminars in African social and political theory led by Professor George Hagan at the Institute of African Studies yielded important insights into the internal dynamics of African history. Historians Kofi Baku and Irene Odotei provided valuable guidance and inspiration during this project's infancy. Yaw Bredwa Mensah and James Anquandah invited me to their archeological digs, expanded my knowledge about West African material culture, and discussed with me in depth the methodological challenges of my own research. Desmond Appiah, Ekua Arhin, Albert Edmond, Maya Harris, Fiker Kebede, Theresa Kwakye, David Stevens, David Stimson, and Sean Theus accompanied me through the harvest, Harmattan, and rainy seasons in the tropics.

The University of California Santa Barbara's Center for Black Studies funded my research with a dissertation year fellowship. While I was at the center, the faculty in the department of black studies prompted me to plunge into the history of an ocean people thousands of miles away. Cedric and Elizabeth Robinson served as models of integrity and generosity. Avery Gordon, the late Kofi Buenor Hadjor, Otis Madison, Christopher McAuley, Jacob K. Olupona, Oyeronke Oyewumi, Gérard Pigeon, and Earl Stewart offered their mentorship at critical moments. Sylvia Curtis and Alyce Harris helped me track down materials in UC Santa Barbara's library. Above all, Douglas and Kryah Daniels and Claudine Michel made my year in Santa Barbara feel as close to home as possible.

The history department at the University of Memphis provided me with an intellectual home and financial support during an important phase of this project. In particular, then chair Kenneth Goings offered steady leadership, and Beverly Bond set a fine example as a teacher/scholar. The friendship of Harry Bryce, Paul Heron, Ramona Houston, Mukti Khanna, and Rajmohan Ramanathapillia allowed me to stay grounded and place my scholarship in perspective. Their commitment to social change fired my own. My dear friends Dennis and Rebecca Laumann, whom I first met in Ghana, provided me with many hours of conversation and laughter over great food, especially at Lotus.

My year as a postdoctoral fellow in the Center for the Advanced Study of Africa and the Atlantic World at the University of Virginia's Carter G. Woodson Institute for African and African-American Studies was one of the most enjoyable and valuable of my life. I was fortunate to be surrounded by a group of colleagues who read my work, pushed me to think more deeply, and offered their personal kindness. I am deeply honored to have worked alongside Wallace Best, Reginald Butler, Jeffrey Fleisher, Scot French, Jerome Handler, Meta Jones, Wende Elizabeth Marshall, Joseph Miller, Isabel Mukonyora, Dylan Penningroth, Jemima Pierre, Hanan Sabea, Scott Saul, Robert Vinson, Bryan Wagner, and Corey D. B. Walker.

Since my move to Colorado, friends and colleagues have helped me press forward with this project. My colleagues in the history department, particularly Ruth Alexander, Ann Little, and Doug Yarrington, have been stalwart supporters. The financial support of the College of Liberal Arts allowed me to accept a postdoctoral fellowship at UC Riverside. More than the big skies and majestic landscape of Colorado's front range, Adrian Gaskins, Rachel and Vincent Harding, Arthur McFarlane, and Linda Potter offered me refuge.

This book has been woven together with threads from a number of sources. The history department at UC Riverside awarded me its first P. Sterling Stuckey Postdoctoral Fellowship in African-American History, which helped me to deepen and expand my work. The John Nicholas Brown Center for the Study of American Civilization awarded me a fellowship that funded my research in archives in Providence, Rhode Island. Vikki Vickers of Weber State University invited me to present a portion of my manuscript as part of their history department's lecture series. Michael Gomez, who sets a standard for me of scholarly excellence and intellectual depth, graciously invited me to present my work at New York University's African Diaspora Forum.

I would like to thank Deborah Gershenowitz of NYU Press for taking such keen interest in this project and to Kimberley Phillips and Daniel Bender for including my work in the press's Labor, Culture, and History series. Gabrielle Begue has been very helpful at an important stage of this book's production. I would also like to thank Peter Wood and an anonymous reader whose comments on an earlier draft made this a stronger book.

Four teachers have played an immeasurable role in my personal development. First, Shawki Haffar guided me through the forest into the clearing. His steady hand, words of inspiration, and spiritual guidance allowed me to hear the ancestral call. Sterling Stuckey—gentleman and scholar—has been unwavering in his support. As his apprentice, I was initiated into a world of Boundless Riches. Finally, my parents and first teachers, Herman and Frances Knight, have kept the faith. This book is a humble offering in return.

Introduction

For every European who crossed the Atlantic from the six-teenth to the early nineteenth century, four times as many Africans made the journey. This mass, forced migration of people from Africa shaped the historical development of the New World in profound ways. Along with small farming, mining, artisan labor, cattle ranching, and fur trad-ing, plantation agriculture stood at the core of colonial American mate-rial life and was the basis of competing European claims on the Western Hemisphere.[1] Throughout the Anglo-American plantation-based colonies, English indentured servants and Native American workers were the first to raise crops for export. Yet for a number of reasons the British turned to black labor in their American possessions, particularly when other labor pools faltered. Colonial elites started with small numbers of black workers who toiled next to Indian and English laborers in the Chesapeake region and the Caribbean islands, and over time slavery spread like a virus over the Anglo-American colonial landscape.[2] While slaves engaged in a wide range of work, the bulk of their labor was geared toward cultivating cash crops for European markets. Envisioning the profits to be gained from large-scale agricultural production, the English Company of Royal Ad-ventures, which formed in 1660 and was the parent of the Royal African Company, proclaimed in 1662 "that the English Plantations in America should have a competent and a constant supply of Negro-servants for their own use of Planting."[3] Looking increasingly to forced African labor, British American plantations yielded profits from export crops that en-abled them to buy more people, a cyclical process that resulted in "the Africanization of the Americas," as the historian Ronald Bailey terms it.[4] This book explores the Africanization of the Americas by focusing spe-cifically on the role of Africans in agricultural and craft production in the Anglo-American colonies and early United States.

Under the watchful eye and avaricious demands of the colonial elite toiled a force of unfree laborers, particularly from West or West Central

Africa. First complementing and in most cases replacing indentured servants, enslaved workers from Africa cultivated the sugar, tobacco, indigo, cotton, and rice fields of the Anglo-American world. And while planters owned the land, hired overseers, and employed managers to maintain production, the process depended heavily upon the daily work of enslaved Africans. This book argues that Africans not only added physical might but also transplanted agricultural and craft *knowledge* into American soil. In parallel to work practices in West or West Central Africa, the enslaved raised food crops and nonfood crops, including cotton, indigo, and tobacco. In addition, some Africans in the colonies transmitted nonagricultural work skills, such as experience in fishing, woodworking, blacksmithing, textile production, and pottery. The Anglo-American colonial project, it will be argued, mobilized Africans not only for their brawn but also for their knowledge.

The Anglo-American colonies took on a distinctive African character and were deeply interconnected through trade and migration. The sheer number of Africans imported into the colonies indicates their role in plantation development. Up to 1820, approximately 850,000 white immigrants ventured across the Atlantic for the Anglo-American colonies. Holding positions as commercial, political, religious, or landed elites, working as artisans, doing domestic chores, toiling on plantations, or tilling small farms, they sought to turn the Americas into a replica of England.[5] In contrast, during this same time period, over two million Africans landed in the British American colonies. They entered agricultural fields, labored in artisan workshops, and worked on the docks, rivers, and coasts of the islands and mainland. The vast majority of this population landed in the Caribbean islands, with almost one million captives from Africa arriving in Jamaica. An intercolonial trade dispersed them to other American colonies, including those on the North American mainland.[6] So if we look at the Anglo-American plantation world from the perspective of the Atlantic crossing alone, the colonial project had essential African dimensions.

As a consequence of this mass, forced migration, the New World colonies held by the British incorporated a large influx of African workers. They first endured the Atlantic crossing aboard "floating prisons."[7] They then entered new environments and worked under a nightmarish and deadly work regimen, which meant that planters needed to constantly replace their slave labor force. As a consequence, from the middle of the seventeenth century onward, Africans served as important actors in the British American colonies. For example, from 1655 to 1684 the slave population in Barbados increased from 47 to 70 percent of the island's population, and most of them had been raised in Africa. The pattern continued well into the eighteenth century.[8] On September 18, 1712, the ship *Pindar* landed in Barbados, carrying 292 captives from the Gold Coast, who were bought for sugar and were most likely destined to enter into the cane fields to produce even more.[9]

In Jamaica, the slave population expanded steadily after the British claimed the island in 1655: between 1662 and 1673, it increased from 13 to 50 percent of the island's inhabitants, and twenty years later to approximately 85 percent. The growing African population prompted anxious colonial officials to encourage English immigration to the island, as well as to form a militia to deter slave rebellions. Royal African Company officials suggested that for "every Eight Blacks . . . every man should bee obliged to keep one white man." In spite of this tactic, Africans and their descendants continued to outnumber English people on the island and constituted approximately 90 percent of its population by the late eighteenth century.[10] Some of them had been born in Jamaica, yet the African-born population remained substantial. For instance, in 1730 on Colonel Charles Price's Worthy Park estate, 80 percent of the 240 slaves were African born.[11] From the second half of the seventeenth and into the eighteenth century, the British Caribbean had a sizable African population.

While not as large and concentrated as in the Caribbean, the African population in the Anglo-American mainland colonies was substantial as well. From 1700 to 1775, nearly half of the migrants to the mainland were Africans.[12] The bulk went to Virginia and South Carolina, fueling the expansion of their tobacco, rice, and indigo plantations. In South Carolina, the black population outnumbered the white population beginning in 1708, and they remained a majority of the population throughout the colonial period and into the nineteenth century. During the early colonial years, African men and women arrived in South Carolina in relatively equal numbers, so they were able to form kinship ties and bear children.[13] However, by the 1720s, the slave trade shifted and brought increasing numbers of men directly from Africa. The physiological toll of working in the malaria- and yellow fever–ridden rice fields meant that slave populations in the Lowcountry had a high turnover rate, so Africans continued to flow into the colony throughout the colonial era. In 1740, approximately two-thirds of the slave population was African born, and as late as 1780, Africans constituted one-third of South Carolina's slave population.[14] Slavery became central to colonial Virginia's history in the aftermath of Bacon's

Rebellion in 1676. In the wake of this interracial uprising, colonial elites drove a wedge between black and white workers by granting more privileges to English plebeians while ratcheting up the system of racial slavery. They turned increasingly to the slave trade for plantation labor, supplied by the Royal African Company, which brought enslaved workers directly from Africa.[15] As a result, by 1710, over half of Virginia's slave population was African born, and thirty years later they still constituted one-third of the colony's slaves.[16]

Each of the colonies drew its labor force from particular African regions, and these migration patterns changed over time. For example, South Carolina had a substantial West Central African population in the early years of that colony and then received a large influx of people from the Senegambia region of West Africa. Virginia received a majority of its labor force from the Gold Coast, southeastern Nigeria, and the Senegambia region. The African population of Barbados and Jamaica came primarily from three broad regions: the Gold Coast, the Bight of Benin, and the Bight of Biafra.[17] As a result of these migration patterns, the cast of the colonies varied from place to place. In particular, Africans formed ethnic clusters in the mainland colonies, which had concentrations of people from particular regions of West or West Central Africa.[18] Slaves also had different experiences depending on the crops they grew. The sugar plantations of Barbados, Jamaica, and Louisiana differed from the rice and indigo plantations of South Carolina and the tobacco world of colonial Virginia. In the major British Caribbean islands, the intense labor demands of sugar planters sent a startling number of enslaved Africans to quick deaths, so that plantations had to be continually fed by the slave trade; the disease environments of South Carolina's rice fields took a similar toll on its African population. But in Virginia, while planters continued to import Africans, the slave trade was less important to them because of the relatively low mortality rates and more balanced gender ratios in that colony.[19] On balance, the Anglo-American colonies relied heavily upon people brought directly from Africa for plantation labor.

A number of forces bound the British American plantation colonies together despite their important differences. The colonies raised some of the same crops, though at different times and levels of intensity. For example, at different points in their histories, Virginia, Barbados, South Carolina, and Jamaica each raised cotton and indigo. During the seventeenth century Barbados and Jamaica exported cotton and indigo, and in South Carolina indigo became the colony's second leading export by the time of the

American Revolution. In the eighteenth century, slaves in South Carolina and Virginia raised cotton on small scales, particularly during the Revolution, when local cotton textile production replaced English manufactures. Furthermore, while Virginia dominated British American tobacco production, Barbados and Jamaica exported the crop in the seventeenth century, before the sugar revolution transformed the islands.[20] Clusters of crops moved across the Anglo-American landscape over space and time, a process noted by commercial planters. One official looked forward to a more open slave trade and expanded plantation production, assessing the present "Trade of Negro Servants, which so proves Advantageous to the Western Plantations in the several Islands of America, as well as that Continent whose chief Commerce is Sugar, Tobacco, Indico, Ginger, Cotton, and Dying Stuffs."[21] British colonists facilitated agricultural diversification by sending seeds from one colony to another. For instance, settlers from the British Caribbean brought indigo and cotton seeds and ginger roots into South Carolina.[22] So while colonies eventually concentrated on particular export crops, in many cases different colonies produced a similar range of crops.

More importantly, people moved across colonial borders, particularly through an intercolonial slave trade. Colonists from Barbados brought slaves with them to labor in early Carolina's frontier environment. In the first years of the British settlement of South Carolina, slaves entered the colony through the Caribbean.[23] West Indian planters also brought slaves to the Chesapeake, paralleling the forced migration to the Lowcountry. Dozens of Barbadians relocated to Virginia in the late seventeenth century, bringing their slaves along. In addition, Barbadian migrants provided valuable contacts to Virginia planters seeking to buy slaves from the Caribbean islands or more directly from Africa. For example, the Virginia planter William Byrd I traded with British West Indian slaveholders and requested Barbadian merchants to send him "4 Negro's, 2 men, 2 women not to exceed 25 years old." In the early years of slavery in Maryland, planters used their connections in the Caribbean to acquire slave labor.[24] Through this process, the Anglo-American colonial borders bound colonial subjects and slaves to the land yet were permeable enough to permit some movement between colonies.

Along with the movement of people came the flow of commercial goods and ideas across colonial borders. Mainland colonies found markets in the Caribbean for their raw materials and processed goods. Virginians traded lumber, food provisions, and draft animals to Barbados for sugar products, cocoa, and ginger. South Carolinians established comparable trading ties with Barbados, exporting livestock, timber, and food products to the island. In addition to the movement of material goods, some of which were produced with slave labor, colonial officials adopted slave laws from other colonies. Jamaica, Antigua, and South Carolina essentially copied their slave laws from the Barbados codes. Virginians also modeled their slave laws on the Barbados statutes, which had three essential components: defining slaves as chattel, creating mechanisms to police the slave population, and defining slavery in racial and inheritable terms.[25] Through this movement of commercial goods, in many cases consumed or produced by slaves; of seeds for agricultural production; of people through an intercolonial slave trade; and of laws to define, control, and racialize the slave population, the major Anglo-American slaveholding colonies were bound together and developed along parallel lines. And it is within this context of labor mobilization, intercolonial movement, and the trans-Atlantic slave trade that the role of African workers in the British Americas and early United States can be assessed.

This project builds on a growing body of scholarship that views labor as a central component of the slave experience. Recent scholarship on North American slavery has reemphasized work as a defining feature of the slave experience. For example, Ira Berlin and Philip Morgan have clearly shown that work, as the primary purpose of slavery and the way that slaves spent most of their waking time, not only was inherently important but also influenced other aspects of slave life. For instance, slave kinship units evolved differently in relation to different crop regimes. But while these studies explore the intricate relationship between agricultural and slave social life, they leave important omissions. For example, they do not extend their formulations about the centrality of work to African contexts.[26] Other studies of American slavery provide more in-depth discussions of African work practices. Prefigured by Martin Delany's *Condition, Elevation, Emigration, and Destiny of the Colored People of the United States*, a growing body of scholarship has argued that slaves contributed more than just physical labor to American plantation development. In particular, Peter Wood and Daniel Littlefield show that Africans with expertise in rice cultivation gave rise to that crop in colonial South Carolina, and Gwendolyn Midlo Hall makes a similar case for colonial Louisiana.[27] The case that Africans originated rice cultivation in the Americas has been presented most thoroughly by the geographer Judith Carney. In *Black Rice*, Carney argues that slaves, particularly women from West Africa, brought rice production "knowledge systems" to the Americas. These systems included not only seeds but also sophisticated irrigation technology.[28] The scholarship on African skills in the Americas has extended beyond research on colonial rice fields. Scholars have acknowledged that Africans cultivated tobacco before their enslavement in colonial Virginia.[29] Others have argued that some American slaveholders drew upon the expertise of African nonagricultural laborers, whether they worked in the fishing waters of South Carolina, in the Spanish American gold mines, or in the coastal waters of the Atlantic World as swimmers and divers.[30]

This school of thought has recently been questioned by the historians David Eltis, Philip Morgan, and David Richardson. In an article that has generated considerable scholarly debate, they directly challenge Carney's argument about the African origins of New World rice production. On the basis of sources including colonial plantation records, economic histories of Upper Guinea and South Carolina, and numbers generated from the Atlantic slave trade database, they argue that very few slaves, and in particular few women, from Upper Guinea's rice-growing regions landed on New World rice plantations. They add that colonial planters learned water management techniques from other parts of the world, particularly the Netherlands and China. While they argue that hybrid forms of production emerged on New World rice plantations, they suggest that Africans had a limited role in rice production, through "folkways" such as pounding rice with mortars and pestles or covering seeds with the heel of the foot. They claim that rice production in South Carolina and other parts of the Americas can largely be attributed to a combination of factors including colonial entrepreneurship, planter ingenuity, European demand for rice, and the general agricultural knowledge that Africans possessed.[31]

This book argues, in contrast to Eltis, Morgan, and Richardson, that the thesis proposed by Carney, Hall, Littlefield, and Wood can, in fact, be extended beyond rice production. Rice constituted part of a larger set of agricultural and craft knowledge systems that Africans carried to the British American colonies and early United States. For instance, West African agriculturalists who worked rice as a primary crop also cultivated secondary crops including cotton, tobacco, ginger, and indigo. With such knowledge, people from West Africa became valuable assets for colonial slaveholders, whose estates grew a similar set of crops. To demonstrate the wide influence of African workers on New World plantations, this project looks beyond colonial borders and sees a steady movement of people and knowledge around the Atlantic, in particular from Africa and between the North American mainland and the British Caribbean. While clear differences set the colonies apart, it will be shown that Africans shaped both mainland and West Indian plantation development. They grew many of the same crops, if not as primary crops then as secondary crops, and evidence of African blacksmiths, tanners, and woodworkers can be found in Jamaica, South Carolina, and Virginia. Africans, carrying a wealth in knowledge across the Atlantic, left a deep imprint on Anglo-American plantation development in a number of settings.

The sources consulted for this study reflect the trans-Atlantic and intercolonial character of the early African population in the Anglo-American colonies. The project is based on primary sources such as the accounts of European merchants and travelers on the West and West Central African coasts. These texts provide glimpses into the ways that Africans carved their living out of the soil. Some accounts simply mention the kinds of crops that African agriculturalists placed under cultivation, while others offer more nuanced descriptions. After their encounter with West and West Central Africans, European writers described the gender divisions of labor for agricultural production, depicted the range of techniques and tools that agriculturalists deployed, and documented the markets that agricultural products entered. By the eighteenth century, at the height of the Atlantic slave trade to the Americas, European merchants acquired increasingly detailed knowledge about African agricultural practices, so much so that they identified some places, such as the "Rice Coast," with particular crops.

Written and oral accounts of slave plantation development in the New World offer another layer of information about the role of Africans in Anglo-American colonial agriculture. For example, eighteenth-century British and French natural scientists who investigated the agricultural history of the American colonies concluded that particular crops grown by slaves in the Americas had their origins in Africa and crossed the Atlantic aboard slave ships. Plantation inventories, court records, and colonial newspapers made direct references to Africans in the colonies who possessed particular craft skills. And interviews with former slaves as late as the 1930s revealed that some of the enslaved learned their trades, such as leather working, in Africa. Other evidence about the role of Africans in shaping the plantation landscape is more indirect. Records of plantations managers, for example, account for the presence of enslaved workers from particular places in Africa and indicate the kind of work that they performed. So central did slavery become to the Caribbean, the Chesapeake colonies, and South Carolina that colonial religious and political figures, indentured servants, tourists, and free people routinely commented on the subject, leaving behind descriptions of plantation production. Through a close reading of these records, traces of African agricultural knowledge on Anglo-American plantations can be discerned.

This project does not rely solely on the written record produced during the years of the slave trade. I have consulted the findings of African political, economic, and agricultural historians, which reveal the internal dynamics of West or West Central Africa and help to more clearly describe the material and social environments from which Africans who were transported to the Americas emerged. This book draws upon oral histories, modern historical ethnologies, geographical research, and archeological studies. Such sources have been important, for example, in dating the beginnings of tobacco, cotton, and indigo production in West or West Central Africa. Art history, including textiles that have survived for centuries, also provides historical evidence of West African agricultural and craft production. In short, the project heeds the admonition of those who call for an interdisciplinary approach to the study of precolonial West Africa.[32] Similar methods have been deployed to trace the impact of African workers on Anglo-American plantation development. For instance, this book incorporates oral histories and nonwritten evidence, particularly data unearthed by plantation archeologists.[33] Stashed underground, slave material culture bore the clear imprint of people from Africa.

Building upon such material, this book shows that, through their daily activities, Africans acquired a "wealth in knowledge" that they carried across the Atlantic through the slave trade and in many cases transplanted in the Anglo-American colonies. It was not unusual for people in Africa to possess knowledge that extended beyond their primary tasks. For example, African rice cultivators also grew cotton, tobacco, and indigo.[34] So when slaves from West or West Central Africa landed in the British American colonies, they had bodies of knowledge from which they drew in building up colonial plantations. Examining African practices and comparing them to the agricultural and craft practices recorded on Anglo-American plantations reveals the role of slaves from Africa as well as their adaptations to their New World environments.

Working the Diaspora begins by looking at the historical backgrounds of African workers, particularly forms of economic activity in West and West Central Africa during the years of the Atlantic slave trade. In this way, my approach parallels that of scholars who study the religious, ethnic,

and cultural dimensions of the African Diaspora.[35] The first chapter highlights everyday material life in contexts ranging from the daily markets in
Gold Coast towns to the cattle pastures of Central Africa. Since the daily
lives of African captives in the British colonies revolved around material
production, this chapter examines important dimensions of the material
civilizations from which Africans emerged—the urban centers, market
networks, craft production sites, and mining regions within which they
lived their daily lives. It highlights their divisions of labor along gender,
caste, and other lines. While extensive in its breadth, it also looks in depth
at West and West Central African material civilization through focused
studies of particular sites of production, such as the fishing villages of the
seventeenth- and eighteenth-century Gold Coast.

Chapter 2 builds upon the first chapter by focusing on agricultural production in West and West Central Africa and the British American colonies. It first considers the environmental constraints within which African
agriculturalists worked, showing that to make their living out of fragile
environments they developed a range of strategies such as crop mixtures
and rotations. Monocrop production was rare, agriculturalists remained
open to new crops, and African women played an important role in ex-
perimenting with New World cultigens. The chapter then traces the role
of African agriculturalists in staple food production in the Anglo-American world. In the early years of the British American colonies, planters
mobilized mixed labor forces that included Africans, Indians, and English
people, who in many cases had to grow their own food supplies. Chapter
2 explores the interaction between these workers and shows how enslaved
Africans, coming out of environments with a range of agricultural knowledge, survived in the New World in part by drawing upon skills they
brought from the Old.

Chapter 3 extends my discussion of the role of Africans in Anglo-
American agricultural development by focusing on cash crop production, particularly of cotton and tobacco. Each of the major Anglo-American slaveholding colonies raised either cotton or tobacco. Though most
closely associated with the antebellum South, cotton took root in colonial
Virginia, South Carolina, Barbados, Jamaica, and other West Indian islands, and it was grown for either domestic use or export. Furthermore,
tobacco, most well known as a Chesapeake crop, was also raised in Barbados and Jamaica during the seventeenth century. Chapter 3 asserts that
Africans adopted tobacco as a garden crop in Africa. The chapter then
argues that Africans drew upon their experience with the crop to foster

Anglo-American tobacco fields first opened by Indian and English labor. The second half of the chapter looks at cotton production in the British American colonies. It shows that cotton was a central fiber in West African material life and that West Africans drew on their experience with it to play an important role in raising cotton on British American plantations.

Chapter 4 focuses on indigo production in West Africa and the Anglo-American colonies. British American indigo production shifted over time, developing first in Barbados and Jamaica in the seventeenth century and later in South Carolina in the 1740s, with each of the colonies depending on Africans to develop and process the crop. The chapter illustrates the connections between Anglo-American colonies and their reliance on African labor by looking specifically at the Lucas estate in South Carolina. This set of plantation sites was established by a West Indian planter and became a nursery of indigo production, tended by slaves from Africa and the Caribbean. As was true of cotton and tobacco, Africans knew how to raise and process indigo, skills that fostered the development of that crop. The chapter, furthering the previous chapter's discussion of cotton textiles, shows that African textiles were often colored with blue dyes made from locally produced indigo. It was fairly common for West African agriculturalists, particularly women, to grow and process indigo, as a number of writers during the years of the slave trade observed, and enslaved Africans continued these practices on Anglo-American plantations. However, within their new environments they also adopted new forms of indigo production technology, particularly indigo vats designed on South Asian models. The chapter concludes by showing how South Carolina slaveholders built their self-identities on slave-produced indigo.

Chapter 5 furthers my discussion of African workers in the British American colonies by looking at their role in nonagricultural labor. Africans toiled in the mines, fishing waters, and artisan workshops of the British American colonies and early United States, shaping their material culture. While many Africans no longer did the work they had performed before their enslavement in the Americas and others received training from white artisans, many continued their practices on British American plantations. Through this knowledge, such as that among fishers, slaves were able to extract a degree of autonomy from their owners. Chapter 5 shows that while African fishers, woodworkers, miners, tanners, and blacksmiths, like African agricultural workers, played their most important roles during the colonial era, Africans who were imported in the final years of the slave trade or smuggled into the United States continued to have an influence into the nineteenth century.

Chapter 6 shifts the focus of the book by contemplating the relationship between slave work practices and ideologies. In particular, it argues that, since slaves spent the bulk of their time working in the natural world, nature and its metaphors were prominent in their vision of power dynamics and human relationships. Their poetry, folklore, oral history, autobiographies, and other sources reveal that slaves saw the natural world as a metaphor for their own experience as subjects, a domain that offered escape from the confines of slavery, and an object of veneration. For instance, the forests not only created a barrier separating slaves from the outside world but also served as a refuge for runaways. The fields were not only places of work under the scorching sun but also places where slaves had sublime visions.

The forced migration of Africans to the British American colonies had its undeniably tragic dimensions, as many collapsed under the crushing weight of unfree labor in an alien land. Some never made it across the Atlantic, dying of disease in the holds or jumping overboard. Some people were worked to quick deaths under violent plantation regimes. Yet others endured and made their new world look akin to the old through their labor knowledge. More than anyone else, planters reaped the fruits of this labor. This book tells the story.

1

Material Life in West and West Central Africa, 1650–1800

But when all the criteria of civilization have been considered—language and communication, technology, art, architecture, political, economic and social organization and ideological developments—it can be said that the available evidence, however fragmentary or circumstantial, does suggest that the Akan sometime between A.D. 1000 and 1700 progressed rapidly from the level of peasant agricultural communities to the level of urban societies and principalities, culminating in the establishment of an indigenous civilization.

—James Anquandah, *Rediscovering Ghana's Past* (1982)

Needed for more than brute labor on New World plantations, African workers carried agricultural and craft knowledge across the Atlantic that transformed American "material life," a concept defined by economic historian Fernand Braudel. In the first volume of his monumental study *Civilization and Capitalism*, Braudel underscored the significance—then overlooked by most historians—of daily material human needs and economic activities. Looking at economic production in the early modern world, he treated as subjects of historical investigation the foods people ate, the clothes they wore, the tools they used, the markets where they conducted trade, the cities they established, the dwellings they inhabited, and the household furnishings they possessed. Within these structures, human actors lived a "material life," meaning "the life that man throughout the course of his previous history has made part of his very being, has in some way absorbed into his entrails, turning the experiments and exhilarating experiences of the past into everyday, banal necessities."[1]

Given the role that African workers played in material production in the Anglo-American colonies, the concept of material life offers a useful tool with which to explore the historical contexts out of which Africans emerged and to assess their role in New World plantation development. What was the nature of West and West Central African material civilization during the era of the slave trade, how did it come into being, and how did it vary over time and space? What made African material life different from that of other regions of the world? What forces shaped its development? How did Africans perceive the process of material production? This chapter will address these questions, highlighting ways that people in West and West Central Africa produced and reproduced their daily material needs during the height of the Atlantic slave trade. Looking at more than the technical aspects of material production, it will also explore the social, political, and ideological structures through which West and West Central Africans conducted their material lives. In particular, this chapter will demonstrate that Africans acquired a *wealth of knowledge* through their daily life in urban centers or rural communities, their trading practices and social networks, and their fishing, mining, and artisan practices. The people tragically ensnared by the Atlantic slave trade carried this knowledge with them to the American colonies, and their experience provided them with an important compass to navigate their way through their New World environments.

At the advent and during the height of the Atlantic slave trade, European merchants tied into West and West Central Africa's preestablished social and economic networks. Starting with the gold and pepper trade, they turned to buying slaves on the African Coast. In their log books, ship captains generally labeled their captives as generic commodities.[2] However, enslaved Africans emerged from much more dynamic contexts than such terminology suggests. Indeed, African captives had deeply embedded ties with others through local or long-distance trading networks, which underwent significant change during the years of the slave trade. For example, both internal and external factors shaped West African trading networks during the Atlantic slave-trading era. One of the most important internal factors that influenced trading patterns was political decentralization. In 1591, an invasion from Morocco brought the collapse of the Songhay Empire, centered on the Niger Bend. Songhay had previously dominated West Africa's long-distance trade across the Sahara, which tied the West African forest regions to northern suppliers and markets. Merchants in cities and towns such as Timbuktu, Gao, and Jenne and surrounding plantation complexes along the Niger River facilitated long-range commerce. However, with Songhay's demise, economic power shifted west into the Senegambia region, south into the forest and coastal zones, and east into Kanem-Bornu. During this period, Muslim merchant associations such as the Wangara, which survived the collapse of the Songhay Empire, moved a variety of commodities throughout West African and other commercial networks.[3]

Underlying the large-scale commercial networks and long-distance trade of the Wangara and others stood a system of daily market activities carried out by small-scale traders. "Markets were ubiquitous in West Africa," notes anthropologist Elliot Skinner. "The markets served as local exchange points or nodes, and trade was the vascular system unifying all of West Africa, moving products to and from local markets, larger market centers, and still larger centers." Small-scale, local traders set up daily markets that offered foodstuffs and other staple goods, while peripatetic traders moved periodic markets from town to town, returning in three-, four-, five-, or sixteen-day intervals. As agents of West African material life, traders facilitated the exchange of material commodities and, more broadly, ideas and "cultural goods."[4]

Elites and peasants, agriculturalists and artisans, country folk and town dwellers, and women and men encountered each other daily in these urban and rural trading centers, which allowed people to establish or transgress social and cultural boundaries. For example, at the turn of the seventeenth century, peasants, particularly women, traveled considerable distances to trade between the Gold Coast and its hinterland. The Dutch factor Pieter de Marees recorded that on a market day in Cape Coast

> the peasant women are beginning to come to Market with their goods, one bringing a Basket of Oranges or Limes, another Bananas, and Bachovens, [sweet] Potatoes and Yams, a third *Millie*, Maize, Rice, *Manigette*, a fourth Chickens, Eggs, bread and such necessaries as people in the Coastal towns need to buy. These articles are sold to the Inhabitants themselves as well as to the Dutch who come from the Ships to buy them. The Inhabitants of the Coastal towns also come to Market with the Goods which they have bought or bartered from the Dutch, one bringing Linen or Cloth, another Knives, polished Beads, Mirrors, Pins, bangles, as well as fish which their Husbands have caught in the Sea. These women and

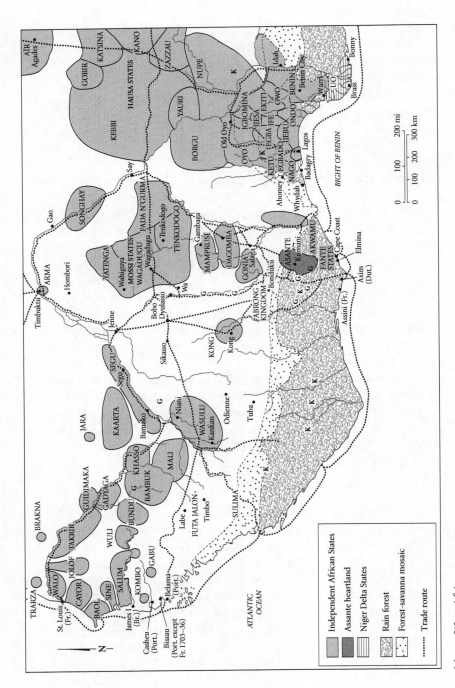

Map 1. West Africa, ca. 1700

N

ATLANTIC
OCEAN

BIGHT OF BENIN

	Independent African States
	Assante heartland
	Niger Delta States
	Rain forest
	Forest-savanna mosaic
·····	Trade route

0   100   200 mi
0   100   200   300 km

TRARZA
BRAKNA
St. Louis (Fr.)
WALO
JOLOF
CAYOR
BAOL
SINE
SALUM
KOMBO
James I (Br.)
Casheu (Port.)
Belama (Port.)
Bissau (Port. except Fr. 1703–36)
GABU
WULI
SULIMA
FUTA JALON
Timbo
Labe
GUIDIMAKA
YAKRUR
BUNDU
GADIAGA
KHASSO
BAMBUK
MALI
KAARTA
JARA
SEGU
Segu
Bamako
Niani
Kankan
WASULU
Odienne
Tuba
Sikasso
Bobo Dyulasso
Jenne
KONG
Kong
Timbuktu
ARMA
Hombori
SONGHAY
Gao
Say
YATENGA
MOSSI STATES
WAGADUGU
Wagadugu
Wahiguya
FADA N'GURMA
Tenkodogo
TENKODOGO
Wa
Gambaga
MAMPRUSI
DAGOMBA
GONJA
Salaga
Bondukú
BRONG KINGDOM
ASANTE
Kumasi
AKWAMU
FANTE STATES
Cape Coast
Elmina
Axim (Dut.)
Assini (Fr.)
AIR
Agades
GOBIR
KATSINA
KANO
HAUSA STATES
ZAZZAU
KEBBI
YAURI
NUPE
BORGU
Old Oyo
OYO
KETU
EGBADO
NAGO
Abomey
Whydah
Badagry
Lagos
IGBOMINA
IJESA
EKITI
IFE
IGBA
IJEBU
ONDO
OWO
BENIN
Benin City
Warri
Itsal
Brass
Bonny
UO

Peasants' wives very often buy fish and carry it to towns in other Countries, in order to make some profit: thus the fish caught in the Sea is carried well over 100 or 200 miles into the Interior.[5]

Guided by these daily rhythms of exchange, West African women linked
specialized areas of food production between the coast and inland.
They also acquired knowledge of multiple environments and economic
activities.

Whereas women generally carried out the trade in foodstuffs, male traders such as the Wangara plied more prestigious commercial goods. They
moved commodities including gold, salt, and kola nuts, used as a stimulant
and to abate hunger and thirst, through West African trading corridors. By
at least the fifteenth century and into the sixteenth century, the Wangara,
an association of Muslim traders from the Niger Bend area, monopolized
the trade between North African salt production centers and West African
kola nut fields and gold mines. Supplying the external demand for West
African gold, merchants mobilized free, slave, or peasant labor in alluvial
or pit mines in Bambuk, Bure, Lobi, and the Akan forest gold fields. Adjacent to these gold-mining centers, peasant and slave labor harvested kola
nuts that stocked kola markets in the savannah, the Sahel, and the Sahara
Desert. Caravans laden with gold and kola nuts moved northward from
the forest region. In exchange, caravans loaded with different commodities, including salt from the North African salt mines of Taodeni, Teguida,
N'tesemt, Idjil, and Awlil, supplied southern markets. According to one estimate, workers at the production centers in the Lake Chad basin yielded
up to thirty thousand tons of salt annually during the sixteenth century,
supporting the daily needs of four to five million people.[6]

Facilitating the flow of commodities, traders exchanged a range of
currencies that circulated throughout West Africa's "vascular system" of
trade. Large merchants, small traders, and consumers used different kinds
of currencies, including gold, cotton cloth, and iron bars, which were
exchangeable at fairly consistent rates over time. At the high tide of the
Atlantic slave trade, West Africans used cowry shells from the Maldive
Islands in the Indian Ocean as currency. During the eighteenth century,
British and Dutch trading firms shipped 25,931,660 pounds of cowries to
West Africa, amounting to approximately ten billion shells that entered
into the system of trade and circulated throughout the region.[7]

Through this ongoing process of trade, West Africans tied together
production centers, towns, villages, and hamlets. They also acquired

experience in managing and transforming the material world, experience
that, though intended for local use, took on particular significance within
the context of the Atlantic slave trade and New World slave labor camps.
Through pathways and "webs" of trade, West Africans brokered and reproduced social and cultural differences. In the process, they reproduced
their material lives in mining centers and agricultural fields, in village
markets and larger urban settings, through trade in gold or cowries, and
by way of local trade or long-distance caravans.[8] Hence, when European
merchants first arrived on the West African coast in the fifteenth century,
they encountered societies with well-established commercial networks.
Over the following centuries, the Atlantic trade tapped into, redirected,
and prompted changes within these market networks.[9]

People from Central Africa who were captured in the slave trade came
from parallel trading worlds. Most of the exchanges of goods in Central
Africa took place on a small scale and were used to cement relationships
with people within one's community. Workers in fishing communities exchanged their catches for staples produced by agricultural labor. Leather
workers and cattle herders from the savannah region of Central Africa
sent their goods to their northern neighbors. Agriculturalists acquired additional protein by exchanging food staples for the game caught by hunters. Salt, iron, and copper workers found outlets for their products. And
while most production was geared toward use within the context of local communities, Central Africans were also bound up in trading relationships with people outside their immediate environs. A small group
of people engaged in commerce as their primary occupation, a trade not
bound to the ties of community and kinship within which much of the
exchange in Central Africa took place.[10]

The exchange networks of West and Central Africa developed along
similar lines, with rotating markets and currencies flowing through each.
In the coastal and central regions of southern Central Africa, a four-day
market system operated, in which traders traveled to four different market villages over a week. In other places, as for one market along the Zaire
River, markets opened once a week. The currencies that flowed through
these markets included shells *(nzimba)* from the Central African coast,
raffia cloth *(lubongo),* and iron bars, a set of currencies comparable to
those circulating through West Africa, where people used cotton textiles,
iron bars, and later cowry shells as currencies. As a sixteenth-century
chronicler of the Congo stated, "Colorful shells the size of chick-peas are
used as money. . . . In other regions, this shell money does not exist. Here

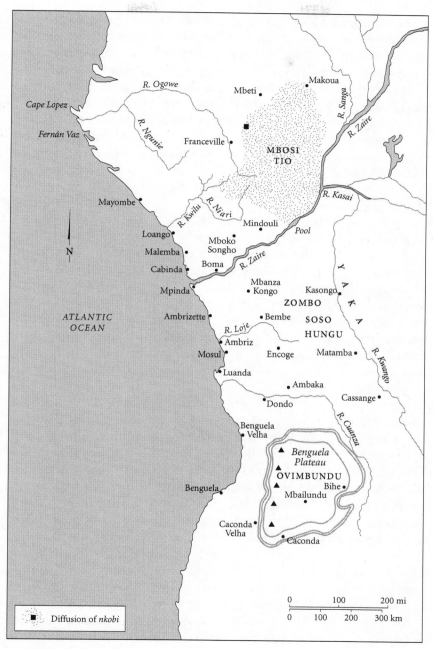

Map 2. West Central Africa, ca. 1700

they exchange fabrics of the type used for clothing, cocks, or salt, according to what they want to buy."[11] In their encounters with people on the Central African coast and in towns such as Mbanza Kongo, Portuguese merchants tapped into these local networks of patronage and trade.

The interaction between Central Africans and European traders altered these internal networks. In particular, the massive infusion of trade goods brought in through the Atlantic trade at Luango, Benguela, Luanda, and other Central African ports provided local elites with the means to expand their patronage networks. By distributing foreign rum, imported Asian and European textiles, and other material goods, African patrons expanded their client base and cultivated allies. Access to these new materials created opportunities for the rise of a new elite. In many cases, patrons entered into debt to acquire the goods they needed to expand their retinue, which enabled them to extend their local power base while also making them vulnerable to the demands of creditors. This system of debt became cancerous, as some local elites further extended the system of credit to less powerful vassals. As African patrons and vassals became overextended on foreign credit in the form of trade goods, many saw that their only way to dissolve their debt was to raid for slaves in neighboring territories or to sell people from within their own domain whom they deemed to be expendable. Through such means, the trading networks of West Central Africa were transformed and generated slaves for the Atlantic slave trade.[12]

In West and West Central Africa, local, regional, and long-distance trading networks linked people across wide expanses, creating a flow of not only material goods but also knowledge. As merchants carried salt from the Sahara Desert into the West African forest, gold and kola nuts from the forest into the Sahara and the Mediterranean World, hides from the Central African savannah to forest agricultural communities, or copper from the Central African mines to its towns and villages, they carried information and ideas about production and the natural world. So people in the regions hit by the Atlantic slave trade had knowledge that was particular to their local social and natural environments, yet they also had an awareness that went beyond what was essential to survive in their immediate surroundings. Out of these environments, networks, and ways of knowing, West and West Central Africans created their material lives.

The web of West African trading relationships connected a population estimated in 1700 to be approximately twenty-five million people, the vast majority of whom lived in rural communities.[13] However, trade bound the countryside to urban areas, which had a long history in West Africa.[14] Through the confluence of external and internal trade, the towns of Timbuktu, Jenne, Gao, Koumbi-Saleh, Niani, and Kano in the West African savannah emerged in the first and early second millennia AD. Toward the end of this period, towns arose in the south, particularly Begho, on the savannah-forest fringe, and Old Oyo and Benin in the West African forest zone. These towns attracted local trade, linked forest and coastal villages to larger trading networks, and served as "ports" of commerce between the West African forest and savannah-zone economies and the Sahara Desert and Mediterranean World.[15] West African urbanization underwent significant change during the years of the Atlantic slave trade. For example, the town of Begho collapsed and Salaga expanded during the eighteenth-century Asante imperial project. Sokoto and the walled town of Katsina grew with the expansion of the Sokoto Caliphate in the early nineteenth century.[16] Furthermore, coastal towns such as Cape Coast emerged as centers for the Atlantic trade. In 1655 the Swedes established a fort in the town, which was seized by the British in 1664. Cape Coast's population grew to approximately three to four thousand people by the early eighteenth century, and its most imposing structure was Cape Coast Castle, which held slaves in its belly in the most wretched of conditions while they awaited a forced passage across the Atlantic.[17]

Hundreds of thousands of people lived in towns along the West African coast, in the forests, and on the savannah, as recorded by a number of nineteenth-century accounts. For example, in southern Nigeria in the 1850s the city of Ibadan had an estimated 100,000 inhabitants, and in northern Nigeria in the 1820s the city of Sokoto had an estimated 120,000 inhabitants (see table 1).[18]

The population figures for West Central Africa similarly are rough estimates; however, the record provides a general indication of the population size of some towns and the region as a whole. Though not as widespread as in West Africa, urbanization emerged in West Central Africa in the early first millennium AD, setting the stage for Portuguese merchants to establish trading partnerships with urban dwellers on their early expeditions to Central Africa in the fifteenth century. In particular, the town of Mbanza Kongo, which became known as Sao Salvador after the arrival of the Portuguese, stood as the economic, political, and religious center of the Kingdom of Kongo. Rising in approximately the fourteenth century, Mbanza Kongo grew with the kingdom and eventually surpassed other Central African towns in population and territory.[19] By around 1630 the

TABLE 1
Estimated Population of Nigerian Towns, 1822–1856

City	Population	Year
Northern Nigeria		
Argonou	30,000	1822–24
Dikwa	25,000	1851–55
Kano	30,000–40,000	1822–24
Katsina	7,000–8,000	1851–55
Kiama	30,000	1825–27
Sokoto	120,000	1825–27
Tabra	18,000–20,000	1825–27
Zaria	40,000–50,000	1825–27
Southern Nigeria		
Abeokuta	60,000	1851
Badagri	5,000–6,000	1846
Ibadan	100,000	1851
Iganna	8,000–10,000	1825
Ilorin	70,000	1853
Koso	25,000	1825
Oyo	25,000	1856

Source: Akin L. Mabogunje, *Urbanization in Nigeria* (New York: Africana, 1968), 64, 91.

town was home to a population of approximately sixty thousand people. In addition, the new Portuguese trading settlement of Loango, like Cape Coast on the Gold Coast, had a population of several thousand people. Smaller towns, which were essentially clusters of villages, had populations between one and two thousand people. These clusters of people stood in the midst of an overall population of ten to twenty million people in West Central Africa during the years of the slave trade.[20]

While people in the towns defined themselves above and against their more rural counterparts, the boundaries between the urban and rural could be porous. For instance, many of the people who lived in Mbanza Kongo farmed within the town's limits.[21] Around the town of Begho, agricultural workers maintained a strong "hunting ethic," and people relied upon fishing, gathering wild plants, and trapping animals for much of their caloric intake.[22] So people in West and West Central African cities and towns interacted across boundaries, worked in multiple economic fields, established local and regional networks, and remained tied to people in the rural hinterlands. Nevertheless, people who lived exclusively in the countryside lived qualitatively different lives from those of their more urban counterparts, who in many cases were protected by a series of walled structures, a prevalent feature of many African towns. For instance, from the eleventh into the nineteenth century, generations of workers constructed and maintained the walls that enclosed the town of Kano. This defensive shield enabled the local elite to more effectively collect revenue, the military to defend urban inhabitants against attack, craft workers to protect their workshops, and the population at large to secure their agricultural fields, craft industries, and food supplies during periods of military siege.[23] Like the West African walled towns, Mbanza Kongo was surrounded by a palisade, and the African Catholic King Afonso I had his subjects add a stone wall to surround the royal and Portuguese quarters in the early sixteenth century.[24] The Portuguese priest Duarte Lopes wrote then about Sao Salvador that "the town is . . . open to the south. It was Dom Afonso, the first Christian king, who surrounded it with walls. He reserved for the Portuguese a place also surrounded by walls. He also had his palace and the royal houses enclosed, leaving between these two enclosures a large open space where the main church was built."[25]

Town walls instantiated social hierarchies, ways of accessing power, and forms of labor organization, as in the West African town of Benin. Within Benin's town walls, urban workers organized along craft lines. Farmers, hunters, traders, soap makers, metalworkers in iron or brass, woodcarvers, potters, bead makers, basket, mat, and textile weavers, dyers, tailors, dressmakers, hairdressers, musicians, medicine makers, administrators, domestic servants, and carriers plied their trades on the streets of Benin.[26] To monopolize their crafts, many of them joined trade guilds, and guild members usually lived in distinct villages, quarters, or town wards. Through these associations, normally composed of family members but open to anyone willing to undergo an apprenticeship, craft workers "were able to control the production of goods, fix prices and also punish guildsmen who violated guild rules."[27] Guilds were not exclusive to West Africa but also became a means by which Central Africans organized labor. Before the Atlantic slave trade, Central African hunters formed protective associations through lineages to shield their crops and settlements. They subsequently organized into guilds to lead the hunt and distribute their game when the Atlantic trade opened opportunities to sell ivory tusks. After giving local rulers and arms dealers their share of the kill, they controlled the sale of the balance to European merchants.[28]

In contrast to the guild system of Lower Guinea and Central Africa, craft workers in Upper Guinea belonged to caste groups.[29] Oral traditions collected during the twentieth century recount that generation after generation passed work practices through caste lines. Individual workers within the major caste groups—smiths, weavers, leather workers, and woodcarvers—specialized in particular kinds of work. Some smiths extracted ore and smelted iron, some forged iron but did not extract ore, and others, usually royal artisans, worked in precious metals, producing gold jewelry and sculptures cast in brass. Some weavers manufactured strips of white cloth; some, known as "kerka" weavers, produced "huge blankets, mosquito nets and cotton hangings" covered with symbolic motifs; and others manufactured cloths with designs based on their knowledge of mathematics and cosmology. Some woodcarvers made sacred sculptures and mortars and pestles out of particular kinds of wood, some built household items and furniture, and some made canoes. Some leather workers specialized in making shoes, some made "straps, reins, bridles, etc.," and others made "saddles, horse collars, etc." The fruits of their labor not only supplied the subsistence needs of farmers and political elites but also entered the market system that connected rural settlements and towns of Upper Guinea with larger trading networks.[30]

Through their networks, West African merchants and political leaders administered trade from the cities and maintained commercial ties with leaders in other towns and cities. For example, after a jihad established the Sokoto Caliphate in northern Nigeria in the first decade of the nineteenth century, its leadership developed regular trading relationships with the south. An early sultan of Sokoto Caliphate, Muhammad Bello, described his empire's commerce with the southern Yoruba-speaking people, observing in 1824, "Yoruba is an extensive province containing rivers, forests, sands, and mountains, as also many wonderful and extraordinary things. . . . By the side of this province there is an anchorage or harbour for the ships of the Christians, who used to go there and purchase slaves. These slaves were exported from our country and sold to the people of Yarba [Yoruba], who resold them to the Christians."[31] This process of trade exported to the "Christians" people who were not merely "slaves" but, though the Atlantic traders might not know it, people with a wide range of practical knowledge of material production.

Whether in empires with large towns or in kinship-based modes of production composed of small villages, "few West African societies were without craftsmen."[32] Their abilities to make tools and extract energy from the natural world made them vital agents in the production of West African material life. Craft workers negotiated within and around frameworks of social hierarchy and power, urban and rural development, and production and trade. They also mastered particular kinds of work skills, inherited and transmitted specialized forms of craft knowledge, maintained clear gender divisions of labor, and managed different scales of production. They worked in different contexts, ranging from rural, small-scale production sites for household and local consumption to urban, large-scale production centers that satisfied tributary obligations or supplied regional markets. And as in other premodern societies, work often carried with it a sacred dimension. Essential participants in precolonial West African life, many West African craft workers were ensnared in wars or enslaved through some other means and sent to the Americas through the Atlantic slave trade.

During the eighteenth century, one of the most important sources of slave labor for the British colonies was the Gold Coast of West Africa. While in the previous century the Gold Coast had been a net importer of slaves who toiled in the region's gold mines, cultivated its farmlands, and carried head-loaded goods along its trading routes, in the late seventeenth century the coast's slave-trading pattern changed with the rise of the Asante Empire.[33] During its expansion, the Asante conquered neighboring states and kinship-based societies and imposed tributary relationships upon its subject territories. The Asante had their foreign subjects work in agricultural fields, set up craft workshops, or march to the coast to be sold to Atlantic slavers. In the eighteenth century, the Asante's armies invaded northern territories and left behind vassal states. Marching northward, the Asante captured territory under the control of the Banda chieftaincy, a largely rural network of agriculturalists and artisans. The Asante attacked the region in 1733 and brought it under their control in 1773, taking possession of the agricultural and craft production centers of the region. Among the workers co-opted or captured and sold by the Asante were women potters skilled in making vessels for storage, cooking, eating, and other quotidian needs.[34] The Asante also conquered the northern states of Gonja and Dagomba, which regularly supplied slaves to the Asante. Pressured to deliver its tribute in slaves to the Asante, the Dagomba state in turn waged wars against neighboring societies to acquire captives. In the mid–nineteenth century and probably earlier as well, they invaded the Bassar region to the east in modern Togo. During such periodic raids, captives from Bassar unwillingly passed through the political fields of the Dagomba and Asante and entered the slave trade.[35]

During this era, workers in the Bassar region operated a large-scale metalworking complex, divided into iron-smelting, iron-smithing, charcoal-making, pottery-making, and leather-working villages. The iron ore–rich region included the iron-smelting towns of Bassar, Kabu, Bitch-abe, and Bandjeli. In the large-scale smelting operation in Bandjeli, orga-nized according to skills and gender divisions of labor, women mined and transported ore from the mines, while men smelted it into iron bloom. Smelters traded the bloom to blacksmithing villages, where both men and women engaged in production. Women pounded the bloom in stone mortars to remove the impurities and then mixed the iron with clay and vegetable fiber. Men working their blacksmith forges fashioned the iron "into hoes, axes, arrowheads, knives, spears, ceremonial bells, and smelt-ing and smithing tools."[36]

Ironworkers plied their trade in dynamic political, cultural, and envi-ronmental contexts. Workers called in ancestral spirits when transform-ing the ore, and the gender divisions of labor were reflected in their craft symbols. For example, male smelters likened their forges to wombs and felt ambivalent toward women. While fearing women's sexuality, they re-vered their reproductive capacity as analogous to the creative process of ironworking.[37] Pressed by external demand, Bassar ironworkers supplied a wide regional trading network, and their industry had a significant envi-ronmental impact. In particular, they risked deforestation from overcon-suming trees to fuel their iron furnaces. From the sixteenth to the nine-teenth century, Bassar expanded production before declining in the face of European competition. At its height, the Bassar trading zone included all of Togo, much of eastern Ghana, and portions of western Benin, cov-ering approximately one hundred thousand square kilometers (38,500 square miles). According to archeologist Philip de Barros, "In terms of people being served, the Bassar trade zone may represent the servicing of a population of well over 600,000," including the Asante Empire, which in its expansion during the eighteenth century increased its demand for iron.[38] Producing iron bars not only for tools crafted by local blacksmiths but also for currency, the labor of Bassar metalworkers fostered regional economic development on a number of levels. And they were part of a larger sphere of African ironworkers.[39]

Like the Bassar ironworkers, Gold Coast fishers served regional mar-kets. They practiced a wide range of skills, managed daily, weekly, and sea-sonal rhythms, organized labor, negotiated political obligations with local elites, and supplied regional trading partners. From the seventeenth into the eighteenth century, the Gold Coast fishing trade was concentrated in a number of towns, including Cape Coast, Mouri, Kommenda, Korman-tin, and Elmina. Off Elmina's shores, coastal fishermen manned around five to eight hundred canoes, which left to fish every morning except Tuesday, the day of rest. Propelled by one or more paddlers paced by the rhythm of work songs, they ventured one or two leagues offshore. Deep-sea fishing teams fished at night, luring fish with torches and catching them with harpoons. In the mornings of January, February, and March, they sailed miles offshore and used lines made of fiber drawn from tree trunks, attached with three or four baited hooks that caught small fish. Close to shore during the nights of October and November, they cast nets of twenty fathoms in length and retrieved them in the morning, before dawn. Others ventured on foot into the ocean at night with a torch in one hand and a basket in the other to catch fish. Pairs of fishermen waded waist-deep into Gold Coast lagoons, marshes, and rivers to sweep hand-held nets through the water. After paying tax in kind and allocating fish for local consumption, traders from the fishing communities marketed the balance to inland farmers in exchange for maize, millet, rice, or other commodities.[40]

People on the Gold Coast learned fishing practices at an early age, gradually acquiring more knowledge about their craft over time. Pieter de Marees observed at the turn of the seventeenth century that cohorts of young males went through an apprenticeship in their craft. Boys between the ages of eight and ten would learn how to "make nets; and once they know how to make nets, they go with their Fathers to the sea to Fish." Before marrying, two or three young men would live together, "buy or hire a Canoe . . . and set out to fish together."[41] Through the course of their work, they acquired not only expertise with the tools of their trade but also a wider knowledge of the environment. They knew the names of scores of fish, and their knowledge also extended skyward.[42] According to one source, a coastal fisherman's knowledge "was certainly extensive, for he could not only give names for the principal planets, constellations and fixed stars, but could also tell what seasonal and meteorological conditions prevailed when they were visible."[43]

In this respect fishermen along the Gold Coast were not unusual among West African coastal workers. In the mid–eighteenth century, the Frenchman Michel Adanson, a correspondent to the Royal Academy of Sciences, recalled that people on the Upper Guinea Coast "pointed to me a considerable number of the stars, that form the chief constellations, as Leo, Scorpio, Aquila, Pegasus, Orion, Sirius, Procyon, Sirius, Spica, Co-anopus, besides most of the planets, wherewith they were well acquainted. Nay, they went so far, as to distinguish the scintillation of the stars, which at that time began to be visible to the eye."[44] Such knowledge had multiple layers—it provided practical guidance for fishermen who ventured to the sea at night, and it also gave them access to forms of spiritual power. Reminded by the winds and waves of the ocean, the life force in the fish, the solidness of the wood in their canoes, the darkness of the night, and the light of the stars, they experienced their fishing not simply as a daily activity but at times as a sacred practice.[45]

Located at the juncture between the realms of the sky, land, and sea, workers in fishing communities were also connected to the labor of local woodworkers, whose skills included timber cutting and canoe building. From the seventeenth into the nineteenth century, woodworkers played important roles in the Gold Coast's material life. In the Birim River Valley, woodworkers drew upon the region's supply of silk cotton trees as raw material to craft military and commercial canoes.[46] At Takoradi, one of the leading canoe-building centers on the Gold Coast in the seventeenth and eighteenth centuries, woodworkers felled trees from their forest hinterland and manufactured dugouts measuring up to thirty feet long and eight feet wide. Meeting the needs of more than the fishing trade, woodworkers also supplied the commercial and political needs of a coastal society that engaged in long-distance sea trade and extensive military operations. Jean Barbot noted in the late seventeenth century that coastal seacraft had the ability to "carry above ten tun of goods, with eighteen or twenty blacks to paddle them," and that the military canoes held approximately "fifty or sixty men, besides ammunition and provisions for fifteen days." He added, "Those Blacks manage them with such extraordinary dexterity in the most dangerous places that it is much to be admired."[47]

Facing the danger of the ocean currents and respecting the Atlantic's power to supply material sustenance yet also take life, coastal fishermen created rituals and symbols of reverence and protection for their work. Relying on more than their "dexterity," the fishers invoked ancestral spirits to support and guide them through the process of material production. In recognition of and supplication to their ancestors, they would "often paint and colour" their canoes or "drape them with ears of Millie and Corn."[48] Contributing their labor to flourishing local and regional trades that connected them to a larger material civilization, Gold Coast fishing and woodworking communities viewed their material life in nonmaterial and symbolic ways, maintaining perspectives and ideas about work and the natural world that captives in the slave trade carried across the Atlantic.

Like craft workers in West Africa, Central African artisans fashioned their material life out of the raw goods of their locales, facing the limitations, tapping into the potential, and making something new of their environments. As in most of the West African forest region, sleeping sickness kept Central Africans from raising large numbers of livestock. However, in parallel to the cattle production in the West African savannah, pastoralists in the Central African southern savannah raised herds of livestock. The Portuguese merchant Pieter Van Den Broecke wrote after landing on the River Congo in the early seventeenth century, "Along the way we saw a large numbers of stock, for example wild animals such as hart, hind, field-fowl, wild pigs, and others too; and particularly, many oxen, cows, sheep, and goats, which were pastured in flocks of 100 by herdsmen."[49] In addition to herding livestock, savannah agro-pastoralists made leathers and hides, finding markets to the north.[50] Hides were among the many goods that circulated in Central African trading networks. Another important trade item was salt. Salt miners extracted the substance from different sites in Central Africa, one of the most important being at Kisama, located south of the Kwanza River, nearly thirty miles from the ocean. In the savannah, salt workers "cultivated salty grasses in marshes, burned them, and filtered the ashes to obtain crystals after evaporation." On the coast and rivers, workers made salt by extracting it from the beds of receded riverbanks or by evaporating saltwater from the Atlantic.[51]

Central African workers made craft goods that remained within networks of household and village exchange or that entered into a broader context. On an everyday level, woodworkers crafted tools for agricultural production, but they also had the skill to carve masks for initiation ceremonies of young boys and girls into adulthood, for divination and healing, for agricultural rituals, and for other occasions.[52] Some artisans became more specialized. With the increase in locally grown and imported tobacco, the demands for locally produced tobacco pipes increased, prompting a shift in the division of labor for pipe makers. Labor became increasingly segmented, with wooden pipe makers increasing their efficiency by having one group of workers craft the stem and another focus on the bowls.[53] Within agricultural communities that produced primarily for local consumption or in craft production centers oriented toward trade, people acquired a mastery of woodworking.

As was true along the Gold Coast and other parts of West Africa, woodworking in Central Africa was tied into other kinds of labor, particularly that of fishermen who daily ventured off the Central African coast in dugout canoes. Van Den Broecke recounted about people near the coastal town of Loango, "The natives are very good fishermen and catch great numbers of fish. There, in the morning, sometimes more than 300 manned canoes go out to sea, and return to land at midday at the height of the sun."[54] Others in West Central Africa tapped the ocean and rivers with harpoons, lines, and nets. Like Gold Coast workers, people in Central African fishing communities ritualized their labor. They worked as clients of local religious and political authorities, to whom they provided an offering before sending their fish to local or more distant markets. According to one account of a fishing community subject to a "countess," "the first fish they catch is immediately sent to the countess, who must prepare it with her own hands. . . . When they reach their village, they eat the fish cooked by the countess, after which they abandon themselves to their customary leaping and rejoicing. After these ceremonies they look forward to a great abundance of fish and the enjoyment of all prosperity."[55]

The most important and deeply respected of artisans were the metallurgists, who worked in either iron or copper.[56] Iron deposits were scattered in Central Africa, particularly in the forests and western mountains, and miners, smelters, and smiths set up regional production centers to transform the ore into metal wares. Artisans made a range of products, including knives, axes, and weapons, and the hoes and iron bars crafted by metalworkers were most in demand and constituted vital trade goods in local and regional networks of exchange.[57] The region also yielded copper, drawing the attention of European merchants on the coast. Van Den Broecke recalled, "There is also much beautiful red copper, most of which comes from the kingdom of the Insiques (who are at war with Loango) in the form of large copper arm-rings."[58] The rings were a final product of a multistage process, in which men mined the rich copper ore deposits at sites such as Bembe, which was about seventy miles south of Mbanza Kongo. Women and young people washed and sorted the ore, and men smelted and crafted the copper into its ultimate form. Through these gender divisions of labor, copper entered West Central African networks, fostered the flow of goods, and cemented social ties between people through gift-giving practices.[59]

As African potters, spinners, woodworkers, and smiths refined raw materials into practical and aesthetic objects, these workers simultaneously transformed their own minds and bodies. Through their labor in the mines and workshops, along the coasts and rivers, and in their housing compounds and adjoining forests, African workers developed a body of knowledge and passed it on to their youth. Young girls learned the craft of pottery from older women making it in their courtyards, and young boys, such as Camara Laye, stood in awe of their fathers who had mastered the art of smelting iron or gold.[60] And while youth were geared toward working within gender divisions of labor, boys might learn something of the crafts performed primarily by women by sitting at their feet, just as girls might catch glimpses of the work done primarily by men. While engaging in work or observing others, they acquired "wealth in knowledge." As Jane Guyer and Samuel M. Eno Belinga argue about Equatorial Africa, people had knowledge "in the arts, music, dance, rhetoric, and the spiritual life as well as hunting, gathering, fishing, cultivation, raffia-weaving, wood-carving and metallurgy."[61]

When merchants from Europe anchored off the coast of West and West Central Africa, they caught a glimpse of the African labor force and their material life. The people whom European merchants encountered along the coast embodied practical knowledge of material production, which involved mastery of the Atlantic coastal currents, fishing, carpentry, metalworking for the tools that carved out the seacraft, lumberjacking to fell the trees for the canoes, agricultural production in coastal and inland communities, and trading practices that tied this knowledge into markets. Their daily life involved setting up apprenticeships, respecting client-patron ties, drawing strength in work through song, naming the bodies of nature from stars to the animal world, and viewing the sacred dimensions of nature and work. This "body of knowledge" was not limited to people along the coast. Experienced with a practical set of skills to manage their environments, people from Africa bought by Atlantic slavers possessed, collectively, a wealth of knowledge. And though the vast majority of them remain nameless in the historical record, they played a considerable role in the New World settings that they entered.

2

Seeds of Change
African Agricultural Workers in the Anglo-American Colonies

Tobacco, cotton, rice, hemp, indigo, the improvement of Indian
corn, and many other important products, are all the result of African skill and labor in this country.
> —Martin Delany, *The Condition, Elevation, Emigration, and
> Destiny of the Colored People of the United States* (1852)

Two generations after the British established their first permanent colonial settlement in the Americas at Jamestown, Virginia governor
Sir William Berkeley "caused half a bushel of Rice (which he had procured) to be sowen, and it prospered gallantly, and he had fifteen bushels
of it, excellent good rice." Behind Berkeley's claims about causing the development of rice worked a team of unfree labor whom he recognized for
their agricultural knowledge. Indeed, Berkeley and through his writings
other colonial elites realized that their slaves brought skills in rice production to the colony. The governor acknowledged, "We perceive the ground
and Climate is very proper for [rice] as our Negroes affirm, which in
their own Country is most of their food, and very healthful for our bodies."[1] Berkeley's testimony indicates that colonial elites did not maintain
complete control over land or labor, so that a space was open for Africans to cultivate a parallel reality. Within the context of a colonial world
that was in flux and experienced periodic crises, Africans in early colonial
settings working next to Indian and English labor were on their own to
survive.

Thus Berkeley's observation opens a window into the world of African
agricultural workers in the Americas. Africans, though enslaved, carried

agricultural knowledge across the Atlantic, shaping the agricultural landscape of the Americas.[2] As the preceding chapter argues, people from Africa emerged from a material civilization that involved urbanization, long- and short-range trade, craft production, and a range of other economic activities. At the foundation of that civilization operated agricultural workers, who transformed forests and savannahs into agricultural fields. The bulk of this chapter will trace the history of West and West Central African agriculture during the years of the Atlantic slave trade, surveying the ecological constraints on, quotidian practices of, and transformations in crop production. In response to their particular environmental and historical contexts, West and West Central Africans developed a host of agricultural strategies. This chapter will then explore the role of Africans in food crop production in the British American colonies. During their early years they worked in the fields next to Native American and English colonists, but over time they played a more central role in producing staple crops. This chapter will argue that through their knowledge of a wide range of crops, ecologies, and practices, African workers shaped the agricultural landscape of the Americas.

An interconnected set of human and environmental factors influenced the course of West and West Central African agricultural history during the years of the slave trade. Agricultural communities faced ecological constraints that affected crop selection, prompted local specialization in particular staples, and stimulated diversification. The social organization of agricultural production also varied, ranging from kinship- to tribute-based modes of economic production. These modes mobilized free or unfree labor, and agricultural production often depended heavily upon the labor of women. Within these social contexts, agricultural workers used different sets of tools and production techniques, making their decisions on the basis of seasonality, crops, soils, or other factors. While during the years of the Atlantic slave trade agricultural production underwent substantial changes in some regions, underlying continuities remained in others as workers passed down knowledge about ecology, soils, crops, field management, drainage, tillage, and crop storage over centuries.[3]

The ecology of West and West Central Africa had a distinct influence on agricultural development in these regions. For example, their forest zones harbored the tsetse fly, which spread the disease trypanosomiasis or sleeping sickness to livestock and thus excluded cattle rearing from much of the forested areas. While some agricultural communities raised livestock to be resistant to the disease, most others did not, and those communities could not rely heavily upon livestock for agriculture. As a result, they used different methods of maximizing returns from the soil—they employed crop mixtures; fertilized their fields with ashes, grass, household waste, night soil, riverbed soil, or millet or rice stalks; farmed on land previously used as cesspits; closely attended to individual plants; allowed land to lie fallow; and cultivated their crops by hand tillage. According to the modern geographers W. B. Morgan and J. C. Pugh, these techniques yielded returns that were "remarkably high."[4]

Not only disease but also climate influenced the agricultural production of these regions. West Africa can be divided according to annual rainfall patterns into the southern (Guinea) and the northern (Sudanic) climate zones. The Guinea zone stretched inland up to two hundred miles from the Atlantic Coast. It spanned western Africa from present-day Guinea into Ghana and also included what are now southern Benin and Nigeria. The Guinea zone had a lengthy rainy season, ranging from seven to twelve months per year, with annual rainfalls in places exceeding 2,000 mm (approximately seventy-two inches). Moving northward, the annual rainy season shortened, with rain falling in a single season, followed by the dry Harmattan season. North of the Guinea zone was the Sudanic zone, which can be further divided into subzones. The southern Sudanic subzone had rainfall for more than six months of the year, with an annual average of 1,500 to 2,000 mm (fifty-four to seventy-two inches) of rain per year and a wider range of temperatures. In the central subzone, the rainy season lasted three to six months and brought from 600 to 1,500 mm (twenty to fifty-four inches) of rain. The northern subzone, also known as the Sahel, received less than 600 mm (twenty inches) of rain in fewer than three months per year.[5]

The West African Sudanic and Guinea climate zones roughly corresponded to its savannah and forest vegetation zones, respectively. The southern savannah, with an annual dry season of up to seven months, consisted of a mix of grasses and woodland. Moving northward, the dry season lengthened, trees were sparser, and vegetation gradually thinned out into the northern and dry savannahs. To the south of the savannah grew a dry deciduous forest, a mixture of evergreen and deciduous trees. From the northern, drier areas of the forest zone to the southern, moister areas, the height and density of the forest increased. The dry deciduous forest gave way in the south to a tropical rain forest, characterized by intense heat, high humidity, multiple levels of canopy, and a general absence of grasses, though other plants may have established ground cover. Similar conditions prevailed along the riverbanks.[6] Prior to and throughout the period under study, the boundaries of these vegetation zones shifted when agriculturalists responded to demographic or political pressure, cleared lands, gradually turned forests into savannah, or abandoned exhausted land that would then lie fallow and revert to grasslands or forests.

West African soil types fell into two categories and differed generally according to climate and latitude. In the southern, humid areas the soil was several meters deep, was protected from erosion by forest covering, and consisted of "loose reddish clay." A thick cover of vegetation made these soils appear extremely fertile; however, their sensitivity would be revealed when the land was cleared for cultivation. Soon after clearance, the heat from the sun generated bacterial activity that disintegrated the soil's organic matter and hence reduced its fertility and crop yields. In the northern areas, tropical ferruginous and brown structured soils predominated. These soils were subject to water and wind erosion.[7] Yet over millennia West African agricultural workers developed techniques to preserve the delicate soils.

The ecology of West Central Africa roughly mirrored West Africa's. In the northern region or equatorial zone of West Central Africa, tropical rain forests predominated, which gave way to savannahs as one moved south. The equatorial zone received heavy rainfalls, in most places ranging from 1,600 to 2,000 mm of rain annually. As in the forest belt in West Africa, the equatorial zone divided its yearly calendar into a dry and rainy season, the latter lasting ten months. This zone had considerable ecological diversity, with landscapes including marshlands, meadows, evergreen forests, and open clearings.[8] Moving south, the tropical rain forest gave way to a savannah-forest mosaic, which received less rainfall than areas to its north. It also had a shorter rainy season, lasting approximately seven to eight months. South of the savannah-forest mosaic stretched savannah lands with a sporadic rainy season that lasted five months. In contrast to the substantial rainfalls of the forest and savannah-forest mosaic, some areas of the southern savannah received less than 400 mm of rain per year. Whereas clay soils rooted much of the forest region, dry sandy acidic soils predominated in the savannahs, which along with the short rainy season limited agricultural production. Hence, most people made their livelihoods from hunting, fishing, and raising livestock.[9] And as in West Africa, the soils of Central Africa, particularly in the forest region, had high iron content and hence low fertility. As one historian describes the Central African forest, "Rich soils . . . are rare." This was the case on

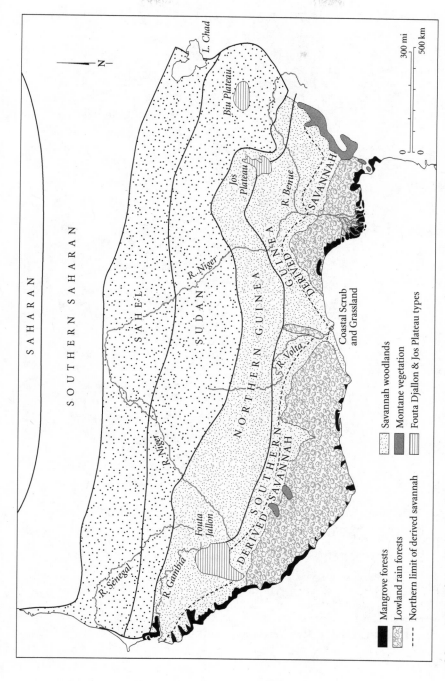

SAHARAN

SOUTHERN SAHARAN

L. Chad

Biu Plateau

Jos Plateau

R. Benue

R. Niger

SAHEL

SUDAN

NORTHERN GUINEA

GUINEA

DERIVED

SAVANNAH

Coastal Scrub
and Grassland

R. Volta

R. Niger

SOUTHERN

DERIVED

SAVANNAH

Fouta
Jallon

R. Senegal

R. Gambia

Mangrove forests

Lowland rain forests

Northern limit of derived savannah

Savannah woodlands

Montane vegetation

Fouta Djallon & Jos Plateau types

N

300 mi

500 km

0

0

Map 3. West African Vegetation Zones

37

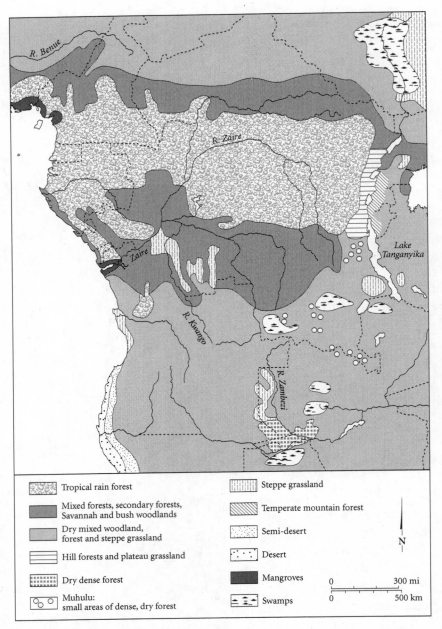

Legend:

- Tropical rain forest
- Mixed forests, secondary forests, Savannah and bush woodlands
- Dry mixed woodland, forest and steppe grassland
- Hill forests and plateau grassland
- Dry dense forest
- Muhulu: small areas of dense, dry forest
- Steppe grassland
- Temperate mountain forest
- Semi-desert
- Desert
- Mangroves
- Swamps

N

0   300 mi
0   500 km

Map 4. West Central African Vegetation Zones

the floodplain of the Zaire River, which swept away organic material and deposited clay soils. And because of the low fertility of the soils, population density tended to be low in comparison to other parts of Central Africa.[10] Moving south toward the Kalahari Desert, the clay soils of the forest and forest-savannah mosaic yielded to sandy soils.[11]

Agricultural workers encountered the uncertainty of their environments as they wrested their well-being from the earth. For example, unusually lengthy dry seasons occasionally turned the soil brick hard, and the following rain, even when heavy, moistened the soil only a few inches in depth. Hence, a series of squalls were needed to mark the beginning of the growing season, after which workers could proceed with their normal routine of cultivation. On the basis of their previous experience and accumulated knowledge, they normally accurately forecasted the timing, intensity, and overall patterns of rainfall, yet it periodically defied their predictions. When the rainy season opened with the usual succession of heavy squalls, moistening the soil deep enough to begin cultivation, a subsequent dry spell might come in to wither their plants. In other years, unseasonably heavy rains might beat the shoots back into the earth. Like peasant communities in other parts of the world, West Africans experienced periodic drought or flooding, which figured into their cultural practices and worldviews.[12] For example, the Ga marked their migration to Accra along the Gold Coast by remembering that they had experienced famine while fleeing from the east, a migration they celebrated annually during the Homowo festival.[13]

While agricultural communities looked to supernatural forces, particularly the ancestors, for help in agricultural production, they took other practical steps to harness the power of their environments and endure the vicissitudes of the seasons. Environmental challenges prompted agriculturalists to manage their environments through practices of what the social anthropologist Paul Richards refers to as "inventive self-reliance."[14] For instance, small-scale agriculturalists deployed strategies such as shifting cultivation, planting particular crops at different seasons, intercropping, and using multiple landscapes. Through these methods, agriculturalists spread out the demands for labor throughout the year, managed soil and fertility levels, reduced demands on labor, and abated the risk of famine if a single crop failed. As a practical matter, agriculturalists developed a number of different storage methods. To avert famines, many communities constructed pits that stored food for several years. To preserve crops until better opportunities arose to sell them in market, they stored staples in woven grass bins for short periods of a few weeks. To guard against the "hunger season" that periodically occurred before their harvests, they stored grains in clay bins and root crops in racks for periods from a few months up to a year. Through these practices, agriculturalists raised a variety of crops, including root crops, rice, millet, maize, tobacco, cotton, and indigo.[15]

Within these ecological contexts and through specific social divisions of labor, agriculturalists cultivated the land, raised a host of crops, and deployed a wide range of agricultural techniques. In the forest zones peasants focused on root production, while in the savannahs cereal crops predominated; however, in many cases, no clear line between these crop zones existed. In the agricultural fields of West and West Central Africa, women played an essential, if not primary, role in agricultural production. Given their importance in staple crop production, they both passed down knowledge from previous generations and adapted to contemporary needs and changes, such as the new crops introduced through the Atlantic trade.

As Africans formed closer ties to European merchants and the Atlantic World, agriculturalists adopted crops from the Americas. On Portuguese ships, maize, groundnuts, and cassava "migrated" across the Atlantic from the Americas. Around the early sixteenth century, cassava took root and by the eighteenth century became a staple crop in Central Africa. Maize also migrated from the Americas to Central Africa, where it was gradually adopted as a food crop, and in West Africa it spread quite rapidly. West Africans also incorporated cassava as a garden plant, slowly learning how to cultivate the potentially poisonous crop before cassava production expanded in the nineteenth century.[16]

The introduction of maize and cassava, and other plants such as tobacco, added to an already multilayered agricultural complex. While agriculturalists normally focused their energies on a particular crop, such as rice or yams, they simultaneously or periodically cultivated other crops as well. Agricultural labor employed these strategies for a number of reasons, such as preventing soil erosion; saving labor, since dense crop growth minimized weeding; averting famine; and maximizing returns from the soil by planting crops that made different demands on it.[17] The effects of these methods caught the eye of European merchants and travelers, who left behind writings about the range of crops that African workers cultivated during the years of the Atlantic slave trade.

European sailors, merchants, and explorers repeatedly testified about crop diversity in West and West Central Africa, as witnessed in their agricultural fields and markets. For example, in the fifteenth century the Portuguese adventurer Alvise Cadomosto observed on the Upper Guinea Coast that its agricultural fields, which were often the domain of women, yielded "various kinds of millet, small and large, beans, and kidney beans, which are the finest in the world."[18] In the seventeenth century the French-man Nicolas Villault observed that from Senegal to the Gold Coast ag-riculturalists raised rice along with other crops. He remarked about the Senegambia region that "this Countrey produces great quantity of *Rice*, of *Millet*, and *Mays*, which is a kind of *Turkish Corne*, they make their bread off, and is not very ill." And on the Gold Coast, he observed that agricul-tural workers cultivated a range of crops, including rice, which agricul-turalists grew in different environments. Villault remarked, "Their Mays or Turky Corne, agrees best with the Hills; the Millet, and Rice, with the Vallys."[19] In the tidal floodplains, uplands, valleys, and marshlands of the Gold Coast and other parts of West Africa, agriculturalists grew rice, which in the words of a Gold Coast proverb "likes to have wet feet."[20]

During the early seventeenth century, the English merchant William Finch saw that rice was a staple crop in Upper Guinea and noted that "they feed also on rootes, and plant about their houses many Plantan-trees, Gourds, Potatoes, Pompions and *Guinne*-Pepper." He added that they grew tobacco and "higher within Land, Cotton, called *Innumma*."[21] Gaspar Mollien later recorded that in the state of Futa Toro agricultural communities not only cultivated rice as a primary staple but also grew millet, cotton, tobacco, and indigo. Furthermore, we are informed that maize was cultivated in Bondu.[22] During his early nineteenth-century ex-ploration of West Africa, Réné Caillié witnessed in one settlement that "when the maize is in flower, they plant cotton between the rows." He also received reports from a merchant that surrounding the city of Kong in what is now Côte D'Ivoire were fields cultivated with "millet, rice, yams, cassava," and cotton.[23]

Sailors and travelers to West Africa alike agreed that agriculturalists rarely grew rice as a staple crop alone. The French sailor Jean Barbot, who voyaged to the West African coast in the late seventeenth century, made repeated references to rice being cultivated with other kinds of crops. Upon reaching the coast of Sierra Leone, he stated that "the land abounds in millet or white maize [*mil ou mahys blanc*] and in rice which they have as their chief food."[24] He observed that down the coast in Sestro (in modern Liberia) "the country greatly abounds in rice and maize on which the natives live" and that nearly 170 miles farther down the coast people "work hard at their agriculture, sowing rice and millet, and collecting *maniguette* which forms their means of trade."[25] Barbot reported of the Gold Coast that "these lands produce a sufficiency of edible products in various places, above all maize, millet *[mil]*, rice, *patates* (sweet potatoes), yams, limes, oranges, coconuts, palm wine, *bordon* (raffia palm) wine," and other produce.[26] Paralleling the accounts by Villault, Barbot, and others, Scottish explorer Mungo Park wrote that at the turn of the eighteenth century agriculturalists in Upper Guinea cultivated millet and rice as staple crops while simultaneously keeping gardens that yielded other plants, including "onions, calavances, yams, cassava, ground-nuts, pompions, gourds, water-melons, and some other esculent plants." Park continued, "I observed likewise, near the towns, small patches of cotton and indigo."[27] The observations by Park and others make clear that people from West Africa who raised rice as a main crop did so in the context of a wider set of agricultural practices. It was fairly commonplace for agriculturalists to move from rice cultivation in river valleys, floodplains, or mangrove swamps to the production of millet, cotton, indigo, peanuts, or tobacco near their housing compounds and in other upland areas.[28]

It was not unusual for agricultural communities in other parts of West Africa, as in the rice-growing region, to focus on a primary staple crop while also cultivating secondary crops. This process facilitated the introduction of new crops, as the region's landscape could maintain older agricultural practices and crops while adopting new ones. Detailed analyses of agricultural practices during the colonial period corroborate the more descriptive writings from the era of the Atlantic slave trade. For example, along the Slave Coast and its interior, agricultural workers intercropped staple cereals such as millet or maize with other plants to minimize competition with weeds for soil nutrients, a technique that concurrently prevented soil erosion under heavy rains.[29] Other West African communities rotated root and cereal crops. In this case, agricultural workers changed crops annually, cultivating yams in the first year, then maize, guinea corn, and early and late bulrush millet in the second. In the third, they might grow early and late bulrush millet and guinea corn, followed in the fourth year by cassava, sweet potatoes, and beans. In the fifth to eighth years, they let the land lie fallow to regenerate its fertility.[30] In the "cereals belt" that spanned the northern, savannah section of West Africa, agricultural workers cultivated millet, guinea corn, and other crops. In some enclaves such as in northern Nigeria, agriculturalists sowed early bulrush millet, called *gero* in Hausa, and harvested it three months later. They then planted cotton under a *dorowa* or *kod* tree, whose leaves functioned as a source of manure for the soil and whose cover provided shade for the arduous task of cotton cultivation.[31] Through such daily practices, West African agriculturalists acquired wealth in knowledge.

It is also clear that during the years of the Atlantic slave trade West Central African agriculturalists cultivated multiple crops. As one authority on the Congo stated about its agricultural workers, "They cultivate twelve species of edible plants, each of which ripens during a different month, so that fresh foodstuffs are available throughout the year."[32] Staple crops included pulses; root crops, particularly yams and cassava, after the latter crop arrived from the Americas; grains such as millet, sorghum, and maize; and "Luco, which is like mustard seed, but larger."[33] Furthermore, agriculturalists rotated crops to delay depletion of the already fragile soils. In crop rotations in Equatorial Africa, women workers cultivated peanuts, which they followed with different varieties of cassava in succeeding seasons before letting the land return to fallow.[34] As part of their material life, they trudged into agricultural fields to wrest their living from the fragile soils, raising multiple crops. People from this context ensnared in the Atlantic slave trade possessed a body of knowledge that they could draw on during their enslavement in the Americas. Schooled in agricultural production, Africans knew a wide range of crops, potentials they drew on to shape the Anglo-American colonies into which they entered.

Facing the challenges of crop production in the forests and savannahs, agriculturalists embodied extensive knowledge about soils, plant life, and intercropping practices, which they combined with tillage and soil management methods. In this regard, women played a particularly important role. In the early eighteenth century, the Catholic friar Laurent de Lucques noted that women in the Kingdom of Congo "had the duty of preparing food and working the land at specific times, and this quickly done. At the first rains they go with their little hoes and loosen the top soil and plant their beans and other legumes on top of it." He added that they took "charge of cultivating the land, sowing, and reaping, to obtain sufficient food for their husbands" and that they also ridged the soils for cereal crops.[35] In the forests of Equatorial Africa, women tilled the soils, prepared and planted root crops in mounds, and planted complementary crops such as maize or sweet potatoes in between the mounds.[36] West African agriculturalists used similar methods for root and grain crops, as revealed in colonial era reports. For instance, within the northern cereals belt, where soils tended to be drier and sandier than in the south, cultivators generally planted their crops in short ridges from soil tilled approximately three inches in depth. To the south in the "roots belt," agriculturalists raised root crops in mounds, rather than in ridges, generally between one and two feet high from heavy and moist clay soils tilled six or more inches deep. In addition, agricultural communities within the roots belt often grew cereals as a secondary crop, with tillage generally deeper and ridges higher than the short ridges of the northern cereals belt. These methods helped to conserve and maximize returns from the soil.[37]

Depending on the ecological, political, and social structures within which they operated, agricultural workers employed one or more methods of soil management. These methods included floodland cultivation, tree cultivation, permanent cultivation, mixed farming, rotational planted fallow, shifting cultivation, and, most prominently, rotational bush fallow. These practices clearly varied over space and time. For example, during the seventeenth century the kinship-based Balanta changed from upland yam cultivation to lowland rice cultivation in response to opportunities created by the Atlantic trade and supplies of iron from European merchants. This transformation allowed them to survive under the intense pressure of the slave trade.[38] While the Balanta adopted paddy-rice cultivation, others in West Africa practiced floodland cultivation, which involved the "planting of rice, sugar or maize in riverain alluvium as water levels decline, in most cases at the end of the rainy season." A similar technique, called the *decrue* method, was used for sorghum cultivation on the Niger and Senegal floodplains. As noted by geographer J. T. Harlan, "When the floodwaters recede in the early dry season, seeds are planted in the mud and the crop is grown on stored moisture, without rain or irrigation."[39] In the upland areas, they used different methods of cultivation to grow cotton or other crops.[40]

Other agricultural workers practiced shifting cultivation by building temporary settlements, cultivating the surrounding land until it was exhausted, and then moving to other areas. This system predominated in the Central African forests and in parts of West Africa. Agriculturalists selected land on the basis of the "type, height and density of plants it supports" and when possible chose areas with a distinct dry season, which made it easier to clear the ground cover with fire. Upon selecting a settlement site, workers burned the extant ground vegetation to both open the land for cultivation and return nutrients to the soil. They used a minimum amount of tillage and raised a small number of plants, which in some cases they intercropped. For instance, some communities grew "yams at the top of a mound, maize on the sides, and cassava in the trough."[41] After cultivating a plot of land for one or two years they let it return to fallow, and after several years of cultivating fields adjacent to their settlements they moved to another settlement site near fallow land.

One of the most common cultivation cycles was rotational bush fallow. In this method, agricultural workers divided the land around their settlement into rectangular cultivated plots and larger fallow plots. In the land under cultivation, they interplanted cultigens. Though intercropping diminished yields from individual plants, it enabled the growth of a high density of crops, yielded high returns from the plot as a whole, protected the soil from water erosion, and reduced the tasks of weeding. At the beginning of the rainy season, they planted their primary crop, which required maximum amounts of water and mineral resources, and then followed with secondary crops. Having placed soils under cultivation for several years, they allowed the land to revert to fallow, which took different forms. In the more humid areas of West Africa, woody fallows developed from tree shrub seedlings or from the remains of root crops. When agricultural workers in the roots belt returned fallow land to cultivation, clearance normally required several weeks of heavy labor that included cutting, uprooting, and then burning the vegetation. Within the drier regions, grassy rather than woody fallows required less arduous labor to clear—cutting the grass and burning the remains to open the field for cultivation. Once the workers cleared the soil, having allowed it to rest long enough to regenerate its fertility, they returned it to the cultivation phase of the agricultural cycle.[42]

Agricultural workers often accompanied the rotational bush-fallow system with a system of permanent cultivation adjacent to or within household compounds. On these compound lands, also known as "kitchen gardens," they grew items to complement their primary food source and enhance their quality of life. In the early nineteenth century, Réné Caillié observed in several West African villages that the people cultivated tobacco, onions, beans, or cotton in small gardens next to their dwellings.[43] Fertilizing their compound plots with "household refuse, ashes, crop remains and animal manure," they grew not only tobacco and cotton but also particular kinds of yams that needed a great deal of attention, manuring, or watering; food reserves such as cocoyam, sanio bulrush millet, or fonio; relishes, including okra and peppers; and fruit, timber, and oil palm trees.[44] In the forests and savannahs of West Central Africa, women grew crops in their gardens, where they employed fertilizers and rotated crops to preserve the soils. These kitchen gardens were "important because they served as experimental stations to test new plants."[45] From the Senegambia region to the Niger Delta, and into the Central African forests and savannahs, agricultural communities maintained similar practices of keeping kitchen or tobacco gardens adjacent to their houses.

Through intense periods of land clearance, timing of work on the basis of natural cycles, and painstaking attention to crops, agricultural labor transformed these communities' landscapes. Forests yielded to one kind of crop and then another, which gave way to forests again. And as agriculturalists entered production, they were transformed in the process. Workers faced the challenges posed by their natural environments and remained open to change and innovation during the course of the Atlantic slave trade. They practiced a wide range of skills, including knowledge of rainfall patterns, soils, plants, tillage methods, crop rotations, and garden production, using their knowledge to transform their surroundings. In some instances, agriculturalists incorporated crops from the Americas. Others, such as the Balanta, adopted crops and agricultural techniques from neighboring West African societies. Their constant effort was clear to contemporaries such as Olaudah Equiano, who noted in his autobiography, "All our industry is exerted to improve those blessings of nature."[46]

While they labored, agricultural workers "embodied" agricultural knowledge, established connections with larger social networks, and created local bonds with each other and the land under cultivation. By way of trading ties or tributary obligations, their labor, depending on their political and economic circumstances, entered what the anthropologist Elliot Skinner has described as any of three different larger social spheres: the production of "subsistence crops, from which surplus food was taken to be sold in the markets; production for the nobility, some of which was also drawn off for sale; and specialized production for the market."[47] And as they negotiated the terms of market- and tribute-based production, some agricultural workers, particularly free labor, infused the process with kinship-based ideas.

For example, on the Gold Coast at the turn of the seventeenth century, agriculturalists worked within both kinship- and tribute-based relations of production. At the beginning of the growing season, free agricultural workers obtained permission from local elites to cultivate land to provide for their kin. Accompanied by their slaves if they had any, they cleared with fire the overgrowth on the allotted field, which had been fallow for several years and covered with a considerable amount of vegetation. They then used cutlasses to mix the ashes into the soil and allowed the land to rest for eight to ten days. Before they cultivated their own fields, they first had to cultivate the field of the local elite. During this labor, agricultural workers joined together to clear and sow the field, for which the elite reciprocated by feting them with food and drink. Upon completing their tributary labor, they invoked ancestral spirits to provide a fruitful growing season, formed a circle around a fire, and "enjoy[ed] themselves with food and drink . . . singing and making merry." In the following days, they moved together from field to field, celebrating at the end of their task in the same way, with "each giving a treat to his helpers according to his ability."[48] From this act of reverence, they entered the daily task of work in the fields; through their efforts they established their connection to the land and continuously shaped and reshaped the material landscape of the Gold Coast.

On the Slave Coast, a similar set of forces shaped agricultural production at the onset of European trade. Agriculturalists such as the Fon-Ewe raised a combination of New and Old World crops, including maize, sweet potatoes, cocoyams, ginger, millet, and sorghum, which became part of their daily material lives.[49] They sold some of their produce in local markets, which were often run by women.[50] During the early eighteenth century, a Dutch commercial agent in the Slave Coast town of Whydah was informed that the market's ginger "comes from a place called Fou or Foin, about 20 miles from here. It is being brought here on every market day, that is twice every nine days, in small bits. The Foin Negroes bring it as a kind of medicine."[51]

The social divisions of labor emerged through kinship- and tribute-based contexts and also unfolded along gender lines. In many cases, West African women played central roles in agricultural production. For example, it was probably they who undertook the task of incorporating American crops, adapting them in their gardens, and integrating them into larger agricultural fields.[52] They either did most of the agricultural work or labored in partnership with male workers. For example, on the banks of the Benue River, men and women engaged in different phases of production. They raised an array of crops from both the Americas and West Africa, including cotton, indigo, gourds, groundnuts, guinea corn, rice, and yams, the staple crop.[53] Each day, agricultural workers moved from their compounds to work in the fields and then returned to their homes after work. During the land clearance phase, women, men, and young people worked en masse to remove trees and other ground cover, preparing the soil for cultivation. During the tillage phase, men went into the fields together, if necessary drawing assistance from neighboring compounds to carve the soil into mounds for yam seedlings. In the planting phase, women chose the seed yams, joined men to plant them in the top of the mounds, and maintained and weeded the fields daily. And during the harvest phase, women unearthed the produce, selecting yams for consumption and the following year's seed.[54] These seasonal rhythms not only involved the technical and social dimensions of production but also provided metaphors for spiritual concerns, as embedded in beliefs related to the natural world and harvest festivals.

Agricultural products went toward a number of ends, including immediate consumption, exchange, political protection, and ritual purposes. Agriculturalists who produced surpluses sold them to people in neighboring communities. For example, like people on the Gold Coast, people on the western coast of Central Africa set up markets for produce from inland cultivators.[55] And as in West Africa, Central Africans propitiated political authorities and spiritual forces before engaging in agricultural production. In the words of the historian Georges Balandier, Central Africans generally regarded "nature as a source of vital products whose acquisition requires knowledge, skill, and the consent of the generative or guardian 'forces.'" In some parts of Central Africa, political subjects followed elites to the fields to engage in public ceremonies that invited the seasonal rains. Such elites or diviners under royal authority had ritual knowledge through which they guaranteed the fertility of the soil, and they conducted ceremonies to bless the first fruits of the harvest. In other cases, agriculturalists cultivated a sacred field that helped guarantee an abundant harvest.[56]

Africans carried to the Americas through the slave trade came from such contexts. Some lived in towns and engaged in craft production, but most resided in rural settings, working primarily in agriculture. They knew soils, plant life, and the timing and duration of the rains. They knew how to cultivate a variety of crops. When by the seventeenth century Atlantic traders brought maize, tobacco, and cassava to Africa from the Americas, agriculturalists readily incorporated them into their fields. These crops added to an agricultural knowledge that included irrigation techniques, cyclical patterns of cultivation, and methods of soil management. Moreover, they knew different methods of tillage and crop storage. Hence, African captives brought a wide of range of agricultural and craft knowledge into the Atlantic World.

While working in their agricultural fields, West and West Central Africans reproduced knowledge or "cultural capital." Cultural capital, as defined by sociologist Pierre Bourdieu, takes different forms. One form, objectified cultural capital, consists of "cultural goods . . . which are the trace or realization of theories or critiques of these theories, problematics, etc."[57] In essence, intellectual and artistic efforts produce objectified cultural capital that takes the form of material objects, owned individually or collectively. West African agricultural workers created and recreated objectified cultural capital in the form of work tools, gardens, cultivated fields, crops, food storage spaces, and other objects. Objectified cultural capital appeared fixed, dead, concrete, and static but possessed life hidden within it. As they lived and worked, agriculturalists created objectified cultural capital and in the process transformed themselves. Through their work activity, personal agency, and unintentional internalizing of their social and material worlds, they embodied their surroundings. As Bourdieu notes, "all cultural goods," and one might add cultural performance and cultural activity, "particularly all those which belong to the childhood environment[,] exert an educative effect by their mere existence."[58] In the process of cultivating agricultural fields, selling, storing, or paying taxes with their surplus, traveling from home to market, collecting herbs from the forest, and passing by ironworking, pottery, or weaving workshops, agricultural workers produced, reproduced, and embodied different kinds of cultural capital. Without realizing it at the time they acquired it, captives of the slave trade possessed cultural capital that provided them with the means to survive and come to terms with their new environments in the Americas.

The first phase through which Africans transmitted cultural capital to the Americas was the Atlantic crossing. The horrors of the Middle Passage and the demands that American slave labor camps placed on their bodies meant unimaginable losses for captives from Africa. Marched in some cases hundreds of miles to the African coast, worked on plantations or held captive in pens, lodges, or castles before being forced aboard slave ships, stripped of their clothing and forced beneath the deck, guarded by the ship's crew, and subjected to the sights and smells of death around them, Africans experienced the Atlantic slave trade as a waking nightmare.[59] The nightmare was not over when they landed in the Americas, thousands of miles away from their places of birth. In the New World, they were worked to death. The pain of the Middle Passage and enslavement burned in the consciousness of the Africans like the branding irons that marked them as property. Yet those who lived through this ordeal survived by creating something familiar. Indeed, slave ships transmitted seeds that Africans used to make sense of their experience in the New World.

African agriculture literally fed into the Atlantic economy, with slave ships being provisioned on the African coast. African captives transported to the British American colonies had to survive the Atlantic crossing with at least a minimum amount of food, which slavers bought on African shores. The Upper Guinea Coast supplied slave ships with the West African red rice *Oryza glaberrima*, which fed captives for the Atlantic crossing and provided survivors with seeds to cultivate in the Americas.[60] And in the early eighteenth century, after the Portuguese carried groundnuts to West Africa, the staple was "brought from Guinea in the negroes ships, to feed the negroes withal in their voyages from Guinea to Jamaica."[61] West Africa supplied ships with other produce, including pepper, coconuts, maize, palm oil, beans, plantains, oranges, and yams. For example, in 1677, Captain Robert Doegood of the Royal African Company dropped anchor near New Calabar to buy slaves for the Royal African Company. In cold, calculating fashion, he and the "King of New Calabar" negotiated and set prices for trade. Doegood agreed to pay one iron ring for nine yams, thirty-six copper bars for a male slave, and thirty copper bars for a female slave. Daily, canoes went back and forth between the coast and Doegood's ship *Arthur,* carrying food provisions and slaves bound for the island of Barbados.[62]

Where root crops were prevalent slavers bought them, and where cereals were staples they supplied slave ships. In Lower Guinea, where root crops predominated, slave ships were supplied with yams. For example, in 1728 the ship *Judith* docked at the Gold Coast port of Annomaboe, where it was provisioned with yams.[63] The ship *Providence*, trading in slaves on the West African coast in 1757, recorded buying 5,900 yams, which must have been a fraction of what was needed to complete its slaving voyage.[64] Speaking about the slave trade at Calabar, the sailor Jean Barbot, perhaps overestimating the amount of food required, suggested in the early eighteenth century that "a ship that takes in five hundred slaves, must provide above a hundred thousand yams."[65] In some cases, captives shaped the choice made by ship captains to provision ships with yams. Barbot noted that "the Calabar slaves value this root [yams] above any other food, as being used to it in their own country." However, he added that some captains tried to avoid using yams as food because of their tendency to rot.[66]

For slaves from the coast the yams may have been a painful reminder of home, and for captives from inland areas where cereal crops predominated, their new diet perhaps added to an already jarring experience. As maize spread on the Guinea Coast, British slavers provisioned their ships with corn as well as palm oil, salt, and malaguetta pepper.[67] In Upper Guinea, slavers fed their captives with a range of crops, including manioc, millet, and rice. And some ship captains and crews put their female captives to work milling rice before they even landed in the Americas.[68] The material life of slave ships, which relied on African staples to feed captives aboard them, transmitted resources that slaves drew on in their New World environments.

Though staple crops grown in West Africa supplied slave ships, the power relationships and material life on board the ships still contrasted sharply to Africans' previous experiences, which led some to revolt or refuse to eat. Barbot wrote about slaves that "they are also sometimes brought to revolt when provisions are lacking, which almost always happens on ships which make a lengthy passage."[69] Olaudah Equiano and other captives aboard his ship reacted to their experience by rejecting demands to eat, and as a result he along with his mates suffered severe punishment.[70] This tension between captives and shipmasters was also enacted on the ship *Florida*, commanded by Captain Samuel Pain. The *Florida* carried 360 slaves and left from the West African port at Calabar. Pain observed in the course of the Atlantic crossing that "they now began to sicken very much, and sometimes we threw overboard 4 or 5 in a day; their common distemper was the flux, with a swelling in their limbs. Their opinion is that when they dye, they go to their own Country, which made some of them refuse to eat their victuals, striving to pine themselves, as [the more] expeditious way to return home." The *Florida* lost 120 captives during the Atlantic crossing. Through intimidation and sheer will to survive, most of the enslaved ate their provisions.[71] Yet the context of the slave ships and the relationships of domination embedded within them clearly nourished the captives' longing for home.

Over time, the survivors of the Atlantic crossing tried to reproduce that sense of home in their gardens and provision grounds, raising crops brought from Africa. Early authorities on the British Caribbean pointed out these connections. In the late eighteenth century, British natural historian Charles Bryant wrote in his 1783 text *Flora Diaetetica: Or History of Esculent Plants* that sorghum was "cultivated in Africa under the name of Guinea corn. . . . The grain is there made into bread, and is otherwise used, and is deemed wholesome food. From Africa the Negro carried them to the West Indies, where they were sown for their use." The French naturalist Richard de Tussac, who surveyed the landscapes of Saint Domingue and Jamaica, drew similar conclusions. He wrote, "Under the plants of major importance which have been introduced to the Antilles and which are naturalized, the yam must rank first; the genus of this plant is native of the country, but the kind I am going to describe, like the prickly yam or yam of Guinea, have been brought from Africa by the Negroes." He added, "The yam is an important commercial subject for the free Negroes and the slaves, who cultivate them in their gardens, sell them at the markets found on Sundays in all villages of the country."[72] Recounting the history of African crops in the Caribbean, Tussac and Bryant provide a glimpse into the flow of African agricultural practices across the Atlantic through the slave trade.

The transplantation of African crops into the Americas constituted part of a larger process through which Africans entered a different material and social environment. During the first half of the seventeenth century, Africans in Barbados and other islands encountered Indian and English laborers, who laid the agricultural foundations of the Anglo-American colonies. To survive, they grew a host of cultigens from the New and Old Worlds. For example, on the island of Bermuda in the early seventeenth century, tenant farmers and indentured servants worked tobacco as an export crop, but they also raised their own foodstuffs.[73] Colonial planters developed similar economic strategies in Barbados, where English laborers and a small number of Indians raised cotton and tobacco for export. However, landowners also had their unfree workers raise their own food, which included Native American plants such as sweet potatoes, maize, and manioc.[74] As the historian Hilary Beckles states, these workers "paved the way not only for the subsequent emergence of the revolutionizing sugar industry, but also for the plantations' large-scale absorption of African slaves."[75]

During the transition to slavery and sugar production in the British Caribbean, Africans inhabited fields opened up by and, in many cases, worked alongside Indian and English people. They leveled the forests with axes and fire and planted Old and New World crops. Before the colonial era, the island of Barbados had relatively dense forests with multiple layers of canopy, but the development of commercial farming transformed it. The English transplanted cultigens from England and other parts of the world and also relied on Native American crops for their survival and

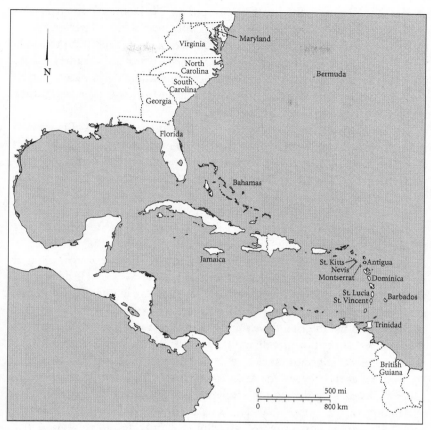

Map 5. Major Anglo-American Slaveholding Colonies

to trade.[76] For instance, in the middle of the seventeenth century, Africans on William Hilliard's sugar, cotton, and tobacco estate toiled alongside English servants and Native American laborers, who raised not only export crops but also maize, cassava, and plantains.[77] This world would not have been completely unfamiliar to slaves, given the history of African agricultural practice. During this era, Africans were in the process of adopting New World crops, and many slaves would have been experienced with cultivating both root crops and cereals. Furthermore, it is possible that some Africans had experience with sugarcane cultivation. For instance, at the turn of the seventeenth century Pieter de Marees recorded sugarcane for sale at Gold Coast markets, and Jean Barbot made similar observations later in the century, remarking, "In some places here one finds sugar cane."[78] Thus the agricultural work that Africans performed in early Barbados would not have been completely alien. Yet within the context of mass sugar production and with scores of workers heading out to the fields to raise export crops, the expectations that slaveholders had of their slave population would have been jolting to them, even when they had prior experience raising sugarcane.

With planters or their overseers standing in the shadows, British Caribbean workers daily went into the sun to work the agricultural fields and face seemingly incessant demands to produce export crops and perform other kinds of work. Barbados, after its early years of concentrating on cotton and tobacco, had an economy in which sugar and slavery dominated, and the island became a model for planters in Jamaica and other islands.[79] For contemporaries, sugar and Barbados became synonymous. In the mid–sixteenth century, the Jesuit priest Antoine Biet observed of Barbados that "the wealth of this island consists of sugar. Sugar cane or reed is planted in the countryside as far as the eye can see." He added that the island produced so much sugar that "every year over two hundred ships are loaded to transport it to all parts of Europe." When he made his observations, the island was undergoing its transition to slavery as its primary instrument of mobilizing labor. Within this world of coercive labor, the mills that ground the cane during harvest time perhaps reminded slaves of what they experienced on a daily basis, with the pressure on the sugar stalks passing through the rollers paralleling their daily grind.[80]

Making nearly impossible demands on their labor force to produce sugar, the planter class in many cases failed to provide sufficient food provisions. Thus Africans survived by raising their own crops. With sugar being so profitable in Barbados from the middle of the seventeenth century onward, planters geared most of their labor to the sweetener and offered little in the way of food supplies to their labor force. "There is no nation which feeds its slaves as badly as the English," Biet recounted, because "for all meals the slaves get potatoes which serve them as their bread, their meat, their fish, in fact, everything."[81] Slaves, most recently arrived from West or Central Africa, had to procure their own food, yet because of the pressure to produce export crops they often had limited opportunities to do so. As one contemporary noted, slaves had to "maintain themselves without burdening their master," who generally found it more important for slaves to cultivate and process sugar than to raise foodstuffs.[82] Ironically, to muster the energy to survive the demanding labor of sugar production, slaves worked on the margins, adopted crops and agricultural practices set up by Indian and English labor, and relied on knowledge they carried from Africa to meet their everyday needs.

Into the eighteenth century, slaves in Barbados raised African food-stuffs. They cultivated yams, which they grew in mounds and stored underground or in their garrets. According to natural historian Griffith Hughes, agriculturalists took special care with harvesting the root crops, which could be easily bruised and spoiled.[83] By the middle of the century such crops were well established, as the young George Washington observed in Barbados, where he noted the cultivation of "gunia Corn (which greatly supports their Negros) Yams plantens Potatos & rice."[84] Over time, these practices declined on the island. Because of the scarcity of land in Barbados, many of the island's slaves did not have access to grounds to raise their own crops; however, on islands that had more abundant land or were less reliant on sugar exports, slaves raised their own food. As Africans entered the Caribbean islands, they integrated their crops into fields opened by English, Spanish, or American Indian labor. For instance, by the middle of the eighteenth century, in the market of St. John, Antigua, slaves brought crops raised on their grounds, including "Greens, Yams, potatoes, Oranges, Limes, Lemon," and other foodstuffs.[85] The Bahaman Islands raised a similar mixture of crops, which included "Cotton, corn, Potatoes, yams, Peas, Casava, and other Provisions."[86] This was particularly the case in Jamaica.

In the second half of the seventeenth century, after the British seized Jamaica from the Spanish during Oliver Cromwell's Western Design, colonists on the island relied heavily on American crops for food provisions. In the first couple decades of British occupation on the island, Jamaican agriculturalists raised New World crops such as cassava, plantains, maize, and potatoes as staple foods.[87] The shift to slave labor transformed the agricultural landscape, with Africans continuing to grow staples planted by Indian and English labor while simultaneously introducing African crops. On the margins of export crop production, slaves cultivated small plots of land and in them created agricultural landscapes somewhat like those they had created in Africa. Concurrent with the practices of inventive self-reliance through which women in West and West Central Africa adopted American crops into their agricultural fields, Africans in the Americas introduced African crops in the British Caribbean. In Jamaica, Africans cultivated rice in land they staked out. "Rice is planted here by some Negros in their own Plantations, and thrives well, but because it requires much beating, and a particular Art to separate the Grain from the Husk, 'tis thought too much troblesom for its price, and so neglected by most planters," the British naturalist Hans Sloane explained.[88] African crops became important enough that they were produced for export, as was the case with sorghum, known at the time as "Guiney Grain."[89] Hence, under the pressures to raise their own food and produce cash crops, Africans in the British Caribbean cultivated crops with which many were familiar.

Slaves also drew on their own agricultural techniques and practices. They would have been familiar with the Native American practice of slash-and-burn or swidden agriculture, which was a widespread form of land clearance and fertilization among tropical agriculturalists.[90] In the early eighteenth century, British Caribbean slaves used these methods to raise their food provisions. The British natural scientist Hans Sloane noted in the early eighteenth century, "After seasons, i.e. three or four, or more days of Rain, all manner of Provisions, Maiz, Guinea Corn, Pease, Patatas, Yams, Plantains, etc. are planted. The Ground, after these Grains and Provisions are gathered, is cleared, before they expect a new Season, of the remaining weeds, stalks, and Rubbish, which are put in heaps and burnt."[91] Like agriculturalists in the South American or Central or West African forests, Caribbean slaves practiced this method to return nutrients to the soil and preserve labor, which would have been particularly important given the intense labor demands of export crop production.

Well into the nineteenth century, Africans expanded agriculture in Jamaica, where they tended to raise food provisions in the mountains. Since land near the rivers and coasts was reserved for export crop production, slaves trudged into the mountains with their tools in hand to cultivate food for their own consumption and also for sale. In these plots, Africans deployed the crop mixtures that had evolved in the seventeenth century. In the early eighteenth century, the historian John Oldmixon wrote that next "to each hut there is a little Plot or Garden set out, where the Negroes plant Potatoes, Yams, Cassavia Roots, &c.," which they used as foodstuffs or traded in local markets.[92] In the late eighteenth century, Jamaican slaves cultivated maize, plantains, yams, guinea corn, peas, and small amounts of rice. They also raised kola nuts, which colonial historian Bryan Edwards described as "an African Fruit, introduced by the Negroes before Sloane's time, called Bichey or Beffai."[93]

As the island churned out exports by working some slaves to early deaths, planters continued to demand slaves from Africa. They along with American-born slaves were forced primarily into cash crop production, but they also worked provision grounds where they raised multiple crops. This was the case among slaves on the Greenpark and Springvale estates. At the end of the century, the labor force was mixed between American and African-born slaves, including ten Angolans and ten workers from the Gold Coast bought by the plantation owners in October and November of 1793. They replaced workers who had died from a host of ailments, including measles, inflammation of the bowels, "dropsy," pleurisy, "worm fever," consumption, and suicide (one woman was said to have "hanged herself"). The ones who lived and worked in cash production were forced to grow coffee, but the estates' slaves also raised guinea corn, maize, and yams.[94] During this period, Africans also labored on the Somerset plantation. Slaves named Cuffee and Coromantee Molly toiled along with others to cultivate forty acres of guinea corn, forty acres of plantains, and six acres of yams.[95] Raising the West African staple sorghum as a primary and secondary food crop was particularly important within the context of New World slavery. The crop, when compared to others, was more drought resistant and productive in less fertile soils, such as those in the mountains where planters reserved land for slave provision grounds.[96] So for Africans exhausted from sugarcane or coffee production, guinea corn offered both a familiar and a relatively efficient food source.

When they walked to their provision grounds, slaves passed their counterparts from neighboring estates on routes that crisscrossed each other. This enabled slaves to communicate with each other and forge ties with people from other plantations.[97] Furthermore, these worlds offered a space for African agricultural production, as was the case on the Somerset Vale estate in St. Andrew's Parrish in Jamaica's Blue Mountains. On this sugar and coffee estate, slaves did a wide range of work such as planting, weeding, and harvesting sugarcane, making lime, building livestock pens, clearing and repairing roads, making bricks, making posts and rails for fences, and building thatched houses. As was customary on many other Jamaican plantations, slaves worked their provision grounds on Sundays. On the "Old Negro Ground," "Jack's Old Ground," "Dolly's Old Ground," "Jacob's Old Ground," and "Quashe's Old Ground," slaves cultivated multiple food crops, including guinea corn, maize, yams, and peanuts, which were common in different regions of West and West Central Africa during the years of the slave trade. They raised foodstuffs biannually, beginning the planting season during the rains of November and April. Also, slaves on the Somerset Vale plantation used similar crop rotations, sowed root crops in mounds, and followed root crop production with cereals on the same soil.[98] Their work became more important during the era of the American Revolution, when food supplies from the mainland could not reach the British Caribbean islands, which were forced to substitute imports by increasing domestic food production on slave provision grounds.[99]

Even after the slave trade to the British Caribbean was abolished and during the apprenticeship period, Africans left an imprint on the landscape. On the Green Valley estate, apprentices produced coffee for the landowners but also had plots of land where they grew yams and "Congo peas."[100] Over two centuries, Africans in the Caribbean built on foundations established by Indian and English laborers who had first cleared the fields and raised foodstuffs. Slaves integrated African crops into their provision ground rotations, used land clearing and fertilizing methods prevalent in Africa and other tropical environments, and built mounds to sow their root crops. While engaging in staple food production, Africans transformed the agricultural landscape of the British Caribbean, a process that had parallels on the North American mainland.

In the early years of slavery in colonial North America, Africans who landed on tobacco plantations entered polyglot worlds, encountering English and Indian people in the fields. During colonial Virginia's infancy, it was commonplace for Africans to work alongside English and Indian laborers. Under the headright system, planters received fifty acres of land for every laborer they brought to the colony, and colonial records indicate that a number of planters received land grants for importing both English and African labor into Virginia. For example, on March 3, 1673, the Surry County courts granted Arthur Allen 2,000 acres of land for bringing in servants as well as slaves, named Simon, Emanuell, Tony, Comsee, Stephen, Mingo, and Mathew. On July 2, 1678, the court granted Frank Mason 1,100 acres for importing the slaves "Cudge, Hector, Frank, and Maria," "Twig, Soffe, Peter, and James," and fourteen servants. On July 6, 1680, the court granted William Simons 400 acres of land for bringing in six servants and two slaves, named Frank and Elias.[101]

York County records also indicate an ongoing interaction between black and white labor. In 1685, the English servant woman Sussana Shelton suffered twenty lashes for giving birth to a child of the slave Will. In 1649, the York County estate of James Stone claimed the indentures of five servants and also held two slaves, named Mingo and Emmanuel.[102] In 1661, the York County estate of the late William Hughes was worked by the English servants William Barton, John Clarke, George White, Thomas Arnupp, Mary Shelly, Thomas Collier, John Lambert, William Cuerton, and Alice Richardson, as well as "One Negro woman" and "One negro girle of about 5 yeares old."[103] The inventory of the late John Hansford listed four slaves, named Silver, Julian, Penney, and Besse, as well as servants William Collis, John March, Edmund Lockwood, Thomas Walker, John Lucas, Andrew, Mary Bennett, and Ursula Naylor. In 1668, the estate of John Croshaw possessed three English servant women, one English servant child, five slave women, one slave man, and two slave girls. And in 1669, Mathew Collins acquired a 650-acre headright for importing twelve servants and "Maria a Negro."[104]

Having originally introduced English colonists to tobacco, Indians had a continued role in its production on colonial Virginia plantations, laboring with African and English workers. For example, in 1671, Arthur Jordan of Surry County returned to Rowland Place three runaway slaves, "One Negro, one Maletto, and one Indian."[105] In 1678, Robert Caufield received a 350-acre headright for himself and six laborers, including "Jacob an Indyan" and "James a Negro."[106] In 1683, the Charles City County Court, assessing the property of Benjamin Harrison, adjudged "Sambo a Negro Servant" to be seven years old and "Franck an Indian Girle Servant" to be ten years old. The colonial planter James Blamore mobilized both Indian and African labor, as indicated in a court case brought by the slave Mingo. After Blamore died, his former slave Mingo claimed in the Charles City County Court that the executor of Blamore's estate Thomas Harrison "unjustly detains him a slave contrary to the last will and testament" of Blamore. As the case proceeded, it became clear that Blamore had ordered that "four year after my decease that my Negro man and Indian boy be free. If the law will then admit otherwise I give the Negro to my executor," naming Harrison and his wife Elianor to be executors of his estate. Mingo timed his case poorly, for Virginia had recently passed a law restricting slave emancipation, so the court decided against him. The fate of the Indian slave on Blamore's estate is uncertain.[107] These examples indicate that in the early years of colonial Virginia African slaves worked in forced labor camps next to Indian and English labor.

In colonial Virginia and Maryland, Africans experienced continuity by transplanting agricultural knowledge from Africa and finding similarities with English and Indian agriculture and experienced change through the process of adapting to new tools and environments. In the early years of colonial staple food production, the English acquired through observation, trade, and force the agricultural models, crops, and labor of Indians. A number of features defined food crop production among the indigenous population. They cleared the fields using swidden or slash-and-burn techniques, which they followed with other agricultural practices. Native American communities mobilized women's labor in their agricultural fields, where they grew multiple crops of maize. They intercropped other plants such as beans and squash, which "have qualities that make them mutually symbiotic." Agricultural production was labor intensive, requiring workers to till mounds as beds for the crops and to constantly weed the fields.[108] Slaves entered this world, which was different from their material life in Africa in some respects but alike in others. African women in Virginia, in particular, had grounds to connect with Indian women in the agricultural fields. In West and West Central Africa, they incorporated maize into their fields, and captives from maize-growing regions saw a familiar sight in Virginia. Perhaps for this reason, during a time of scarcity when only wheat was available the slaves of William Byrd became weak and asked him "to allow them Indian corn again, or they could not work."[109] Like people on the Middle Passage and in the British Caribbean, Africans in colonial Virginia shaped the contours of food consumption.

This process continued with the growing influx of slaves from the Caribbean and directly from Africa. During the years of Atlantic trade through which Africans adopted New World crops, West and West Central Africa fed colonial Virginia with slaves who had been exposed to American agriculture before being taken captive. Some, such as the two captives that William Byrd I sought to enslave on his plantation in 1686, never made it to Virginia plantations alive. Others survived, fought off diseases such as smallpox, and lived off the land. The survival of slaves was not guaranteed, nor was the productivity of their crops, which depended not only on human labor but also on acts of nature. For example, in the spring of 1686 Byrd feared that he would lose his corn and tobacco crops to heavy rain.[110] When the weather was more favorable to agriculture, food production in Virginia revolved around maize production, as indicated in the records of colonial planters.

Slaves in Virginia used labor-intensive methods to till the soil and intercropped New World plants. These practices caught the eye of William Hugh Grove, who entered the mainland aboard a slave ship. Grove noticed in Virginia that slaves cultivated a wide range of food crops besides the tobacco they produced for planters. As Grove recalled, planters allowed slaves to "plant little plottes for potatoes or Indian pease, {?} wch they do on Sundays or night for they work from Sun rising to setting 6000 plants of Tobacco wch wil make 1000£ beside their share of corn is a slaves task."

They also cultivated pumpkins and ginger. To till the soil, added Grove, "they don't generally plow ye land but manage it with ye Broad Hough."[111] Bent over cereals, legumes, and root crops and tending the soil with hoes rather than plows, African and Indian agricultural workers had parallel practices.

While the bulk of food production revolved around maize, slaves incorporated the American sweet potato into their diet because of its availability and its similarity to West African yams. To protect their crops from rotting, slaves from southeastern Nigeria dug root cellars, a practice common to African, English, and Indian agriculturalists. This storage method continued into the nineteenth century, as Frederick Douglass noted about his grandmother Betsey Bailey. As a nurse, agriculturalist, and fisherwoman, Bailey held the respect of her fellow slaves. Douglass noted that she "was a gardener as well as a fisherwoman, and remarkable for her success in keeping her seedling sweet potatoes through the months of winter, and easily got the reputation for being born to 'good luck.' In planting time Grandmother Betsey was sent for in all directions, simply to place the seedling potatoes in the hills or drills; for superstition had it that her touch was needed to make them grow." Like African priestesses who received offerings for blessing the agricultural fields of their clients, Betsey Bailey garnered a portion of the crops from the slaves she helped. She also stored her crops in root cellars. Douglass recalled that in the dirt floor of her two-story cabin was "a hole so strangely dug in front of the fireplace, beneath which grandmamma placed her sweet potatoes, to keep them from frost in winter."[112] Born to "good luck," Betsey Bailey was revered by her fellow slaves for her agricultural knowledge, which she had inherited from previous generations.

A similar process unfolded in early colonial South Carolina, where English, African, and Indian laborers worked the agricultural fields. British colonial planners directed the unfree black and white workers to plant a number of food crops and told them that "the proper season to plant corn & Beanes & Pease you will be informed by ye Natives." As in Virginia, colonists depended upon Indians for their knowledge and for food provisions, with the native population helping them "cleare and plant their land." Over time, the early agricultural fields would reflect the diversity of the labor force, with American crops such as tobacco, potatoes, and maize being grown in addition to Old World crops including sugarcane, English peas, wheat, ginger, and yams. One colonist noted within the first decade of the colony's settlement that "Guiney corne growes very well here."[113]

Indeed, many people remarked on the introduction of African crops into the Lowcountry. Thomas Jefferson recounted that "the African negroes brought over to Georgia a seed which they call Beni, & the botanists, Sesamum." African descendants in coastal Georgia made similar observations. For example, Rosanna Williams recounted that her African-born father would "plant mostly benne and rice." Emma Hunter also remembered that her grandmother planted benne.[114] Africans introduced other crops into colonial North America as well. The early eighteenth-century British natural historian Mark Catesby stated that guinea corn "was at first introduced from Africa by the Negroes."[115] Other colonial elites procured African crops via the Caribbean. For example, one colonial South Carolina planter received a sample of yams from a West Indian planter.[116] As in the Caribbean, slave gardens and provision grounds were essential to slaves, and they used them as sites to transplant African crops in the Lowcountry.[117]

Either by way of West Indian networks or directly from Africa, African crops and the people who grew them shaped the agricultural landscape of the major slaveholding colonies of the mainland. However, African labor's influence did not end at the level of crops. The most important of these contributions would be their rice production knowledge system, which consisted of experience with an indigenous West African red rice (*Oryza glaberrima*); water and saline level management skills that involved constructing banks and sluices; expertise with rice cultivation in tidal floodplains, inland swamps, and upland areas; and the production of tools such as the long-handled hoe (*kayendo*), mortar and pestle, and woven fanner baskets for separate phases of production.[118] The rice fields of colonial South Carolina and elsewhere in the Americas resulted from the expertise that West Africans brought across the Atlantic, leading planters to actively seek out slaves from the Senegambia region of West Africa, commonly known by colonial elites for yielding people experienced in rice cultivation.[119]

As with other crops, rice production was contingent upon a number of factors, including labor and the proper environmental conditions. The South Carolina indigo and rice plantation owner Peter Manigault wrote in 1768 that "the rice was planted, and after it was up, was great part destroyed by a kind of Caterpillar."[120] In some years, such as in 1762, it could be stifled by drought, while in 1771 it was harmed by excessive rain.[121] Yet rice production continued. Throughout the eighteenth century, particularly in the second half, South Carolina planters funneled slaves directly from West Africa onto their rice plantations. In 1765, the South Carolina planter Peter Manigault wrote, "I bought some of the New Negroes early in the Spring. I directed 30 Acres of Rice more than was planted last Year, to be planted at each of the Savannas by which means I hope you will make 150 Barrels of Rice extraordinary, to help pay for the Negroes." And in 1771, he wrote, "I bought 55 fine Gambia Negroes of Brewton. They consisted of 20 Men 20 Women and 15 Boys & Girls, & they are all settled at the Savannas."[122] Slaves from Upper Guinea's rice region also toiled on the Ball family plantation, where on their Cominge plantation Gambian slaves named Hamshair, Paul, Black Jack, Will, Harrey, Quash, London, Scipio, Doctor, Portius, York, Polydore, Eboney, and Natt were enslaved.[123]

Africans in the Carolinas had other skills that were mobilized to open up plantations. Slaves came from the Senegambia rice region, and they also emerged from places such as the Akan or Central African forests, where they had periodically cleared forests to open up fields for agricultural production.[124] Africans from these regions held knowledge that would be important on the Carolina frontier. They continued to practice swidden agriculture, which was described by Catesby. He witnessed that after slaves cut down trees, the timber was "piled in heaps, and burned, the trunks being left to rot. . . . In the meantime maize, rice, etc. is sown between the prostrate trees." The ashes fertilized the soils, which in West and West Central Africa were so thin that they demanded agriculturalists to use hoes rather than plows as their primary tool, a practice that slaves continued in the Carolinas. Catesby remarked that slaves used no "other tillage than with an hoe, to raise the earth where the grain is dropped." The Scottish woman Janet Schaw, who visited colonial North Carolina on the eve of the American Revolution, recounted that "the only instrument used is the hoe."[125]

Over time, the process of agricultural production changed, and plantations synthesized different agricultural practices. One clearly sees this in the South Carolina backcountry at the time of the American Revolution. On the estate of Samuel Matthias, slaves raised English garden crops including lettuce, cabbage, and mustard plants, and they also cultivated Indian corn. They worked the fields with plows, something Africans and their descendants learned in the New World. Yet they simultaneously continued to work the fields with the more labor-intensive hoe, which was not a central tool in English agriculture, and they raised potatoes in mounds, so that their fields resembled the root crop fields of West and West Central Africa.[126]

In conclusion, African agricultural workers were accustomed to using a combination of methods to produce crops on fragile soils. These methods included keeping kitchen gardens, using crop mixtures, clearing the fields with slash-and-burn agricultural methods, fertilizing the soil with the ashes, and employing hand tillage to manage the fields. During the years of the slave trade, West and West Central African agriculture underwent significant change, incorporating crops from the New World. The agricultural knowledge slaves had acquired in their home environments in Africa as part of their daily lives proved important in their process of adaptation to the Americas. In cases where their owners gave them little or no food, they had the skills to survive. And in the process they enriched the economies and transformed the material landscape of the English colonies. The following chapter will further explore this question by looking specifically at the role of Africans in American cotton and tobacco production.

3

Cultivating Knowledge

African Tobacco and Cotton Workers
in Colonial British America

> Slowly but mightily these black workers were integrated into modern industry. On free and fertile land Americans raised, not simply sugar as a cheap sweetening, rice for food and tobacco as a new tickling luxury; but they began to grow a fiber that clothed the masses of a ragged world.
>
> —W. E. B. Du Bois, *Black Reconstruction* (1835)

The remains from slave quarters and burial grounds point to the role that Africans played in material production in the British American colonies. West and West Central Africans, working in the Anglo-American tobacco fields, left behind tobacco pipes that have been unearthed in the Chesapeake region and Barbados. In the tobacco colony of Maryland, slaves placed a tobacco pipe in the grave of a departed woman to take on her ancestral journey. And while tobacco had faded as an export crop from Barbados, slaves still cultivated and consumed it on a small scale well into the eighteenth century. There, slaves left a pipe in the grave of an African diviner, which he carried into the ancestral realm. Produced in Africa or the Americas, the pipes carried distinctive African motifs. Paralleling the presence of clay pipes, an artifact unearthed from a colonial South Carolina archeological site represents the work of Africans in the Diaspora.[1] On the colonial South Carolina Howell plantation, slaves left behind an African ceramic spinning tool.[2] These findings, significant alone, indicate that Africans in the Anglo-American colonies had experience with cotton and tobacco cultivation. African captives entered colonial worlds where Indian and English workers grew these crops on a commercial scale, yet in every case Africans took over the primary role of raising them. And as with their knowledge of staple food production, Africans brought cultural capital to the New World that fostered cotton and tobacco production in the Anglo-American colonies.

The slaves who crafted these material goods lived in a violent world of mass agricultural production. While Africans by no means transplanted their agricultural knowledge into the Americas wholesale, the written record clearly indicates that many enslaved people from Africa had previous experience with tobacco and cotton. During the years of the Atlantic slave trade, agriculturalists in West and West Central Africa incorporated tobacco production and consumption into their daily lives, integrating the American crop into their routine agricultural practice and social life. Tobacco consumption expanded in West Africa from the sixteenth century onward along parallel and at times converging paths. Along one route, tobacco grown on American plantations entered West Africa through the Atlantic trade. At the turn of the eighteenth century, it was not unusual for Portuguese, French, or English merchants to find markets for American tobacco on the Gold or Slave Coast, where in some cases they traded the leaves for slaves.[3] While imports from the Americas met part of West Africa's demand, local tobacco production expanded concurrently. "Tobacco is planted about every mans house," noted the British merchant William Finch, who arrived in Upper Guinea in the early seventeenth century.[4] Shortly thereafter, the British commercial agent Richard Jobson noted about people in the same region that "onely one principall thing, they cannot misse, and that is their Tabacco pipes, whereof there is few or none of them, be they men or women[,] doth walke or go without." Echoing Finch, Jobson added that tobacco "was ever growing about their houses."[5]

In the seventeenth and eighteenth centuries, tobacco plants and seeds moved through established trading networks and became part of West African material life. In the shadows of the British trading and military castle at Cape Coast in the late seventeenth century, women traders sold "Country tobacco" in the town's bustling market.[6] People in what is now southeastern Nigeria, Olaudah Equiano tells us, grew "vast quantities" of tobacco.[7] A British official noted in the 1760s about the Senegambia region "that it abounds in prodigious quantities of Wax, Rice, Cotton, Indigo, and Tobacco," and the Scottish traveler Mungo Park made similar observations at the end of the century.[8] The maintenance and expansion of tobacco culture required skilled cultivation, which was described by a nineteenth-century observer in the Senegambian town of Nomou: "The people take great pains in cultivating it. They first sow the seeds in beds, and when the plant has attained a certain growth, they transplant it; for this purpose they prepare the ground by two diggings, and dividing it into little squares, the plants of tobacco are there placed at a distance of eighteen inches asunder; they are watered twice a day, there being wells for that purpose near the plantations."[9] The way that Senegambians transplanted tobacco from seedbeds to other fields paralleled rice production methods. And African women's skills in crafting ceramic bowls for eating and cooking rice dishes translated into making tobacco pipes, for while they imported some clay pipes through the Atlantic trade they also relied upon local manufacture. Drawing on practical and artistic skills that they employed to produce earthenware, sculptures, and other forms, local potters shaped and fired clay pipes for tobacco smoking from the seventeenth century on.[10] First cultivated as a garden crop near their housing compounds, later developed on larger scales and stuffed into locally manufactured tobacco pipes, tobacco was part of the material life of West African workers.

Concurrent with its spread in West Africa, tobacco entered the Central African agricultural world during the height of the Atlantic slave trade. By the early seventeenth century, tobacco arrived in West Central Africa, with women playing a prominent role in its development. As with maize and other American crops, tobacco seeds "were at first planted in little plots near the houses where women could watch their growth."[11] From these garden plots tobacco production expanded, with seeds and plants passing through local and more long-range exchange networks. Some communities came to specialize in tobacco production and by the nineteenth century grew enough for export. And as in West Africa, tobacco transformed other dimensions of Central African material life, particularly clay pipe production.[12] During the years of the Atlantic slave trade, both West and West Central Africans had incorporated tobacco into their daily lives, and it is from such contexts that they landed on American tobacco estates.

Africans moved into environments already under cultivation by English and Indian labor. The tobacco plantations of the early British American islands first relied heavily upon English laborers, who crossed the Atlantic as tenant farmers or indentured servants. In the process of claiming Bermuda after the first British colonists landed on the island in 1609, officials from the Somers Island Company leased land to tenant farmers or had indentured servants sent to the island. In 1615, the English servant

Edward Dun wrote to colonial authorities in England, hoping for a small grant of land to cultivate tobacco, and tobacco fields opened on the island.[13] In these early years of tobacco production in the British Americas, planters also used African workers, and at least one of them had a reputation for his agricultural knowledge. The colonist Robert Rich asked his brother Nathaniel to send a slave named Francisco to the island because of "his judgement in the cureing of tobackoe."[14] Francisco came out of a Central African material environment where tobacco production was spreading, much as it was on the island.[15] So with a combination of English and African labor, tobacco production in Bermuda arose.

Cultivated by English and Native American labor, tobacco grew on a number of British Caribbean islands, including Nevis, Jamaica, and Barbados. It arrived in Barbados in 1626 with the first expedition by the British, who carried Indian laborers along with tobacco plants from the mainland to the island. Tobacco growing expanded in Barbados despite the competition the island faced from other British colonies and the problem of overproduction. Tenant farmers, who were heavily in arrears, argued that the only way to pay off their debts was by growing tobacco. As a result, it remained an export crop for decades, even though colonial elites cautioned against it.[16] Around midcentury Barbados had areas of regional agricultural specialization, with over two thousand acres of land farmed by "poor Catholiquos" who raised tobacco on the northwestern part of the island.[17]

In the following decades, colonial planters relied more heavily on slaves to work the island's tobacco fields.[18] During this period of transition to slave labor, tobacco production was expanding on both sides of the Atlantic, so a number of Africans in Barbados would have had experience with the crop. Some of the tobacco produced in Barbados was intended for local use. Father Antoine Biet noted in the mid–seventeenth century that "tobacco is only produced on the island for the use of the English and the slaves who are given some time off when working, in addition to the meal time, to rest and smoke tobacco."[19] Placing limits on the demands of their owners, Africans received temporary relief from the pain of agricultural labor by consuming some of the tobacco they grew. On other plantations, planters drove their slaves to cultivate tobacco on a scale large enough for export. For example, the African majority on Thomas Modiford and William Hilliard's Barbados plantation worked alongside English and Indian laborers to cultivate thirty acres of tobacco land. But while tobacco provided an early opportunity for Barbadian planters, it could not compete in quality with tobacco produced elsewhere.[20] As it exhausted the island's soil, one contemporary complained that Barbadian tobacco was becoming "earthy and worthless"; it could not match the quality of competitors such as Virginia, which had a greater supply of fresh lands to grow the crop.[21] By the middle of the 1660s, tobacco was no longer an important cash crop on the island: its value was being outstripped by sugar, and it constituted less than 1 percent of exports.[22] Tobacco exports from Barbados gradually declined in the second half of the seventeenth century as sugar and other crops pushed the leaf off the island as a major export.[23] But before then, a generation of planters had depended on enslaved Africans to carry on production of the labor-intensive tobacco plant, a crop that a substantial number of them probably already knew how to grow and that they continued to grow for domestic consumption into the eighteenth century.[24]

Other British Caribbean islands went down a similar path. Tobacco became one of the commercial crops of Nevis during the early years of the British colony there, and by the second half of the seventeenth century in Jamaica tobacco was said to be "so good, that the Merchants give Six pence a Pound for it, and buy it faster than the planters can make it."[25] The island continued to produce tobacco on small scales after the decline of indentured labor there and the expansion of the African labor force, with slaves producing it into the eighteenth century. Describing the skills required to grow tobacco, the naturalist Hans Sloane wrote that the slaves planted it alongside indigo, and he described its requirements:

It is sown in Beds: when the Leaves are about two Inches long, the Plants are drawn, and planted at four Foot distance one way, and three and an half another, then they are kept clean, and when grown about a Foot high, and going to shoot out their Stalks or Tops, the top of the Stalk or Bud is snipt off. That day seven night the Buds rising *ex alis foliorum* on the sides, are snipt off likewise, and seven days thence the other Underbuds. It stands some time longer, and then the Stalks and Leaves are cut off, hang'd up in a Shed, and if wet weather come, a Fire is made in it to hinder the Corruption of the Tobacco. Some time after the Leaves are stript off and preserv'd in great heaps from the injuries of the Air till 'tis made fit for the Market.[26]

Sloane added that the slaves' tobacco-related skills were not limited to methods of cultivation but extended to a knowledge of its medical uses. He reported how an African woman, described as "a Queen in her own

Country," had treated a "Chego," a flea that infects the skin and plants eggs that can multiply if not removed, by piercing "the Skin with a Pin above the swelling, and carefully separat[ing] the Tumour from the Skin, and then pull[ing] it out, putting into the Cavity whence it came, some Tobacco Ashes which were burnt in a Pipe she was smoking. After a very small smarting it was cured."[27] She had most likely learned this skill from an Amerindian woman.[28]

Slave-based tobacco production continued in the British Caribbean into the eighteenth century, with colonists mapping tobacco onto their possessions. In the 1720s, one of the Bahaman islands was said to be a "fine Island for oranges, Lemons, pomgranatts, ffiggs—cotton Tobacco Indigo."[29] Planters on the island of St. Vincent, where sugar production predominated, still devoted five hundred acres to tobacco production in 1783.[30] Building on precedents set by Indian and English laborers, the constant waves of African forced laborers who landed in the Caribbean continued to make tobacco a viable crop, one that they had had experience growing before landing in the Americas.

The first wave of forced migrants to early colonial Virginia from Africa worked in the maize and tobacco fields next to Indian and English laborers. As in the Caribbean, Chesapeake planters used their enslaved Africans not only for their physical labor but also for their experience with tobacco cultivation, so Francisco of Bermuda probably had Virginia counterparts. When planters in Virginia made the transition from indentured servitude to slavery after Bacon's Rebellion in 1676, they imported over one hundred thousand slaves from the Senegambia region, the Bight of Biafra, the Gold Coast, and West Central Africa. Nearly half the slaves brought to Virginia came from the Bight of Biafra, and a similar percentage from the Senegambia region landed in Maryland in the eighteenth century.[31] And as demonstrated above, merchants on the West African coast and figures such as Olaudah Equiano recounted that tobacco production was fairly widespread in these regions. As a result, planters would have had to provide little to no training in tobacco production to slaves from these parts of Africa.

Like food crops, tobacco had seasonal rhythms of production. The labor force went into the fields in March to prepare the land by felling trees and burning brushwood on the soil, a practice similar to Amerindian and West and West Central African land clearing and fertilizing methods. By May, they sowed the seeds in the soils nourished with the remaining ashes. They then weeded the soil and transplanted the plants after they were about two inches high. Concurrently, workers prepared the soil that received the transplanted plants by "digging holes of about a foot square, and as deep, three feet apart every way, in rows." Then laborers returned the loosened soil into the holes, building hills into which they transplanted the young plants. Over the following months, workers weeded the plants, "topped" and "succoured" them (i.e., removed their top and secondary leaves), and finally judged the proper time for cutting them. Under the management of their owners or overseers, they then cured and "stripped" the leaves and packed them into hogsheads for the market.[32]

With the transition from indentured servitude to slavery, British American colonial tobacco plantations continued to thrive, with many workers bringing experience with the crop across the Atlantic Ocean. By the seventeenth century, tobacco had become an Atlantic World crop, not only because of tobacco shipments from the Americas to Europe but also because of the spread of tobacco seeds and the crop's cultivation in Africa. During the years of the Atlantic slave trade, African agriculturalists, particularly women, from the Senegambia region to West Central Africa incorporated tobacco into their agricultural fields. From these African tobacco-growing regions, Virginia, Maryland, and other Anglo-American colonies drew a substantial portion of their labor force for their tobacco plantations. Africans not only maintained and expanded tobacco production in the colonies but also shaped other areas of tobacco plantation development. For instance, they applied their experience as woodworkers and boatmen to the commercial development of tobacco.[33] Drawing on their woodworking skills and knowledge about storage units, coopers made barrels for the dried tobacco and carpenters constructed curing barns and sheds to store the hogsheads before planters shipped them off.[34] In a system of unfree labor that maintained a high level of production and quality of tobacco, Africans and their descendants fostered the economic development of the British colonies. And they left reminders of their role in the agricultural fields through tobacco pipes that they interred with the dead.

During its development into a plantation economy, colonial Virginia revolved around tobacco and slavery much as the British Caribbean revolved around sugar and slavery. On the margins, slaves cultivated food crops, raised staples, and used agricultural techniques from West and West Central Africa. And while cotton plantations boomed in the antebellum South, the Anglo-American colonies produced cotton as well, both for domestic consumption and for export. The production of cotton, like that of tobacco, rice, maize, and guinea corn, was familiar to West

Africans. Several accounts written during the years of the Atlantic slave trade reveal the extent of African cotton textile production. Cotton cultivation and textile production date back well before the fifteenth-century arrival of the Portuguese on the Atlantic coast of Africa, and by the time they began trading on the Guinea Coast, cotton already pervaded much of West Africa. Like tobacco and food crop production in the Americas, cotton cultivation in the British colonies was stimulated by the labor of Africans who had mastery over the crop.

Cotton and its products helped define the political, economic, social, and cultural life of West Africa, from the Senegambia region to the Bight of Biafra and from the coast into the interior. African cotton production caught the attention of European traders who saw from West Africans' agricultural fields, workshops, markets, and clothing styles that these people were accustomed to cotton, even though they also imported textiles from European merchants. Many of them, through trade, observation, and interaction along the Guinea Coast, came to reflexively associate West Africa with cotton.[35] European merchants encountered cotton crops and cloth production during their early years of contact with West Africans. For example, the Venetian merchant Alvise Cadamosto wrote in the mid–fifteenth century that in the Senegambia region "the chiefs and those of standing wear a cotton garment—for cotton grows in these lands. Their women spin it into cloth of a span in width." Cadamosto recounted that men also spun cotton, and he added that men and women traveled from a radius of up to five miles to sell cotton produce, thread, and textiles at coastal periodic markets, open on Mondays and Fridays.[36] Also, the Portuguese sailor Pacheco Pereira suggested that the Gola produced cotton farther down the coast in Sierra Leone and Liberia.[37]

Early English merchants made similar observations along the coast. Richard Jobson, representing the British after they increased their ties with West Africa, left a record of cotton cultivation in Upper Guinea. He reported that "with great carefulness, they prepare the ground, to set the seedes of the Cotton wooll, whereof they plant whole fields, and coming up, as Roses grow, it beareth coddes, and as they ripen, the codde breaketh and the wooll appeareth, which shewes the time of gathering."[38] While something of a novelty to early English traders, cotton was fairly commonplace in West African material life. Hoping to take advantage of this, European trading companies sought to develop cotton plantations in West Africa, where the crop was already well established on its own terms. These efforts failed, primarily because Africans effectively resisted outside efforts to control trade, land, or labor. At this moment, effective European control over African labor could be had only in the Americas.[39]

Though they realized the extent of local textile production, European merchants sought to tap into West African markets, selling textiles to its commercial and political elites. But despite the opening of its markets to Asian and European textiles, West African cotton cultivation and textile production remained viable.[40] The European trade failed to dislodge local production, which was carried out on a wide range of scales and required specific production techniques and skills. For example, textile workers in the coastal village of Keta just to the east of the Volta River produced textiles on a small scale in the early eighteenth century, a time of significant social change. During this period, pressures from the Akwamu and Asante states to the northwest, waves of migration into the region, and opportunities for trade with Europeans on the coast altered gender and ethnic relationships in Keta and neighboring communities.[41] Yet in the face of these commercial and political transformations, textile workers continued to carry out textile production within the context of kinship units. In 1718, a Dutch commercial agent witnessed "a large number of children and men constantly busy spinning cotton" on spindles "of about a foot in length." He added, "They said they collected this cotton in order to maintain their children." Within this social arena of kinship relationships, youth came to embody textile production skills.[42]

Keta's textile production was carried out largely in response to kinship demands, but in other parts of West Africa textile workers produced for regional markets or to fulfill taxation requirements. In the Gonja state, fabrics entered internal and regional markets and satisfied levies imposed by the Asante Empire during its eighteenth-century northern expansion. In meeting market and political demands, textile producers worked within gender divisions of labor, with women producing the raw cotton and thread and men weaving it into fabrics. For instance, in the Gonja town of Bole, women collected and ginned the cotton, which was locally grown or acquired from the town of Bonduku to the west. Using a tool called a *karadea*, women textile producers spun the cotton fibers into yarn and took it to local male weavers, who accepted some of the yarn as payment for their workmanship.[43]

Women were instrumental in West African textile production. More often than not, African women performed the labor of cotton cultivation and spinning. For example, textile production in the city of Kano depended upon the labor of free and unfree women to cultivate the raw materials and transform the cotton into thread. One observer in the early nineteenth century described the task of ginning the cotton, stating that the women placed "a quantity of [cotton] on a stone, or a piece of board, along which [were twirled] two slender iron rods about a foot in length."[44] Whereas in Keta men played a role in spinning cotton, in Senegambia women working within their household compound spun locally cultivated cotton into thread; according to one estimate in the eighteenth century, the most productive workers spun enough cotton thread in one year to make six to nine garments. They turned the thread over to male artisans who wove it into five- to six-inch strip cloths, which when sewed together created cloths measuring three by one and one half yards. Women were also responsible for growing, cultivating, and processing indigo, dyeing the cloth, and entering the cloth into trade.[45]

While a clear gender division of labor restricted women from occupations such as weaving, some women exercised considerable social power and could accumulate substantial wealth through the textile trade. As accounts from the nineteenth century suggest, women traders traveled throughout the countryside to buy cotton from local peasants, thereby achieving a degree of autonomy not realized by women bound to labor for others.[46] And modern ethnography shows how women exercised power by managing cotton production, which they did through distinct gender and class divisions of labor. For example, in some Senegambian communities one's social status depended upon, among a number of factors, membership in one of three basic classes: *rim e* (free persons), *nyeenybe* (persons of skill), and *rimaybe* (bondspersons). The *rim e*, especially the Muslim clerics, controlled the vast majority of the land, cultivated primarily by *rimaybe*. Also, *rim e*, particularly women from the major cleric households, controlled cotton production and devoted their premium land to that crop. To cultivate, harvest, and process the cotton, *rim e* mobilized *rimaybe*, with women undertaking "all stages of production, from planting to weeding and finally harvesting, except for clearing of land." After the harvest, they ginned and spun the cotton into thread, and the free women sold it to local weavers in exchange for cloth, which free women in turn marketed or used to consolidate their patronage networks.[47]

From Senegambian villages and towns and from other regions, the labor of textile producers moved into local and regional West African markets. For instance, Senegambian communities exported their textiles by way of the Atlantic to Gold Coast markets.[48] Other textile producers traded over land. In the state of Wuli, where according to Mungo Park "the chief productions are cotton, tobacco," and other crops, the town of Sansanding housed a bustling textile market. The town, with a population of approximately eight thousand people, was located about ten miles from the town of Sego on the Niger River. In Sansanding's market, traders exchanged salt from the Sahara and beads from the Mediterranean for gold dust and West African textiles. Within this regional trading network, Sansanding specialized in textile production and through trade along the Niger was linked to Sego and Timbuktu. Within the towns, "each craft was the monopoly of an ethno-professional corporation." Workers from some towns had a monopoly on leather working, while workers in Sansanding held the monopoly on indigo dyeing. Interwoven through trade, these production centers exchanged raw materials, finished products, ideas, and knowledge.[49]

Like Sansanding, Kano supplied an extensive regional textile market. "The market is crowded," one early nineteenth-century English traveler recalled, "every day, not excepting their Sabbath, which is kept on Friday." Kano's regulated market stocked luxury items such as writing paper, silk, swords from the Mediterranean world, and West African crafts.[50] German physician Heinrich Barth, who surveyed West Africa in the mid–nineteenth century, "enumerated and described twenty different types of cloth made in Kano and other towns." Giving a sense of its scale, he stated that textile exports from Kano brought in an estimated three billion cowry shells in revenue. To place this in historical perspective, he stated that an annual income for a prosperous family was fifty to sixty thousand cowries.[51] Kano's textile industry fed into distant markets and required support from the agricultural sector of the economy, particularly supplies of cotton, indigo, and food staples.

Between Kano and the Bights of Benin and Biafra to the south, textile production and markets dotted the landscape. Cotton markets flourished in the city of Benin, the capital of the Benin Empire that in the sixteenth century and, later, in the eighteenth and nineteenth centuries supplied labor to American plantations. The empire's agricultural and craft workers supplied the Benin market with "much Cotton yarn, from which they make many clothes to clothe themselves."[52] Some used cotton for lamp wicks that lit the evening markets of coastal towns. Dutch merchants along the coast took note and hoped to tap into this textile market. Scouting prospects to export West African cotton, a Dutch trader along the Slave Coast stated that "cotton can be found everywhere, and a large quantity could be had if the Negroes did not use it themselves for weaving of cloth of various qualities."[53] People on the Benin Empire's periphery also grew the crop. "We have," noted Olaudah Equiano about his community, "plenty of Indian corn, and vast quantities of cotton and tobacco." He added that they produced cotton textiles, some to be used as bed linens and others for dress, consisting of "a long piece of calico or muslin." Equiano added, "This is usually dyed blue, which is our favourite colour."[54]

West Africans encountered cotton textiles in their daily lives, particularly in the large markets and trading networks that connected the landscape. During the years of the Atlantic slave trade, West Africans were surrounded by cotton.[55] In environments that ranged from the southern rain forests to the savannahs in the north, West African workers, often women and in many cases unfree, raised cotton for domestic consumption, trade, or tributary demands. The assiduous toil of cotton cultivation taxed their bodies while cotton cloth covered them. Cotton made up essential fibers of West African material life.

Paralleling the production of cotton in West Africa, cotton expanded in the British American colonies from the early seventeenth well into the eighteenth century. While sugar, rice, and tobacco became the most important exports from the Anglo-American colonies, cotton was also produced both for local consumption and for European markets. Cotton grew in southern European countries such as Spain, where Moors introduced it in the tenth century, and Italy, where it was introduced in the early fourteenth century, but it did not have a long history in England. By the middle of the sixteenth century, some English families cultivated and spun cotton for household consumption, but cotton was not very widespread.[56] So most English colonists in the Americas would have had little familiarity with the cotton plant. However, during the early years of their colonial projects, they looked to cotton as a possible commercial crop.

In the early years of their colonial project in Barbados, the English tapped into the knowledge and labor of Amerindians to raise cotton. Amerindians entered the island during the initial colonization of Barbados in 1627, carried out under the direction of the merchant William Courteen and Captain Henry Powell. Along with fifty Englishmen who migrated to the island, Powell enticed "32 Indians from the mayne" there "to assist and instructe the english to advance the said plantation." Powell also carried tobacco, sugarcane, potatoes, manioc, and cotton to Barbados.[57] Early authorities on the island complained that the island would not be able to maintain cotton as an export, with the planter Daniel Fletcher suggesting that most of the island would "not bear cotton" and that merely "one acre in ten" would yield the crop.[58] But despite such pessimism from some quarters, the island continued to produce cotton, cultivated by Indian, English, and African labor, and by 1640 cotton production was among the colony's most important enterprises.

At the same time that cotton production expanded in Barbados, the African workforce on the island increased. For example, the Barbados planters William Hilliard and Thomas Modiford relied upon slaves, who, as in West Africa, cultivated cotton alongside other crops on the partners' five-hundred-acre estate. Their ninety-six slaves, as well as three Indian women and their offspring, and twenty-eight "Christians," managed pasture land, raised food provisions, and cultivated two hundred acres of sugar, five acres of ginger, and five acres of cotton. The mixed labor force operated Hilliard and Modiford's four-thousand-square-foot carding house.[59]

The Hilliard and Modiford estate was but one of many cotton plantations in mid-seventeenth-century Barbados, when slave labor dominated the island, as the German indentured servant Alexander Heinrich von Uchteritz attested. Uchteritz, who worked in Barbados in 1652, later recalled that in the hills "they plant entire fields in cotton" and that "sugar, tobacco, ginger and cotton" were "produced in great quantities." It is significant that slaves grew cotton in the hills, for cotton is generally an upland, dry-soil plant. Uchteritz added, perhaps with a degree of exaggeration, that while English and Native American servants lived on Barbados plantations, "slaves must do all the work."[60] With many of them bringing experience with cotton cultivation from West Africa, the island's labor force sped up the development of that crop. Producing their own food, toiling on sugar plantations, or raising cotton, slaves proved to be a valuable asset to planters in several ways. As Father Antoine Biet stated about Barbados slaveholders, "Their greatest wealth is their slaves." In this way, Barbados slave society was not unlike parts of Equatorial Africa where people with knowledge constituted the basis for wealth.[61]

Slaveholders' control over their slaves yielded cotton exports. Even with the ascendancy of sugar production in the mid–seventeenth century, Barbados continued to produce cotton. In the 1660s, cotton fields, located primarily in the south and southeast of the island, covered over 15 percent of its 135,000 acres of arable land.[62] In 1665 and 1666, Barbados exported approximately 749 metric tons of cotton, valued at over 21,000 pounds sterling. Over the next three decades, exports declined, with the island exporting an estimated 78 metric tons (3,800 pounds sterling) in 1688, 1690, and 1691 and approximately 127 metric tons (8,000 pounds sterling) in 1699 and 1700. In the first three decades of the following century, mass cotton production was eventually phased out.[63]

Soon after colonizing Barbados, Englishmen turned to other Caribbean islands to extend plantation agriculture, particularly cotton, tobacco, and indigo production. For example, in May 1632, officials from the Company of Providence Island instructed Thomas Punt to recruit English labor to build plantations on the Bahaman Islands. Punt carried out the orders. He first passed through Barbados and other West Indian islands on the way to the Bahamas "to procure cotton seeds" and other provisions.[64] Decades later, British colonists in Barbados migrated to the Bahamas, taking slaves with them. For example, John Dorrell and Hugh Wentworth had established a plantation on New Providence Island by 1670. Their estate consisted of eight Africans and five English servants, and within a few years they had carved out a plantation. The island elite soon boasted about the possibilities for lucrative plantations, reporting that they were self-sufficient in food production and noting that the island was amenable to indigo. Dorrell and Wentworth also reported that the island "produceth as good Cotten as ever grew in America and gallant Tobacco."[65] Given this experience using slave labor, the Bahaman elite hoped to "persuade the people to plant provisions and ground for cattle and planting tobacco, indigo, and specially cotton."[66] While the Bahamas later became more oriented toward the sea and profited from salt manufacture, shipbuilding, turtling, timber production, and trading rather than agriculture, the slave population affected the islands' early economic development.[67]

In Jamaica, in contrast, elites turned not to the sea but to the land and looked to cotton as a commercial crop. By the early 1670s, Jamaican planters had established at least three cotton plantations, and as the century progressed cotton estates proliferated on the island. Favorable reports about Jamaican cotton arrived in England, leading the British geographer Richard Blome to write about the island that "cotton here hath an especial fineness, and is by all preferred before that of the Carribbee Isles."[68] Africans cleared the land and cultivated the soil, production grew apace, and cotton plantations dotted the island. Contemporary mapmakers indicated that by the middle of the 1680s cotton estates spread across the northern and southern coasts, with a concentration of cotton plantations in St. Elizabeth's parish, in the southwestern corner of the island.[69] By the end of the century, cotton plantations worked by African women and men ringed the mountainous island.

The input of labor from West Africa enabled Jamaica to develop a reputation for its cotton, which was sent to protected markets in England and on the North American mainland. As one writer observed, "The cotton not inferior to any in the Indies, they find by experience, it grows in the worst of land in the island, so it be within three or four miles of the sea in the southside, it being there warmest; the great product, and returns from New England, make it very profitable, especially to the middle sort of planter, that cannot compass a sugar work."[70] British geographer John Ogilby reported Jamaican cotton to be "very firm and substantial, and preferr'd before any that grows in the neighboring islands."[71] The Jamaican governor Thomas Lynch reported to the Lords of Trade and Plantation that "much cotton, sugar, indigo, &c. is made in the Island" and figured that "every Negro's labour that produces cotton . . . is worth twenty pounds to the Customs." He added, "It is impossible to hinder the importation of Negroes, for the Island is large and slaves as needful to a planter as money to a courtier, and as much coveted."[72] Yet another contemporary postulated that "if the Planters were furnished with Negroes from Africa, Answerable to their Industry, . . . four times the Sugar, Indico, Cotton, etc. would be Imported every Year."[73] Using African labor, Jamaican planters continued to export cotton into the eighteenth century. As a 1757 map of Jamaica by the French cartographer Jacques-Nicolas Bellin indicates, cotton production was concentrated in the northern parishes, particularly in St. Anne's and St. Marie's, signaling a shift from the more diffuse distribution of cotton plantations of the previous century.[74]

British Caribbean cotton production extended into the British Leeward Islands as well. Confronted by the capital- and labor-intensive demands of sugar production, British colonists with more modest means migrated to these islands hoping to establish a foothold in the Caribbean by investing in small-scale cotton estates. Cotton required less in start-up costs and though it was oriented toward economies of scale did not require as large a slave labor force as sugar. So operating on a comparatively smaller scale, colonists in the British Leewards turned toward cotton and slaves from Africa to work their plantations. For instance, planters in Anguilla and Tortola reaped the fruits of the labor of slaves, who outnumbered the free population by 1.5 to 1 by the early eighteenth century. On the basis of slave labor, the islands produced approximately one million pounds of cotton at midcentury.[75] On a consistent basis, ships laden with cotton left the British Caribbean islands; this enabled planters to buy more slaves who grew more cotton, a process that proved to be a boon to colonial elites throughout the eighteenth century. And with knowledge of the crop, African workers in the British Caribbean spun out worlds of cotton.

As cotton production expanded in the British Caribbean, the crop shaped the daily life, visual landscape, and contests over power on the islands where cotton grew. Throughout the British Caribbean, Africans and their descendants cultivated and ginned different varieties of the crop. In Jamaica, slaves cultivated a wide range of cotton seeds, including "Common Jamaica," which bore strong but coarse wool and was the least valuable; "Brown Bearded," which yielded finer fibers, had seeds that were tightly attached to the fibers, and was generally planted along with Common Jamaica; "Nankeen," similar to Brown Bearded cotton but with a different color fiber; "French," which produced fine fibers; and "Kidney or Brazilian," which generated plants with seeds that were easy to remove.[76] In the Bahamas and Anguilla, slaves cultivated Sea-Island cotton.[77]

Over the seventeenth century, enslaved Africans were fundamental to the rise of cotton plantations in the Anglo-American world, and by the following century colonial planters further systematized their fields and labor forces for mass cotton production and export. In allocating labor, they took a number of factors into consideration. They required slaves to cultivate sugarcane between October and December and to harvest it sixteen months later from January until May. During sugar's slack period from May through September, slaves cultivated cotton along with maize and other food crops.[78] As one planter noted, "Dryness, both in respect of the soil and atmosphere, is indeed essentially necessary in all its stages; for if the land is moist, the plant expends itself in branches and leaves, and if the rains are heavy, either when the plant is in blossom or when the pods are beginning to unfold, the crop is lost." For that reason and because of the demands on slave labor for sugar production during other times of the year, cultivation began in May so that the plant would mature after the heavy rains of the hurricane season had subsided. As with sugar production, planters envisioned their fields in linear form, suggesting that the ideal cotton plantation should have straight rows set eight feet apart with the plants being grown every four feet. Africans workers on the British Caribbean cotton plantations engaged in ongoing weeding of the soil and also "topped" the plants by breaking off an inch of the growing stems to increase the number of branches.[79]

They also employed gins to separate the seed from the fiber. While in West Africa workers manually rolled metal rods over cotton to gin the fiber, Caribbean cotton estates adopted mechanical gins from India. "The Instrument by which they separate the Seeds and Filth from the Cotton," noted Hans Sloane, "stands as a turning Loom, and is made of two, long, small, round, Cilinders of Wood, on which are three or four small Furrows; these have more or less Space between them, as the Master desires, but generally are so close, as only to suffer the fine Cotton to go thro', whereas the Seeds are kept back, and the Cotton is drawn by one of these Cilinders, and thrust away by the other, they being turned by the Feet two contrary Ways, one from the other."[80] Tapping into a global flow of labor and information, British Caribbean plantations combined agricultural and mechanical knowledge from across the Atlantic to yield cotton exports.

African workers in the Caribbean, already familiar with intercropping practices that included cotton production, helped transform Caribbean landscapes, and their know-how generated fortunes for British American colonial elites. Hoping to use their knowledge of cotton production to their advantage, some of the enslaved grew cotton in their provision grounds or garden plots, thereby adding to the material life of the slave quarters. For example, as in the markets of West Africa, Caribbean slaves used locally produced cotton for candle wicks.[81] And while they used cotton for domestic consumption, their efforts to market the crop met with planter resistance. Fearing competition from slaves or concerned that slaves might pilfer cotton from the main cotton fields, colonial assemblies throughout the British Caribbean prohibited slaves from selling cotton. For instance, in the late eighteenth century, Barbados levied fines on white colonists who bought ginger or cotton from slaves.[82]

Through their agricultural practices, Africans shaped the British Caribbean material landscape. As in West Africa, slaves cultivated combinations of food crops such as rice, maize, root crops, and sorghum to maximize yields from the soil. African workers in the Anglo-American colonies cultivated food for subsistence, and the fruits of their labor also entered into the larger Atlantic economy. On the margins of the sugar estates, they also grew cotton and tobacco, cultivating them for domestic consumption and as cash crops. In essence, the cultural capital that Africans embodied and carried across the ocean ultimately enriched Atlantic merchants and British Caribbean planters, and this process happened concurrently on the North American mainland.

During the first decades of colonial Virginia, the British tried a number of experiments with cotton, importing seeds from the Caribbean and the Mogul Empire. For instance, Governor Berkeley ordered his workers to plant tobacco, indigo, and "a considerable area of land in flax, hemp, and cotton."[83] Berkeley's slaves, who told him that they knew how to grow rice, probably had experience with cotton, indigo, and tobacco, which were raised simultaneously in West Africa's upland fields. Virginia's small-scale experiments with cotton continued into the late seventeenth and eighteenth centuries. And though tobacco dominated the colony's agricultural and social landscape, cotton grew in its shadows, particularly in periods when overproduction of tobacco led to a drop in prices and weakened the region's ability to import textiles from Great Britain. During such crises, colonial leaders hoped to substitute imported goods with local products. For instance, Edmund Andros, appointed governor of Virginia in 1692, embarked on plans to raise cotton and promote local textile manufacturing. Furthermore, under the administration of Lieutenant Governor Alexander Spotswood (1710–22), the colony became more self-sufficient in textile production. Addressing the Council of Trade, Spotswood noted that parts of the colony "have been forced into the same humour of planting cotton and Sowing Flax, and by mixing the first with their wool to supply the want of coarse Cloathing and Linnen, not only for the Negros, but for many of the poorer sort of house keepers."[84]

While Virginia's leaders saw domestic cotton textile production as a path to independence, cotton production depended, ironically, on slaves. On the plantations of Landon Carter, Thomas Jefferson, and George Washington, slaves, particularly slave women, produced textiles.[85] They were most likely supplied by locally grown cotton, which slaves grew in the interstices of the tobacco production schedule. After slaves cleared the fields for tobacco cultivation in early spring, prepared seedling tobacco plants, and transferred them to the furrowed soils in May, they in some cases shifted their labor toward cotton cultivation. As William Hugh Grove noted in his 1732 account of Virginia, "Cotton is planted Early in ye Spring in July & beginning of Aug." Taking advantage of the warmer and moister climate of the season, slaves worked the crop until the boll ripened and became ready to be harvested in October.[86] So as on Caribbean sugar plantations, Africans on Virginia's tobacco estates cultivated cotton during the slack periods.

Across the Chesapeake Bay on the Eastern Shore of Maryland, African laborers performed similar work on the colony's tobacco plantations. To meet the needs of their families, slaves apportioned small plots of land for cotton production. The Revolutionary economic booster Tench Coxe recounted that his mother Mary Francis had told him that "the cultivation of cotton, *on the garden scale—though not at all as a planter's crop,*—was intimately known and familiarly practised, even among the children of the white and black families, in the vicinity of *Easton* in the county of Talbot, on the Eastern Shore of Chesapeake Bay, so early as the year 1736."[87] During this era, when an influx of people entered Virginia and Maryland from the Senegambia region and the Bight of Biafra, colonial plantations experimented with small-scale cotton production. Used to growing cotton or wearing cotton textiles, African workers in the Chesapeake reproduced familiar worlds.

They played a comparable role in colonial South Carolina. Looking to precedents in Barbados, Jamaica, and other British Caribbean islands, the early settlers of South Carolina viewed cotton as one of several crops with commercial potential. Though some colonial planners thought that producing cotton in South Carolina would produce a glut in the world market, colonists persisted in their hopes and promoted cotton cultivation for domestic consumption or as a commercial crop. Scouting his prospects, Joseph West reported in 1671 that "the planters that came now from Barbados doe say that they doe not question but the ground will produce as good ginger, Cotton &c as they have in Barbados." The early British colonist Maurice Mathews recounted that "Guiney Corne growes very well here, butt this being ye first I euer planted ye perfection I will not Auer till ye Winter doth come in, ginger thriues wll butt ye perfection &c. Cotton growes freely butt ye perfection &c."[88] The demise of cotton cultivation in Barbados fueled hopes for cotton production in South Carolina. For example, in the early eighteenth century one observer found that in the colony, "Flax and Cotton thrive admirably."[89] Africans forced into the colony in the earliest years of British settlement constituted from one-fourth to one-third of the colonial population in the 1670s, and they performed a considerable amount of the field work.[90]

Over the late seventeenth and early eighteenth centuries, the slaves' largest contribution would be in transplanting rice production knowledge systems from Africa, but they also cultivated cotton on small scales to meet domestic clothing needs. For example, slaves on the Lucas estate raised cotton for the plantation. Eliza Lucas's plantation records indicate that the estate held workers from the Gold Coast and a carpenter named Sogo, probably from Africa. They raised a combination of crops, as Lucas wrote to her father on the efforts on the plantation in July 1740. She reported the estate's efforts to "bring the Indigo, Ginger, Cotton and Lucerne and Casada to perfection."[91] Within four years, cotton production had expanded so much that the plantation overseer requested two cotton cards and reported, "We shall have Cotton to make a good part of the cloaths but a grate deal of trouble for want of a gine." Indeed, her slave Sogo built the plantation's cotton-weaving loom.[92] Though it had first been primarily a rice plantation, the estate mobilized its African and American-born labor force to produce cotton.

Lucas was one of several Lowcountry planters who used their slaves to raise cotton. During the wave of forced migration from Upper Guinea to South Carolina and Georgia, the region's slaves churned out cotton. By midcentury it was well rooted, leading the doctor and naturalist Alexander Garden to note that "*Gossipium*, grows extreamly well, and yields very fine Cotton," and to add that slave women, particularly elderly women, played a prominent role in spinning the fiber.[93] In some cases, it is clear that planters hired white artisans to train their slave labor force in textile production. For example, during the early years of the American Revolution, one planter reportedly hired a white woman to instruct slaves on how to use the spinning wheel and a white man to train slaves in weaving.[94] In other cases, the work that slaves did in the Lowcountry more closely paralleled West African patterns. As in the Senegambia region, slaves grew rice and cotton simultaneously in the Lowcountry. Henry Laurens reported that on his Broughton Island, Georgia, plantation his slaves grew "fine Rice, Corn, Pease, Hemp, and Cotton."[95]

During the Revolution, cotton production expanded in South Carolina and Georgia, where Africans and their descendants grew cotton and subsistence crops to survive the crisis. For example, the South Carolina planter Ralph Izard, who was in Europe on the eve of the Revolution, requested that his plantation manager Henry Laurens have his slaves plant cotton to make their own textiles, given the colonial boycott on English imports. John Lloyd reported to Izard that "cotton is produced in such plenty, *that considerable quantities may be bought*. Mr. Heyward, who I suppose has as many negroes as any gentleman in the State—makes clothing sufficient for their service." And while one colonial figure suggested that workers from France be sent to the colony to set up cotton manufacturing, most of the work done during the Revolutionary period in cotton production was performed by the enslaved.[96] Shortly after the war, the United States considered a range of economic alternatives to help the new nation stay afloat and maintain its independence from Great Britain. Having found themselves dependent upon fluctuations in British markets for tobacco and rice during the colonial era, the leaders of the new republic searched for other exports. Among a number of available choices, they looked to and eventually decided upon cotton production to meet the nation's commercial needs.[97] Prompted by technological innovations in cotton processing and manufacturing, the United States could also look to a history of cotton cultivation in the colonial era. In worlds dominated by rice, indigo, wheat, and tobacco, indentured servants, free farmers, and enslaved workers produced cotton for domestic consumption or for export. These initial experiments, in which African workers played a significant role, established foundations upon which the new nation eventually built.

In a number of different contexts, the enslaved in the North American mainland colonies reproduced African agricultural practices. Africans and their descendants in North America, as in the Caribbean, raised crops and employed production methods that turned the agricultural scene into one that resembled West Africa. Some colonial officials took note, acknowledging the contributions of Africans to colonial agriculture, while others more unwittingly relied upon it. Through the cultural capital and knowledge systems that they embodied, Africans shaped the agricultural landscape of the colonial British North American mainland in several ways. They grew food crops, tobacco, and cotton. They also produced textiles, and their knowledge of that craft included indigo production, the subject of the next chapter.

4

In an Ocean of Blue

*West African Indigo Workers in
the Atlantic World to 1800*

The forests gave way before them, and extensive verdant fields,
richly clothed with produce, rose up as by magic before these
hardy sons [and daughters] of toil. . . . Being farmers, mechanics,
laborers and traders in their own country, they required little or
no instruction in these various pursuits.
—Martin Delany, *The Condition, Elevation, Emigration, and
Destiny of the Colored People of the United States* (1852)

Between 1740 and 1770, colonial South Carolina emerged as
one of Great Britain's principal suppliers of indigo, used foremost as a
blue textile dye. In 1750, South Carolina exported approximately eighty-
seven thousand pounds of indigo, which soon gained a reputation as a
middle-grade commodity, next in quality to the highest grade produced
in Guatemala and the French Caribbean. Between midcentury and the
American Revolution, a period that coincided with an increased importation of enslaved workers from West Africa, the colony's indigo exports
expanded more than tenfold to over one million pounds per year.[1] How
did this transformation happen? What factors shaped the development of
indigo production in colonial South Carolina? In what ways did indigo
shape colonial South Carolina? What were the legacies of indigo production in South Carolina? This chapter will address these questions by viewing South Carolina indigo plantations within the contexts of British commercial expansion and the larger Atlantic World, examining the role that
West African indigo workers played in their development, and considering their historical legacies, including material and ideological ones.

Among the ideological consequences of the development of South Carolina indigo plantations has been the depiction of Eliza Lucas Pinckney as the principal agent of indigo production in South Carolina. For instance, according to the agricultural historian Lewis Cecil Gray, whom many later researchers have followed, "The credit for initiating the [indigo] industry is due Eliza Lucas, who had recently come from the West Indies to South Carolina, where she resided on an estate belonging to her father, then governor of Antigua."[2] One colonial historian has written, "Eliza Lucas (later Pinckney) especially labored to introduce West Indian indigo cultivation." Furthermore, this scholar argues that Lucas was one of many innovators "within a wider network that included Carolinians, West Indians, and Britons."[3] As the mother of American revolutionary heroes Thomas Pinckney and Charles Cotesworth Pinckney, Eliza Lucas has been the subject of biographies, children's books, and a novel for her reputation as an innovator in indigo and a mother of the American Revolution.[4] Such depictions make the slave labor force invisible, leading one prominent authority on American slavery to state, "Unlike the Africans who had grown rice prior to their capture, the slaves assigned to indigo production brought no knowledge of the task with them to the New World and often had to be directed by white artisans; still their on the job training gave them a special expertise in the intricacies of making the blue dye."[5] These interpretations obscure a number of important factors that led to the development of indigo in South Carolina, a process related to rice production.

While the colony struggled for decades to find a viable export comparable to Caribbean sugar, it found a saving grace in rice, a crop that African workers transplanted into the colony's soil.[6] As rice took off, colonial planters had the means to buy even more slaves. With increasing flows of labor from Central and West Africa and expanding exports of rice, coastal South Carolina attracted planters and prospective planters, and the Lucas family entered the colony in this spirit. By 1713, John Lucas of Antigua owned in absentia a number of Carolina rice plantations. In 1738, John Lucas's son George left Antigua to live in South Carolina. His political aspirations soon called George Lucas back to Antigua, where he served as its governor, leaving his daughter Eliza with the authority to manage his property for him. She managed three plantation sites: one at Wappoo, where the family lived; one at Garden Hill on the Combahee River, a fifteen-hundred acre property that produced pitch, salt pork, tar, and other commodities; and one, a three-thousand acre rice plantation, on the Waccamaw River.[7] As noted earlier, a number of sources credit Eliza Lucas with developing indigo into a major cash crop in South Carolina. Though previous generations in South Carolina had tried and failed to do so, her estate sustained indigo production and offered resources and models for neighboring plantations. The Lucas plantation was significant; however, the innovations that occurred there and elsewhere in South Carolina can best be explained by broadening the field of view. Other factors that enabled the rise of the colony's indigo industry included changes in the supply structure of indigo to Great Britain from India, inputs of knowledge from India, West Africa, and the Caribbean, and the opportunities created by a wartime crisis.

Hoping to add to their supply of indigo from India, the British turned to the Americas for the dye, which they sought to export along with other staple crops. Shortly after British colonial settlement on the island of Bermuda, colonists planned to develop indigo. For instance, the colonist Robert Rich set English laborers to work on indigo plants in his garden, though he admitted, "I stand in great need of one whose judgment is better than my one [sic], for the making of it." He requested written instructions about the crop; however, it never became a major cash crop on the island.[8] It did become a cash crop shortly after the British claimed Barbados, which, within its first two decades under colonial rule, produced indigo for export. By the 1640s, Dutch traders in Barbados bought indigo with slaves, some of whom, ironically, produced more indigo for export. In spite of the sugar revolution at midcentury that transformed the Barbados export economy, the island continued to produce small amounts of indigo into the 1660s. As either the secondary or primary labor force, Africans in Barbados cultivated and processed indigo, a labor-intensive crop.[9] And many of them carried knowledge of indigo across the Atlantic, which fostered the development of the dye in Barbados and elsewhere in the Anglo-American world.

At the inception of the Atlantic slave trade, West Africa was one of many indigo manufacturing centers in the world. In addition to southern Europe, India, China, South America, and other areas, Africa had a long history of indigo production during the early modern era. Archeological research has uncovered fragments of indigo-dyed blue textiles that date indigo production in what is now Mali to at least the eleventh to twelfth century AD. For centuries, blue textiles were used to clothe not only the living but also those who had recently passed into the ancestral realm. Their physical remains, preserved for eight to nine centuries in the caves of Mali's Bandiagara Cliffs in the Dogon region, testify to the long history of indigo production in West Africa.[10] This early tradition established precedents for later developments in West Africa, and plantation owners in the Atlantic World tapped into this pool of knowledge.

During the years of the trans-Atlantic slave trade, indigo was developed throughout West Africa despite the disruptions caused by the traffic in human cargo and the influence of European imports on West African industries. In some cases, Atlantic commerce clearly influenced the development of West African textile production. For instance, some West African textile workers added a novel dimension to their craft by weaving thread from imported textiles into their cloths. In the late seventeenth century, the Englishman Thomas Phillips, who was on the west coast of Africa in the late seventeenth century, remarked, "The Whidaw cloth is about two yards long, and about a quarter of a yard broad, three such being commonly joined together. It is of divers colours, but generally white and blue. . . . To make these Cloths, especially the blue streaks, they unravel most of the sayes and perpetuanoes we sell them."[11] By the mid–seventeenth century, European and Asian textiles shaped African textile production, yet as noted earlier the imports were unable to dislodge West Africa's textile industry. At this time, imports constituted only 2 percent of West Africa's clothing needs, and indigenous textile production far overshadowed the influence of European imports.[12] This was not lost on European merchants, many of whom sought to tap into West Africa's textile and related crafts. For example, as early as the mid–sixteenth century, Portuguese merchants initiated an indigo trade on the coast of Sierra Leone.[13]

Though West Africans used different kinds of dyes in their cotton textile industries, the most prevalent was indigo, sustaining the production of blue fabrics in a number of cloth production centers. Concerning textile production in Benin, the Dutchman David van Nyendael wrote at the turn of the eighteenth century, "The Inhabitants are very well skill'd in making several sorts of Dyes, as Green, Blue, Black, Red and Yellow; the Blue they prepare from Indigo, which grows here." Also, representing the Dutch West India Company in the early eighteenth century, Ph. Eyten observed indigo for sale in the Slave Coast port town of Whydah.[14] In the early seventeenth century, Pieter de Marees noted that in Senegal the male elders would "wear a long cotton Shirt, closed all around, made like a woman's chemise and with blue stripes," a style also prominent among elites in Ardra, as surviving textiles from the mid–seventeenth century show. On the basis of firsthand accounts of mid-seventeenth-century Benin, the Dutch geographer Olfert Dapper remarked, "The women wear over the lower part of their body a blue cloth, coming to below their calves." And in the interior town of Jenne, it was reported, "the Priests and Doctors wear white Apparel, and for distinction all the rest wear black or blew Cotton."[15] The prevalence of blue textiles, from Senegambia to the Slave Coast and into interior regions, reveals the wide distribution of indigo production throughout West Africa.

Agriculturalists who raised indigo cultivated it in tandem with other crops. In particular, it was commonplace for rice cultivators to grow indigo, which often stood in the fields next to cotton. The landscape of West Africa's rice region, which varied from the damp floodplains and swamps to drier upland fields, accommodated indigo cultivation, which is suited to drier soils. Several eighteenth- and nineteenth-century sources testify to the relationship between these crops. Michel Adanson, a French naturalist who surveyed the geography of the Senegambia region in the mid–eighteenth century, observed, "The higher grounds were covered with millet; and there also the indigo and cotton plants displayed a most lovely verdure." In contrast, rice was "almost the only grain sown at Gambia in the lands overflown by the rains of the high season. The negroes cut all these lands with small causeys, which with-hold the waters in such a manner, that their rice is always moistened."[16]

These patterns continued into the following century, as rice fed into indigo production. After the Frenchman Gaspar Mollien passed through the state of Futa Toro in the early nineteenth century, he noted that the crops included "large and small millet, cotton, which is very fine, excellent rice, indigo, and tobacco." He added that "the country comprised between the Rio Grande, the Gambia and the river Geba, bears the name of Kabou; it is very fertile; the inhabitants cultivate rice, millet, and maize, and a little indigo and cotton." Richard Lander noted that from Boosa "the soil improved greatly as we drew near Yaoorie; and immense patches of land, cultivated with a variety of corn, also with rice, indigo, cotton, etc., were attended by a drummer, that they might be excited by the sound of his instrument to work well and briskly." Clearly, rice cultivation was often bound to indigo.[17]

Agricultural workers used similar methods to process cereal crops and indigo. Rice and millet growers, particularly women, used mortar and pestles to remove rice grains from their hulls, and they employed similar techniques for indigo production.[18] This was the case in the Senegambia region, according to a number of accounts. Adanson remarked that after the indigo was harvested, workers pounded the leaves "in a mortar to reduce them to paste."[19] According to William Littleton, a commercial agent who worked on the Senegambia coast for eleven years during the eighteenth century, workers would first cultivate indigo and then "cut it, pound it in a wooden mortar, and hang it up in the form of sugar loaves." Cultivating and then transforming the indigo leaves into indigo balls was one step in the dyeing process.[20]

The final production of blue textiles required a number of other techniques and tools, and the indigo, after being pounded in the mortar and dried, went through another phase before it was ready for use. To turn the leaf into a dye, Africans fermented indigo in an alkaline solution of ash water. The Dutch merchant Ph. Eyten recounted in the early eighteenth century that in the village of Keta, on the border of the Gold and Slave Coasts, "they first soak the leaves and then make balls of them about the size of a fist, which they then put away. In this way, they seem to keep them in a good condition for more than a month."[21] In the eighteenth century, the British factor William Littleton added a more detailed description of this process. After the indigo was pounded, indigo workers would "infuse it in water, or a lye made of ashes." To make the solution, they burned wood, ash used for cooking, and ash and ash water left over from previous dyeing on a sieve in a clay kiln. Next, they placed wood, old indigo leaves, and the ashes in a pot that had a hole in the bottom. Into this pot, which sat atop another pot with a hole in its side, they poured water that dissolved the salt from the ashes and passed through the bottom hole. Craft workers collected the ash water in a pot that they placed through the side of the bottom pot and transferred the water to a dyeing pot or vat. They then dissolved the indigo balls in the solution, readying the vat for dyeing.[22]

As with rice cultivation and processing technologies, indigo was produced through gendered divisions of labor, and, though in some places men dominated the craft of dyeing, indigo production and the dyeing process throughout much of West Africa were women's arts. This was noted in the late eighteenth century by Mungo Park in the Senegambia region, where women monopolized indigo dyeing, a division of labor that endured into the following centuries and transformed under pressures of colonial rule.[23] Requiring agricultural development, woodcarving, pottery production, and other kinds of work skills, West Africa's indigo and blue textile industries represented several layers of knowledge. The Atlantic slave trade swept through these areas of West Africa, carrying people with experience in indigo production to the Atlantic islands, the Caribbean, and the North American mainland. It is possible that indigo, though a secondary crop, had a wider distribution in West Africa than rice, given that it was grown from the Senegambia region to the Bight of Biafra and from the forest zone to the savannah. West Africans counted blue textiles as part of their material life, so the alchemy of indigo would not have been a mystery to slaves held captive on Atlantic World plantations.

Whether involved directly in their development or indirectly through trading or other kinds of relationships, West Africans carried indigo production knowledge systems into the Atlantic. Slaves grew the crop in the Atlantic Cape Verde Islands in the early eighteenth century. As in West Africa, indigo workers made the dye "by pounding the Leaves of the Shrub, while green, in a wooden Mortar, such as they use to pound their Maiz in . . . and so reduce it to a kind of Pap, which they form into thick round Cakes, some into Balls, and drying it, keep it 'till they have Occasion to use it for dying their Cloths."[24] However, it would remain a minor crop on the island; colonial indigo production was much more important in the Americas, being launched there in the sixteenth century by the Spanish and expanded by the French and the British in the seventeenth.

Anglo-American colonial indigo development arose through the global movement of people, seeds, commodities, and ideas, and the British tried to create opportunities that they witnessed others reap. With the Dutch East Indies Company and the Spanish getting a jump on the global indigo and blue textile trade in East Asia and the Americas, England sought as early as the late sixteenth century to compete, entering along with the French and Dutch into trade in the Levant and trying indigo on small scales in different colonial American settings. The Spanish, deploying Indian and African labor, set up indigo workshops, or *obrajes de tinta*, a model that other colonists would follow, particularly on the island of Barbados.[25] For its labor supply, Barbados turned to Dutch slavers, who in the mid–seventeenth century delivered the majority of the island's African workers. In particular, the Dutch operated a lucrative traffic in slaves from the indigo- and textile-rich Senegambia region to Barbados plantations.[26]

By the mid–seventeenth century, indigo production expanded in Barbados, and its African laborers transferred their knowledge of the crop and related woodworking skills to the island. The testimony of Felix Christian Spoeri, when compared to contemporary accounts from West Africa, reveals this process. Having worked on the island as a doctor and veterinarian for brief spells in 1661 and 1662, Spoeri noted that after indigo was cultivated and harvested, "the plant is put in hollowed-out trees or troughs and water is poured over it. They let it lie there until it is quite soft and smooth, and then pound it with pestles until all is crushed." He continued, "Then they strain it and fully press out the left overs. The juice is then poured up to a hand's width high, into clean vessels, and is dried in the sun."[27] The development of indigo in Barbados, in part a result of the experience of West African workers, helped buoy the confidence of British colonists in the crop's viability, needed because of previous failures with the crop.[28]

By the 1670s, indigo faded to relative insignificance in Barbados as the island was swept up in the sugar revolution that made it, according to one source, "Crown and Front of all ye Carooby Islands." From the late seventeenth into the eighteenth century, most other British Caribbean islands also became dominated by sugar plantation barons. With capital converted from trading or small-scale farming and with credit extended by Dutch or English merchants, the sugar revolution recurred throughout the Caribbean. The islands received a steady influx of enslaved African workers who supplanted indentured servants, replaced those who perished from disease or the rigors of forced labor, and changed the labor force's size and character.[29] On many of the islands, sugar was nearly as important as it was in Barbados, yet planters elsewhere in the British Caribbean continued to see indigo as a viable secondary export crop.

Within the first decade of the British occupation of Jamaica in 1655, the island included indigo among its exports, a product cultivated by both black and white workers. Early Jamaica had a small slave labor force that worked in the fields next to indentured servants. And while the early African population of other colonies such as Barbados consisted of both West and Central Africans, imports of slaves to Jamaica came primarily from West Africa, particularly from the Slave Coast and the Bights of Benin and Biafra. Because it could not absorb the approximately 3,800 slaves imported into the island between 1656 and 1665, many were dispersed to other islands. Yet by 1662 hundreds of slaves populated the island, toiled alongside indentured servants, cleared the forests, and cultivated indigo and other crops for export or subsistence. With the allure of profits from the dye, Jamaican elites invested in slaves and indigo production technologies, so that in the final two decades of the century and into the next, indigo exports steadily increased in volume.[30]

By the late seventeenth century, when sugar production expanded on the island, Jamaican landowners without enough capital to invest in sugar enterprises made smaller investments in indigo production. This became particularly important to the mother country, given changes in the structure of indigo production in India, one of England's principal indigo suppliers in the seventeenth century. The cost of indigo in India went up in the late seventeenth and early eighteenth centuries. This happened in part because of increased demand for indigo in Indian and Middle Eastern textile industries and also because of increases in road tolls and tribute collected from peasants.[31]

Searching for cheaper indigo, the English looked to Jamaica and other Caribbean islands to meet their demands. In 1671, Jamaican sugar works numbered fifty-seven, and during the rest of the seventeenth and into the eighteenth century sugar and its by-products remained Jamaica's largest and most lucrative export. Yet amid the island's sugar-fed transformation with a substantially larger African population, Jamaica continued to include indigo among its exports. From 1671 to 1684, the number of indigo plantations increased from nineteen to forty, with many of them concentrated in Clarendon Parish, along the Mino River (see figure 1).[32]

Jamaican indigo plantations raised two kinds of indigo, some of which also grew in West African agricultural fields. The first, labeled "French" indigo, was *Indigofera tinctoria*. Grown throughout the Mediterranean World and western Asia, *I. tinctoria* was one of the many crops that crossed the Atlantic during the colonial era. More important in Jamaica than "French" indigo, a plant called "Guatimala" by some contemporaries yielded higher-quality indigo. Guatimala indigo, or *Indigofera micheliana* or *guatemalensis*, was one of several genuses that yielded indigo, and during the sixteenth and early seventeenth centuries both Native American and African workers refined the plant into dyes in toxic *obrajes de tinta* or indigo workshops. Of the nearly eight hundred species of *indigofera*, *I. tinctoria*, *I. suffruticosa*, and *I. micheliana* or *guatemalensis* became the most prominent and sought after for commercial indigo production in the Americas.[33]

West African agriculturalists grew similar kinds of indigo. In addition to *Lonchocarpus cyanescens*, an indigo-bearing plant grown in southern Nigeria, Sierra Leone, and the Côte D'Ivoire, at least two species of *Indigofera* were cultivated in West Africa. Through indigenous agricultural development and ongoing trading relationships and interaction with North Africa and the Atlantic World, *Indigofera tinctoria* and *Indigofera*

Figure 1. P. Lea, "A New Mapp of the Island of Jamaica" (1685). Geography and Map Division, Library of Congress.

guatemalensis spread throughout West Africa.[34] Experienced with different varieties of indigo, West Africans workers, though slaves, fostered its development in the British Caribbean. Yet their work experience with it changed in significant ways.

To rationalize slave-based production, Jamaican indigo planters recorded cultivation techniques, employed accounting methods, and introduced technologies that on the one hand facilitated the development of economies of scale and on the other imposed strict requirements and demands on labor. In West Africa during the slave trade era, indigo cultivation, processing, and dyeing were generally done within closely adjacent fields and workshops. The indigo produced in Jamaican forced labor camps was shipped across the Atlantic to English markets, where it fell into the hands of local dyers. Hence, most labor was devoted to the agricultural fields, which demanded meticulous cultivation. In fields allotted to indigo cultivation, the enslaved first weeded the land and then, usually in March, tilled "small trenches of two or three inches in depth, and twelve or fourteen inches asunder; in the bottom of which the seeds are strewed by hand, and covered lightly with mould." Indigo required constant weeding and, in Jamaica, yielded from two to four cuttings. By the mid–eighteenth century, planters figured to make twelve to fifteen pounds of indigo annually per worker, and later in the century they calculated that on average four indigo workers could cultivate five acres of indigo land as well as produce their own food provisions.[35] This, to the planter class, was the ideal output from their slave labor force.

Organizing the development of indigo works to produce the dye on a large scale, colonial planters introduced technologies that demanded that some slaves adapt to different kinds of work. In their combining of large-scale agricultural production and refinement, indigo and sugar production resembled each other. In fact, while most indigo plantations specialized in the crop, others, such as the Lucky Valley and 7 plantations, produced indigo along with sugar, corn, and ginger and depended on slaves not only to cultivate the fields but also, with white artisans, to work as carpenters.[36] These craft workers were needed to build indigo vats, a central feature of indigo production in the Caribbean by the 1660s (see figure 2). In the early seventeenth century, Dutch and English merchants learned indigo production techniques in India, where specialists made the dye by "steeping the plant and agitating the liquid with 'great staves.' They skimmed off the clear water above the precipitate in stages, until the paste thickened enough to be spread out on cloths and partially dried in the sun."[37] By the

Figure 2. From Jean Baptiste du Tertre, *Histoire générale des Antilless habitées par les François*, vol. 2 (Paris, 1667–71). Indigo production in the French Caribbean. John Carter Brown Library, Brown University, Providence, Rhode Island.

second half of the century, colonists transferred these technologies to the Caribbean.

Within this wider context of movement and trade, Jamaicans integrated knowledge from global sources. Indigo went through a series of vats to be transformed into an exportable dyestuff. After the crop was cultivated and harvested, it was

> steept in proportionable Fats 24 Hours, then it must be cleared from the first Water, and put into proper cisterns; when it has been carefully beaten, it is permitted to settle about 18 Hours. In these Cisterns are Several Taps, which let the clear Water run out, and the thick is put into Linnen Bags of about three Foot long and half a Foot wide, made commonly of Ozenbrigs, which being hung up all the liquid Part drips away. When it will drip no longer, it is put into Wooden Boxes three Foot long, 14 inches wide, and one and a half deep. These boxes must be placed in the Sun till it grows too hot, and then taken in till the extreme Heat is over.[38]

The production of indigo, as illustrated in Jean Baptiste du Tertre's study of the seventeenth-century Caribbean, also required workers to pound the indigo leaves in mortars with pestles before they were steeped.[39]

Synthesizing several fields of knowledge, including African agricultural knowledge and woodworking skills and South Asian indigo-processing technology, Jamaican indigo plantations supplied Great Britain's growing demand.

Though indigo became a profitable enterprise for many, planters also faced risks, and some lost their investments. The plant was subject to infestation and, like other plants, could fail because of unexpected, inadequate, or excessive rainfall. In some cases, perhaps as a result of sabotage by slaves, the indigo could spoil because it was steeped for too long. In other cases, the water was agitated too much or drawn off prematurely. Furthermore, the scale of production created clear hazards for the slave labor force. Even Bryan Edwards, the staunch defender of the institution of slavery, acknowledged "the high mortality of the negroes from the vapour of the fermented liquor (an alarming circumstance, that, as I am informed both by the French and English planters, constantly attends the process)."[40]

Through the knowledge they brought to the Americas and in spite of the toll that slavery in the Americas took on their bodies, African workers placed their imprint on the indigo exported from Jamaica. The African labor force, many coming with indigo cultivation and processing skills, made adjustments to their new environment and indigo production technology. In Barbados during the mid–seventeenth century, Africans used indigo-processing technology that they brought from West Africa. However, by the late seventeenth century the planter class elsewhere in the English Caribbean introduced new technologies that allowed for large-scale indigo manufacture, such as working with larger vats, hanging the indigo to dry in the sun in burlap sacks, and dividing the final product into standard-sized blocks for export. Slaves from Africa who processed the dye had to adapt to these newer techniques.[41] However, Africans' woodcarving skills, experience in indigo cultivation, and other kinds of indigo production knowledge sped up the development of indigo production in the Caribbean.

When the British expanded into the Carolinas, they established linkages with the Caribbean that provided not only models but also capital and labor for the development of indigo on the mainland. For instance, in September 1670, Captain Nathaniel Sayle, son of Carolina's governor, brought to the colony on his ship the *Three Brothers* three white servants and a black family of three, individually named John Sr., Elizabeth, and John Jr. Similarly, other colonists were called upon to "tranceport themselves sarvants negroes or utensils the Lords proprietors of the province of Carrolina."[42]

Hoping to begin indigo production on the mainland, English colonists went through Barbados for instructions and seeds before setting sail for Carolina. Around 1670, the ship captain Joseph West had instructions to stop in Barbados to procure "Cotton seed, Indigo seed, [and] Ginger Roots" to take to Carolina to begin a plantation using contracted Irish workers. This first attempt ended in failure because they missed the planting season. West reported in 1670 that their crops were "blasted in October before they could come to perfection." Despite this loss, many remained confident that plantation agriculture would take root in Carolina.[43]

Persistent colonial efforts, mobilizing African and European labor, brought small-scale successes that accumulated over time and slowly extended indigo culture into Carolina. Shortly after the colonial project began, the trader Maurice Mathews found that "Cotton growes freely. . . . Indigo for ye quantity (by the approbation of our western planters I speake it) I haue as good as need be." Colonial Secretary Joseph Dalton indicated that "as for Indicoe wee can assure ourselves of two if not three Cropps or cuttings a yeare, and as the Barbados Planters doe affirme it is as likely as any they have seen in Barbados."[44] Indigo production continued into the late seventeenth century, but it tailed off by the second decade of the following century. By 1710, Carolina imported an increasing number of African workers while exporting, according to one contemporary observer, "about seventy Thousand Deer-skins a Year, some Furs, Rosin, Pitch, Tar, Raw Silk, Rice, and formerly Indigo."[45]

With the interaction between people on the mainland and the islands continuing well into the eighteenth century, the mixed slave and indentured labor force gave way to one that was primarily African, and rice became the colony's staple crop. However, immigrants in early eighteenth-century Carolina looked to profit from the indigo industry, as illustrated in contemporary reports and publications about the agricultural prospects of the colony. For example, Peter Purry's 1731 advice manual hoped to lure prospective Swiss immigrants to come to Carolina and raise "Vines, Wheat, Barley, Oats, Pease, Beans, Hemp, Flax, Cotton, Tobacco, Indico, Olives, Orange trees and Citron trees."[46]

The Lucas family of Antigua entered South Carolina within this larger context of Atlantic commerce and colonial expansion. When the family established itself in South Carolina, it built upon precedents both there and in the West Indies. Aware of indigo development in the Caribbean, including her native Antigua, which exported indigo in the early eighteenth century, Eliza Lucas wrote her father for indigo seeds from the island, which he sent to her. In July 1740 she told her father about the "pains I had taken to bring Indigo . . . to perfection, and had great hopes from the Indigo (if I could have the seed earlier next year from the West India's) than any of the rest of the things I had try'd." The following year, after a frost destroyed most of the indigo crop, she wrote, "I make no doubt Indigo will prove a very valuable Commodity in time if we could have the seed from the west Indias [in time] enough to plant the latter end of March, that the seed might be dry enough to gather before our frost."[47]

Lucas did not depend only on indigo seeds from the Caribbean; she also looked to the islands for skilled craft workers to make indigo vats. In 1741, her father sent a worker to construct these vats and to oversee the process of indigo manufacture. The estate first employed Patrick Cromwell and then his brother Nicholas, both from the island of Montserrat, but Eliza dismissed them both, suspecting that they had sabotaged the operation out of a fear that she and possibly other Carolinians would compete with their home island. In response, Governor Lucas of Antigua looked elsewhere in the Caribbean for skilled labor.[48] In particular, he turned to the French West Indies for workers experienced in indigo. In the seventeenth and eighteenth centuries, a heavily African workforce produced indigo in the French islands of Saint Domingue, Guadeloupe, and Martinique. Often working on small plantations of from ten to twelve workers, they mastered the different stages of production, including cultivation, building of vats, and reduction of the plant to dye.[49] Certainly aware of the French Caribbean model and hoping to establish indigo manufacturing on his Carolina estates, Governor Lucas "sent out a negro from one of the French islands" to supervise the process. Soon after, the Lucas estate added indigo to its exports of rice, pitch, salt pork, and tar.[50]

While mobilizing Afro-Caribbean labor, the Lucas estate received other inputs of labor from West Africa. A 1745 inventory of slaves on the Garden Hill property, a site of indigo production beginning in 1744, listed thirty-five men, sixteen women, seventeen boys, and eleven girls, including workers named Quamina, Quashee, Quau, Quaicu (appearing twice), and Cuffee. Their names indicate origins from the Gold Coast of West Africa, its interior, or its periphery, where indigo-dyed textiles were produced along with a range of other agricultural and craft goods. A number of areas produced cotton textiles, including the states of Bono and Akwapem and the town of Begho and its hinterland. Swept through in the first half of the eighteenth century by Asante armies, who in turn sold the captives to European slave traders, these areas supplied Carolina with slave labor. With workers from the Caribbean and West Africa who brought expertise in indigo production to the colony, the Lucas estate created a template for others to follow.[51]

Building upon the Caribbean model, the Lucas estate provided an example to South Carolina planters who sought to move into indigo production. This became particularly significant because the War of Jenkins' Ear (1739–41) between England and Spain blocked international trade routes. As a result, Carolina planters looked for economic alternatives and, like previous generations, turned to indigo production. By midcentury, indigo was South Carolina's second largest export, with 87,415 pounds being shipped from Charleston between November 1749 and November 1750.[52] Lucas listened to the needs of the colony, but for the actual labor Carolinian planters depended upon knowledge from the larger Atlantic World.

Throughout this period, Carolina's indigo plantations drew heavily upon the slave trade from West Africa for their labor force. Estimates of the labor required to cultivate indigo allow a rough indication of the number of Africans engaged in its production in mid-eighteenth-century Carolina. The 1761 pamphlet *A Description of South Carolina: Containing Many Curious and Interesting Particulars Relating to the Civil, Natural and Commercial History of that Colony* estimated the productivity of indigo workers. It reported that each slave cultivated approximately two acres of land per year, producing a total of sixty pounds of indigo while also cultivating food provisions.[53] In 1750, South Carolina exported approximately eighty-seven thousand pounds of indigo. The crop yielded an estimated thirty pounds per acre, and one slave annually cultivated approximately two acres. Hence, one worker produced approximately sixty pounds of indigo per year. From the original group of African workers who helped give rise to indigo on the Lucas estate, indigo spread throughout the colony to involve at least 1,400 workers producing the over eighty-seven thousand pounds of indigo exported from Carolina at midcentury. Slaves produced this indigo while also cultivating enough food for everyone on their plantations.[54]

During the second half of the eighteenth century, indigo production expanded substantially, remaining Carolina's second-most important export. Much as tobacco shaped the culture of colonial Virginia, indigo along with rice helped to define the character of South Carolina's planter class, fields, and slave quarters. Among elite white Carolinians, indigo culture in South Carolina spread through an established network that connected colonial plantations with each other and the wider Atlantic commercial system. Through the slave trade, the migration of free labor, trading partnerships, published works, private correspondence, colonial newspapers, and commercial documents, Carolinian elites participated in a global flow of labor and knowledge that stimulated the development of indigo in Carolina and supplied consumer demand across the Atlantic.[55]

Once indigo was established on the Lucas estate, information about how to cultivate and process the crop became more available to literate white Carolinians. Throughout the 1740s and beyond, South Carolina planters could thumb through the pages of the *South Carolina Gazette* and other publications for advice and instructions on how to raise indigo. For instance, Charles Pinckney, who married Eliza Lucas in May of 1744, wrote a series of *Gazette* articles to promote indigo. Writing under the pseudonym of "Agricola," he reasoned that since rice prices were so low, Carolina planters should turn land and labor over to indigo. Quoting Philip Miller's *Gardener's Dictionary*, which in turn drew upon the French missionary Jean Baptiste Labat's account of indigo production in the French Caribbean island of Martinique, Pinckney detailed the characteristics of the indigo plant, reported the processing techniques, and envisioned the extraordinary prospects for indigo production in South Carolina. Other descriptions of indigo were published, and, though accounts differed in some details, by the 1750s information about indigo production was much more available to literate Carolinians. During the colonial period, the written descriptions of indigo then became a kind of currency that circulated among Carolina elites who hoped to capitalize on European demand for high-quality indigo and match the standard set by Guatemala.[56] This intention was aided in 1757 when a group of planters established the Winyah Indigo Society in Georgetown. Modeled after the Charleston Library Society, it served as a clearinghouse for information on indigo and other matters, and it also established a school for indigent white children.[57] Through these circuits, South Carolina set precedents for antebellum southern agricultural journals such as the *Southern Agriculturalist*, Edmund Ruffin's *Farmers' Register*, and De Bow's *Review*. And in their private correspondence with each other, planters also passed on instructions about indigo production. For example, they advised each other on the best soils to grow the crop, which were in upland fields. In 1770, Peter Manigault told Daniel Blake, "It is a mistaken Notion that all good Corn Land is Likewise good Indigo Land, for Corn will grow in much wetter Land than Indigo, & the rich Knolls on your Land, which bear Corn extremely well, are too stiff & too low for Indigo."[58]

South Carolina elites, with time freed up by the profits derived from slave labor, also produced forms of symbolic capital related to indigo that reflected and shaped white colonial identities and promoted the state to outsiders. This is particularly apparent from the cartouches on colonial South Carolina maps, which went through a number of changes. On the first cartouche, printed on a 1757 map by William de Brahm, are two statuesque black male figures removing water from an indigo vat and a third, who seems delighted about his work, dividing indigo into blocks for shipment (see figure 3). In comparison, a second cartouche, published on James Cook's 1773 map of South Carolina, shows four primary characters: a black male figure loading a ship with indigo, two gentlemen overseeing the process, and a Native American male in the corner (see figure 4). Another is from a 1773 Henry Mouzon map (see figure 5). This cartouche emphasizes the technology and efficiency of indigo plantations, indicated by the ceaseless motion of the workers, the presence and cleanliness of their uniforms, and the proximity of indigo fields, vats, and sorting areas. This sense of order is heightened by the presence of white overseers, in contrast to the 1757 illustration, in which they are absent. These images did a number of things simultaneously—they revealed historical processes of material production, displayed clearly defined roles and expectations for black and white males in the colony, and concealed the role of enslaved women in the process of indigo production. In these cartouches, particularly Mouzon's, the artists portrayed South Carolina as an essentially progressive society, a vision that stimulated the desire to introduce rice mills and other machinery into South Carolina after the Revolution. Furthermore, their imagery and placement on maps helped Carolina's elite to legitimate their claims to both land and black labor.[59]

As planters discussed indigo in the pages of the *Gazette*, through their correspondence with each other and foreign merchants and commercial agents, and in the halls of the Charleston Library Society and the Winyah Indigo Society, they also talked about the need to import more slaves into the colony to do the work on their estates. Preferring slaves from the Senegambia region of West Africa, Carolina imported over seventy thousand slaves in the second half of the eighteenth century. When indigo took off in the colony, Henry Laurens and George Austin published an advertisement in the July 1751 *South Carolina Gazette*

Figure 3. William de Brahm, "A Map of South Carolina and a Part of Georgia" (1757). Geography and Map Division, Library of Congress.

Figure 4. James Cook, "A Map of the Province of South Carolina" (1773). Geography and Map Division Library of Congress.

announcing the sale of "a cargo of healthy fine slaves" from the Gambia. Such slaves from the Senegambia region went directly to indigo plantations. Writing to Charles Gwynn in August of 1755, Laurens remarked, "The Indigo Planters whose Crops are good are just now at their wits end for more Slaves. Here is only one Gambia Man with us with 115, the Elizabeth."[60] Planters read in the pages of the *South Carolina Gazette* not only articles about indigo but also notices such as the advertisement on July 19, 1760, for "a choice Cargo of about Two Hundred very Likely and Healthy Negroes, Of the same Country as are usually brought from the River Gambia." They saw the announcement on August 23 reporting "a fine and healthy Cargo of about One Hundred and Eighty Gambia Negroes, just arrived."[61] Or they came across the advertisement for the sale of "about *Two Hundred* very likely healthy NEGROES *(of the*

Figure 5. Henry Mouzon Jr., "A Map of the Parish of St. Stephen in Craven County [South Carolina]: exhibiting a view of the several places practicable for making a navigable canal, between Santee and Cooper Rivers." London: 1773. Rare Book, Manuscript, and Special Collections Library, Duke University.

same country as are usually brought from GAMBIA)."[62] As South Carolina planters geared land to indigo, they had a labor force already accustomed to raising the crop.

Slaves engaged in every aspect of indigo production in South Carolina, from cultivating the crop in light, dry soils to constructing indigo steeping vats, extracting the dye, and making the barrels in which the indigo was shipped. And though planters had published accounts of indigo production available to them as a guide, their African labor force had practical knowledge either with indigo or in complementary trades such as woodcarving. While their experience shaped the outcome of indigo in Carolina, they also had to adapt their previous knowledge to different technologies or found that the skills they possessed were of more limited use. In particular, little dyeing was performed in Carolina, as indigo left Carolina packed in barrels exported across the Atlantic for English dyers.[63]

While African workers brought their experience with indigo to South Carolina, its forced labor system altered the relations of production. This was particularly the case in terms of the colony's gender divisions of labor. In many parts of West Africa during the era of the slave trade, indigo production was controlled by women, who mastered cultivation, processing, and dyeing techniques.[64] In the Americas women were generally excluded from processing and generally worked only in the fields. Yet their expertise was not lost upon planters such as Henry Laurens, whose slave Hagar developed the reputation for her "great care of Indigo in the mud."[65]

In these ways, African workers both drew upon their previous knowledge in shaping South Carolina's indigo plantations and adapted to different means of production and divisions of labor. In contrast to the planter class's ideas and symbols about indigo, the slave community developed their own ideas about indigo, some of which were related to West or Central African cosmologies. Into the nineteenth century, the Gullah attributed spiritual significance to the color blue. Some Gullah householders painted their doors blue with residue from the indigo vats, and some Gullah conjurers gave their patients blue pills, apparently for protection from malevolent spirit beings.[66]

Though indigo was a steady source of wealth for South Carolina during the colonial period, its production went into decline in the late eighteenth century. With the growth of cotton textile production in Great Britain in the early nineteenth century, indigo production expanded in India, where between 1834 and 1847 four million people worked in this industry, coincidentally almost equal to the number of slaves in the United States in

1860. Through a combination of British policies and local practices, Indian peasants were forced to grow indigo rather than rice and fell into a cycle of debt that reduced them to virtual slavery, creating the conditions for the 1859 Bengal Rebellion. Indigo production endured into the twentieth century but was gradually replaced by the production of synthetic dyes in the Western industrialized nations. Meanwhile, in South Carolina during the late eighteenth and early nineteenth centuries, indigo production was replaced by cotton cultivation.[67] Like rice, tobacco, and cotton production, indigo production would be no stranger to African workers in the early years of the Anglo-American colonial project.

5

Slave Artisans

Black Nonagricultural Workers in Colonial America and the Antebellum South

Old Man Okra said that he wanted a place like he had in Africa so he built himself a hut. I remember it was about twelve by fourteen feet and it had a dirt floor and he built the side like a woven basket with clay plaster on it. It had a flat roof that he made from bushes and palmetto and it had one door and no windows. But Master made him pull it down. He said that he didn't want an African hut on his place.

—Ben Sullivan in Savannah Unit, Georgia Writers' Project, *Drums and Shadows* (1940)

On the western coast of Africa, European merchants tapped into skilled African labor to build commercial bases and conduct trade. Ocean-bound vessels anchored offshore, and African canoemen ferried merchants and trade goods between the coast and the ships. Pieter de Marees remarked at the turn of the seventeenth century that most of the canoes were "six foot long and one and a half or two foot wide," but some craft he described as "35 foot long, 5 foot wide and three foot high; the rear was flat, with a Rudder and benches, the whole made and cut out of one trunk."[1] The canoemen who made the trek from the coast to the offshore vessels beat through the waves, which demanded "a great deal of activity and dexterity to carry canoos through without being sunk, overset, or split to pieces, and often occasions the death of many men, and considerable losses of the goods," as Jean Barbot noted at the end of the seventeenth century. He added, "Among the Moors are persons engaged in various occupations, those at the coasts being mostly merchants, fishermen, goldsmiths, canoe-men, house-builders, salt-makers, roofers, farmers, potters, porters, etc.".[2] In the Gold Coast town of Elmina, farmers raised local and New World crops; potters made stylized earthenware; metalworkers cast gold jewelry and brass gold weights or recast European metals; artisans carved musical instruments, bracelets, and combs out of ivory; and salt makers evaporated ocean water in salt pans.[3] Because of its location on the coast and constant interaction with Atlantic merchants, Elmina had a unique history. But its range of artisan activity would have been commonplace in other parts of West and West Central Africa. In contrast to the urban setting of Elmina, the bulk of the slave trade's captives came from rural environments, where agricultural workers and craft workers were interdependent. In the course of conducting their everyday material life, African blacksmiths knew agriculturalists, potters knew weavers, and woodworkers knew fishermen and women. Coming from a world where they were in an ongoing process of transforming the material environment, they carried this sensibility across the Atlantic, where they encountered Indian and English laborers in the waters, fields, and workshops of the Americas.

Agricultural production dominated the daily life of most slaves in the Anglo-American colonies; however, slaves performed a wide range of work beyond the fields. In the British Americas they interacted with English artisans, who came to the islands in significant numbers. Shortly after the British colonized the island of Bermuda, Robert Rich requested his brother Nathaniel to send him an English carpenter and a tailor.[4] Decades later on the island of Barbados, English artisans arrived in fairly large numbers. Between 1654 and 1660, approximately half of the servants arriving on the island were registered as "skilled." This was particularly important for the island's planters, who were transforming the colony from a cotton, tobacco, and indigo domain to a sugar plantation world. Many of these artisans, however, never engaged in crafts but were set to work in the sugar fields.[5] Well into the seventeenth century, colonial elites sought to draw English artisans to Barbados, which the planter William Whaley hoped would be a magnet for "a potter, a cooper and a carpenter or two."[6]

In the early years of British colonial Jamaica, English artisans migrated to the island, with the town of Port Royal becoming a center of artisan activity. In the late seventeenth century, the town was home to English cabinetmakers, tailors, fishermen, bricklayers, carpenters, smiths, sailors, bakers, coopers, tavern keepers, and tanners. In many cases, this middling urban population also owned slaves. For instance, the Port Royal shoe-maker and tanner John Waller owned an elderly slave and hired four white servants. English artisans worked in the countryside, with some planters recruiting craft workers from other parts of the island or England to work on their plantations. And in the early years of slavery in the Brit-ish Caribbean, Africans who worked in the crafts did so in some cases under English apprenticeships.[7]

The material world that Africans entered was also distinctly influenced by Amerindians, who shaped the British Caribbean beyond their contri-butions to tobacco, manioc, and maize production. From the cotton that they cultivated they wove hammocks, a material good that the English adopted. They drew upon forest resources to fashion calabash contain-ers, bark cloth, ropes, chairs, stools, and mortars. English colonists con-sulted indigenous healers, particularly women who knew how to remove chiggers, described by Jerome Handler as "a ubiquitous nuisance in the seventeenth century." The Native American population was known for its expertise in bow and arrow fishing and the hauling in of turtles and crabs. The early historian John Oldmixon wrote, "They are wonderful expert in using their Bows and Arrows. They do not take their Wives with them when they hunt or fish, as some Brasilians do. . . . They are the best Fish-ermen in *America*, either with Hook or Dart, or other Inventions." Among those other inventions were poisons, from places such as the dogwood tree, which, when put in the water, drugged the fish while leaving them still edible. They fished the waters and traveled between Caribbean islands in dugout canoes. "The Men," noted Oldmixon about Indians in the Ca-ribbean, "take a great deal of Pains about the Periaga or Boats, some of which are so large, that they will carry 50 Men." On the land and in the waters, Indians in the British Caribbean colonies tapped into the region's natural resources.[8]

Across the linguistic divide, English, Indian, and African laborers worked in common waters. African swimmers and divers drew the atten-tion of European traders on the West African coast and slaveholders in the Americas. Boys and girls on the coast and near large rivers learned how to swim at an early age, and their skills were particularly useful in the worlds of fishing and commerce. They swam for recreation, catching the eye of European merchants who sat as spectators. In the context of colonial America, where most settlement took place near bodies of water, the abilities of African swimmers and divers became particularly signifi-cant. These individuals played a number of roles, which included diving for pearls off the Venezuelan coast at the turn of the seventeenth century, diving for buried treasure in the Caribbean in the eighteenth century, and swimming in informal sporting competitions.[9] "Excellent Swimmers and Divers they are, both men and women," noted the British colonist Richard Ligon about slaves in Barbados.[10]

Though Africans and their descendants spent the bulk of their time in the cash crop economy, others performed nonagricultural labor on the periphery of that economy. Just as slaves grew their own food in the provision grounds, they produced their own food from the fishing waters, work that would have been no stranger to them and that they performed along with Indian and English laborers. From the slaveholding estate of Colonel Humphrey Walrond of Barbados, workers went to sea. In the mid–seventeenth century, Richard Ligon recalled that "Walrond has the advantage of all the Planters in the Iland; for, having a Plantation neer the Sea, he hath of his own a Saine to catch fish withal, which his own servants and slaves put out to Sea, and, twice or thrice a week, bring home all sorts of such small and great fishes, as are neer the shoar."[11] Over time, fishing became an important site of contestation between slaves and their masters, with slaves claiming the material goods and social movement that fishing afforded them, while their owners and overseers at times fiercely punished such displays of autonomy, as the eighteenth-century Jamaican slaveholder and plantation manager Thomas Thistlewood did to his slaves.[12] British Caribbean colonial elites such as Thistlewood had good reason to feel anxious about their slaves, especially skilled ones, for they had developed a tradition of leveraging their knowledge into other forms of power. In the earliest years of British conquest in the Caribbean, colonial elites had had problems managing their slaves. The seventeenth-century chronicler Richard Blome wrote that after the British launched their Western Design in the mid–seventeenth century to seize Caribbean possessions from the Spanish, "the *Spaniards* quite deserted the *Island*, except it were about 30 or 40 of their *slaves*, who betook themselves to the *Mountaines*, but being afraid of Discovery, and to be pursued to Death for some *Murthers* they had committed, built themselves *Conoas*, and in them fled to Cuba."[13] So along with their skills and knowledge came power that Africans could exercise to contest their enslavement.

Plantations relied heavily upon African laborers to work not only in the fields but in a range of other kinds of activities, and an uneasy relationship evolved between them and colonial slaveholders. Some of the most important work took place in the sugar boiling houses, and Africans, like

English servants, learned it in the Americas.[14] Beyond the boiling houses, slaves performed a wider range of nonagricultural labor. On the Somerset Vale plantation in Jamaica in 1776, they made lime, built mule pens, worked on the roadways, made their own dwellings covered with thatch roofs, made hog sties, fired bricks, and crafted posts and rails for fences.[15] Early in the following century on the Duckenfield Hall estate, black coopers and carpenters worked on the foundation of an old house and also made hogsheads for the sugar produced on the forced labor camp.[16] And along with agricultural production, fishing, and pearl diving, Africans performed artisan work in the British Caribbean. For instance, an "Eboe carpenter named Strap" toiled on Matthew Lewis's Jamaica plantation.[17]

African artisans in the British Caribbean operated in two parallel worlds, one that maintained and expanded the export economy and another that shaped the slave community's material life. Carpenters built fences to hem in livestock or hogsheads for sugar exports, but they also made artistic objects. For example, in Barbados, Richard Ligon met an African named Macow in the groves making a xylophone. Macow had in front of him "a piece of large tempter, upon which he had laid cross, sixe Billets, and having a handsaw and hatchet by him, would cut the billets by little and little, till he had brought them to the tunes, he would fit them to; for the shorter they were, the higher the Notes which he tried by knocking upon the ends of them with a stick, which he had in his hand."[18] The work of African artisans in the British Caribbean resonated even more powerfully through their drums. In seventeenth-century Jamaica, African artisan/musicians made drums out of hollowed-out logs and covered with hides, which they produced until the colonial assembly suppressed the practice. As one observer noted about Jamaican slaves, "They formerly on their Festivals were allowed the use of Trumpets after their Fashion, and Drums made of a piece of a hollow Tree, covered on one end with any green Skin, and stretched with Thouls or Pins. But making use of these in their Wars at home in *Africa*, it was thought to much inciting them to Rebellion, and so they were prohibited by the Customs of the Island." African music echoed in the Diaspora, through the work of both the musicians and the people who made their instruments.[19]

While artisans like Macow and Strap can readily be identified as African born, the origins of other slaves who performed nonagricultural labor is more uncertain. Surely, many were apprenticed to English colonists, yet a substantial number of nonagricultural workers acquired some of their training in West or West Central Africa. The earthenware and clay pipes excavated from Caribbean archeological contexts suggest that African potters, most likely women, grafted English and Indian techniques and forms into their practice.[20] For instance, colonial ranch developers bought slaves from particular regions of West Africa where herding was prominent. Outside the Anglo-American world in St. Domingue, slaveholding stockmen preferred slaves from the Senegambia region, particularly the Fulbe, who had extensive experience with cattle rearing and were more likely to work on the island's ranches than other slaves.[21] This was probably the case in other parts of the Americas, as on the cattle ranches of early South Carolina, Hispaniola, and Venezuela that relied upon slaves from West and West Central Africa for their herding skills. After the Spanish carried livestock to islands such as Jamaica, which the English took over, slaveholders deployed their slaves to tend cattle and other kinds of livestock.[22]

The livestock raised by slaves supported Anglo-American colonial leather production. Concerning seventeenth-century Jamaica, one chronicler reported that the island produced "*Hydes*, of which great quantityes have been Yearly made, and are found to be very large and good."[23] For some of the Africans in Jamaican tanneries, leather working would not have been unfamiliar. For instance, the cattle herders of West and West Central Africa had experience with making hides. By the late seventeenth century, both English and French trading companies bought West African hides, brought from the interior to the Senegambia coast, for European markets. For instance, the ship *Dorothy* bought deer skins and cow hides on the Gambia River. The ship's captain also bought sixty slaves there.[24] Within the Americas, enslaved cattle workers managed the work animals used to manure the fields, power the sugar mills, and supply local tanners who worked the hides into leather.[25]

As colonial estates evolved from small enterprises to more highly developed plantations, their labor forces performed a range of work, including extracting and processing metals. For example, while cattle rearing and cash crops dominated the island of Jamaica from the early years of Spanish settlement into the British period, the island also yielded small quantities of raw metal. "*Copper*, they are assured is in this *Isle*, for they have seen the *Ore*, wrought out of a *Mine* here; and by the *Spaniards* report, the *Bells* that hung in the great Church of St. *Iago*, were cast of the Copper of this *Island*."[26] Though colonial figures in Jamaica did not specifically mention that they tapped into the pools of African metalworking knowledge, it is worth considering that mining practices were fairly widespread in West and West Central Africa. The gold and iron ore mines of West Africa, the iron ore mines of West and West Central Africa, and the copper mines of Central Africa yielded raw materials for smiths, who transformed the raw goods into gold, iron, or copperware. Out of these contexts, Africans, particularly "Mina" slaves from West Africa, entered the mines in the Latin American colonies.[27] Given the process in other parts of the Americas, Jamaican mining operatives might have similarly drawn from a pool of African miners.

African artisans also landed in metalworking centers, such as Reeder's Pen in Morant Bay, Jamaica, where they introduced African metallurgical technology. Established by the British coppersmith John Reeder in 1772, the foundry deployed a mixed labor force of maroons, African and Jamaican-born slaves, and free blacks, who produced iron and brass. In Reeder's words, they were "perfect in every branch of the iron manufacture, so far as it relates to casting and turning . . . and in wrought iron." As in African iron-producing regions such as Bassar, where pottery and iron production coincided, Africans at John Reeder's forge coupled the two industries, as evidenced by the iron slag and the locally produced pottery found at the site.[28]

The material foundations established by Indian and English labor would lead Africans to acquire new knowledge in the British Caribbean. Yet the old coexisted with the new. African swimmers and divers plumbed the waters, and carpenters crafted practical and aesthetic goods. African women made earthenware, drawing upon skills that they carried across the Atlantic while incorporating ideas and techniques from English and Amerindian people. In some cases, such as on the Seville and Drax Hall plantations of early eighteenth-century Jamaica, slaves built "hearths, cooking areas, animal pens, and cleared activity space in the yard area outside the house" on the basis of African models, and slaves contested their owners for control over the layouts of their housing settlements.[29] Perhaps for this reason, an eighteenth-century historian of the British Caribbean argued, "every Plantation look[s] like a little *African* City."[30]

Slavery in the Chesapeake region, as in the Caribbean, revolved around cash crop production, which was supported by a host of nonagricultural workers. Over time, colonial elites filled this need through slave labor. By the time of the American Revolution, wrote the son of George Mason, "it was very much the practise with gentlemen of landed and slave estates in the interior of Virginia, so to organize them as to have considerable resources within themselves. . . . Thus my father had among his slaves carpenters, coopers, sawyers, blacksmiths, tanners, curriers, shoemakers, spinners, weavers and knitters, and even a distiller."[31] The dependence of Chesapeake planters on slavery and the kind of work that slaves performed evolved over time, and in some cases, slaves served as apprentices to English artisans. For example, in the late seventeenth century Joseph Rogers apprenticed his slave Dick to Robert Caufield for four years "to learn the trade of shoemaking." Into the eighteenth century, many slaves learned trades from white artisans.[32]

While some slaves clearly served under apprenticeships to English craft workers, African artisans shaped the material landscape of the Chesapeake in subtle ways. The material remains, architectural styles on plantations, and names of slave artisans indicate that Africans plied familiar trades on colonial Chesapeake estates. By the eighteenth century, housing construction for slaves and slaveholders rested heavily upon slave labor. Slaves built the great houses of eighteenth-century Virginia planters such as Thomas Jefferson. And through their role in housing construction, Africans influenced the region's architectural styles by determining the sizes of rooms, lightening the frames of balloon-frame homes, and building separate spaces for housing and cooking.[33] In the workshops of the Chesapeake, Africans produced material goods. In 1726–27, according to a deposition by Peter Legrand, the colonial planter William Byrd sold four slaves to Brooks Baker, one of them a cooper named Cuffee.[34] In the 1770s, a carpenter named Sanco worked on the Elkhill property of Thomas Jefferson, who also owned slaves named Guinea and Angola.[35]

In some cases, Africans labored in the colonial Chesapeake's metalworks. One African named Mungo was described by his owner Bernard Moore as "a good firer and hammer man."[36] And the names of several slaves at the ironworks owned by the Tayloe family in colonial Virginia suggest the presence of African workers there. In the mid–eighteenth century, Tayloe's Occoquan metalworking site included African workers named Quamina, Congoe, Quagua, Juba, Old Quagua, and Cuffy, the last two being "the most valuable slaves at Occoquan, each appraised at £120."[37] Furthermore, an eighteenth-century sculpture found in the remains of the slave quarters of an Alexandria, Virginia, blacksmith shop bears the mark of a blacksmith from the Senegambia region of West Africa. The sculptor gave the figure a smooth torso, arms reaching forward, and jagged and bowed legs, like a man who was weary from a journey, perhaps from the West African interior to the coast, yet was still strong enough to work the Virginia iron forges.[38]

A parallel process unfolded in the Carolinas and Georgia. For example, South Carolina slaveholders apprenticed their slaves to white artisans. Yet Africans shaped the material world of the Lowcountry through their nonagricultural work skills into the early nineteenth century. Having made the Middle Passage through the Atlantic, Africans in the British colonies and United States remained connected to the waters as fishers, boatmen, and divers. During the last years of the legal international slave trade to the United States, South Carolina merchants rushed to import slaves to supply the growing demand on cotton and other plantations. Between 1800 and 1808, approximately seventy thousand Africans landed in South Carolina, "re-Africanizing" the Lowcountry after the halt of the slave trade during the American Revolution. Ten percent of this number were forced into South Carolina from the Gold Coast, so people from this region of West Africa had a continued presence on South Carolina plantations.[39] As discussed in chapter 1, fishing villages dotted the Gold Coast, and people in the interior fished the rivers. Acknowledging the quotidian nature of Gold Coast fishing practices, French sailor Jean Barbot noted, "Constant practice in fishing makes these Moors very expert in the art, so that they have knowledge of the characteristics of each fish and the season of the year to catch it."[40]

Out of this context, a number of Africans landed in South Carolina during the closing years of the slave trade. They entered plantations such as that of Charles Cotesworth Pinckney, son of Eliza Lucas Pinckney. On his estate, Africans named Cuffie and Quash toiled as fishermen. Pinckney recorded on April 22, 1818, that "Gossport & Quash from the Crescent & January & Bob from the old place are the Fishermen for the ensuing week." On the week of April 29, "Cuffie and Sambo from the Crescent and Adam & Caesar from the Old Place begun fishing today." While they drew upon their skills to ply the South Carolina waters, some of their work practices from Africa disappeared in the New World. For example, Quash and his crew caught fifteen drum fish on April 28, 1818, a Tuesday, which along the Gold Coast was the day that fishermen took their Sabbath. On the Christian evangelist Pinckney's estate, the day of rest would be Sunday.[41]

During the colonial era, when the African presence was strong, and into the antebellum period, slaves had an important presence in Atlantic fishing waters and inland rivers. They encountered resistance, as some white people feared competition with slave labor or the latitude that fishing allowed slaves. For example, the fugitive slave Henry Box Brown recalled that kin to the owner of a neighboring plantation rebuffed his request to fish on the plantation's stream and forced Brown and his brother to throw back the fish they had caught in another river.[42] And in North Carolina, "whites complained that the Negroes had monopolized all the good fishing holes and that they sold their fish in competition with white fishermen."[43] In spite of such opposition, slaves in the colonial and antebellum South fished the Atlantic and the rivers that fed into it.

While the bulk of slave labor occurred during the daytime under the watchful eye of planters, some slaves fished at night, a common practice in West Africa. Along the Gold Coast, people ventured into the Atlantic Ocean in their canoes at night, balanced themselves while holding their torches to attract fish, and snared them with harpoons.[44] Drawing on these practices, Africans in South Carolina worked the coastal waters. One planter during the colonial period provided a description of fishing on the Carolina coast: "The way to catch mullets is to take the cano in the night with a stick of lightwood 3 or 4 foot long well lighted which one must hold in his hand as far as he can reach toward the grass or reed about 2 or 3 foot water where the mullets sleep."[45] Furthermore, the canoes that slaves traveled in bore at least a partial imprint from Africa. As did Native Americans, Africans in South Carolina hollowed out cypress logs to make canoes for coastal and river transportation and for fishing expeditions.[46]

Their knowledge of night fishing afforded the enslaved a bit of latitude from their owners, power that Charles Ball exercised off the South Carolina coast. Ball first witnessed slave fishermen on the Patuxent River in Maryland, near where he lived before being sold by speculators into slavery in the Lower South. With his knowledge, Ball gained a certain amount of independence from his owners. As he describes in his autobiography, he and his fellow fishermen were essentially in charge of the fishing works off the coast of South Carolina. Like people in West and West Central Africa, he made a canoe, crafted seine nets, trained apprentices in the craft, and fished at night. He stated, "Every fisherman knows that night is the best time for taking shad." By fishing at night, a practice that his overseer apparently had not mastered, Ball and his team of fishermen extracted a degree of control over their work; Ball recalled that the fish master "knew nothing of fishing with seine." Nighttime fishing also allowed slaves the opportunity to reserve some of their catch for sale and to give the overseer and owners only a part of what they hauled in. Under the cover of darkness, they essentially leveraged their fishing skills to earn cash and improve their lot. Ball reflected on the dynamics between slaves and masters, saying that "I was in no fear of being punished by the fish-master, for he was now at least as much in my power as I was in his."[47]

Many of the enslaved undoubtedly learned skills from Indian and English laborers, but in some instances African artisans continued their work traditions in the Americas. George Lucas, who owned the South Carolina estate where mass indigo production was launched, held several West African artisans. In 1746, he sold to Charles Alexander of Antigua three coopers named Sogo, Quamina, and Say and two sawyers named Quacu.[48] From Lucas's Antigua estate, he sold an artisan named "Quash a Carpenter, since Baptised by the name of John Williams." Alexander then sold the slaves to the South Carolina planter Charles Pinckney to use on his rice and indigo plantations.[49] In some cases, African artisans worked alongside slaves born in the Americas, as apparently was the case on the South Carolina Taylor family plantation, which included sawyers named George, Primous, Strange, Rentey, Job, and Ceasar; carpenters named Peter and Joe; and coopers named Tringlass, March, and Cudjoe.[50]

In colonial South Carolina, planters mobilized Africans in a range of trades, as indicated in runaway slave advertisements and bills of sale. In his 1788 advertisement, Alex Moultrie described his slave Sam as a bricklayer and, he believed, "of the Eboe country." Sam apparently passed as a free person, which indicates how, as they did in the fishing waters, workers turned skills into autonomy.[51] African artisans, whose day names morphed into English, passed through the hands of different slaveholders. During the eighteenth century and into the early nineteenth century, a number of Africans in South Carolina adopted English names, including Monday, who was a "native of Guinea" and sold in 1803, or "an African boy named Friday," sold in 1809 by Joseph Bixby to William Ranton.[52] In 1789, Mathew Poppin of Charleston bought two coopers named Friday, one from James Potts of Charleston and another from Samuel Adams of Washington. So John Williams was not the only artisan to switch from an Akan day-name to an English name.[53]

Whether in fishing waters or artisan workshops, Africans placed a distinct imprint on the material environment of the North American colonies. In addition to the skills in woodworking, they carried house-building, basket-weaving, and pottery traditions into Virginia and South Carolina. The enslaved population left behind fragments of their material life, from appliqué cloths with African motifs, the foundations of their dwelling places, dugout canoes, and metal ware to clay vessels or Colono ware.[54] Albert Carolina remembered how his grandparents had made a kiln to fire pottery: "Grand-mother was African. She had a little bowl made out of clay."[55] Albert Carolina would have been one of many slaves born in the New World who sat at the feet of African artisans. This was the case with the slave blacksmith Philip Simmons of Charleston, South Carolina, who, though born in the New World, was influenced by African practices. Simmons continued to be inspired by an African aesthetic impulse of being struck by visions and opening himself to improvisation as he made ironwork for urban spaces.[56] Some skilled workers such as Charles Ball turned their skills into greater work and personal autonomy. And their descendants carried this sensibility forward into the antebellum South, where it would undergo changes in form.

The Somerset Place estate in North Carolina was one of many plantations that bridged the colonial and antebellum eras. In the early 1780s, Josiah Collins, a successful merchant from Somersetshire, England, along with Samuel Dickinson and Nathaniel Allen, formed the Lake Company to establish a plantation in northeastern North Carolina. They subsequently acquired over one hundred thousand acres of land next to Lake Scuppernong in a region rich in timber, pitch, tar, turpentine, tobacco, and rice production.[57] With precedents both in the state and in neighboring colonies, the Lake Company turned to West Africa for its labor force, and in 1785 they ordered two ships, the *Camden* and the *Jennett*, to go to West Africa to buy slaves to work the land. In June of 1786, the ships returned to North Carolina, each carrying a cargo of eighty enslaved Africans between the ages of twenty and twenty-five. Collins used his political connections to get the state to authorize construction of a new canal from Lake Scuppernong to the Scuppernong River. With the work performed by the newly arrived African labor force, the canal drained water from the adjacent lands, improved the flow of commodities from the plantation to Albemarle Sound, and supplied water power to mills to be built along the canal. When completed, the canal measured six miles long, twenty feet across, and six feet deep.[58]

In the first decades of the nineteenth century, the Collins family consolidated its hold over the entire estate, controlling a labor force that included Africans who had survived the canal-building project, offspring of the slaves brought from Africa in 1786, and American-born slaves bought by the Lake Company and the Collins family to replace those who had perished in the swamps. By the 1830s, the slave population expanded through childbirth and through purchase because of the nightmarishly high child mortality rates, with from 30 to 40 percent of children dying before the age of ten. Many of the slaves did highly skilled work, particularly in the sawmill, with the rice machines, and in the gristmills powered by water running through the canal.[59]

As in colonial South Carolina, African labor shaped the development of rice production on the Collins estate. In the West African rice region, agriculturalists cultivated rice in marshy floodplains by employing a sophisticated irrigation system. This system included the construction of canals, embankments, and floodgates that allowed workers to control saline levels and the flow of water into and from rice fields. After exhausting the fields through the system of tidal floodplain cultivation, workers converted the fields to cattle pasture.[60] Slaves at Somerset Place used similar techniques of rice cultivation. By 1794, eight years after the original cargo of enslaved Africans arrived, the land was turned to rice cultivation and a rice mill was erected. Later, as the agriculturalist Edmund Ruffin noted during his 1839 visit to the Somerset Place plantation, "Rice was cultivated here by the Lake Company, to considerable extent, and with good success. . . . The successive parallel slopes, ditches, and embankments, formed by the 'leading ditches' which run across the ground, afforded great facilities for flooding the land, and drawing off the water when desired, for rice culture." After the plantation abandoned rice, the land was converted to a rotation between wheat and maize cultivation and cattle grazing.[61]

The Somerset Place plantation was not alone in the way it used its labor force. Frederick Douglass recalled about his years as a slave on Edward Lloyd's estate on Maryland's Eastern Shore that Lloyd's slaves "were an immense fortune." He counted among them those experienced with "horse-shoeing, cart-mending, plow-repairing, coopering, grinding, and weaving." They commanded considerable respect from the youth, who, like youth in Africa such as Camara Laye, deferred to their elders. Regarding this respect for elders, Douglass concluded that "there is no better material in the world for making a gentleman, than is furnished in the African."[62] Slave artisans commanded respect largely because of the knowledge that they possessed and their standing in the community as elders.

The Lloyd plantation was geared primarily toward wheat and corn production, supplying markets in Europe; however, the plantation could not operate unless the slave labor force performed other kinds of work to keep it afloat, and this was not unusual in other parts of the antebellum South where plantation owners had skilled slaves on site. For example, in the early nineteenth century, Samuel Gourdin Gaillard's South Carolina plantation raised cotton as a primary crop; however, it also produced maize, peas, and rice. And the estate demanded other kinds of work from its slave labor force. They handled two dozen work mules, fifty cattle, nearly a dozen oxen, and nearly as many horses. They made their own clothing, taking cotton and indigo from their raw forms and turning them into dyed textiles. And as Gaillard recalled, among the slaves several were "a second generation from Africa."[63]

The Somerset Place, Lloyd, and Gaillard plantations adhered to a larger pattern—they raised primary export crops but also had the slave labor force perform other kinds of labor on the margins. For instance, their seemingly incessant work extended from the export crops to the garden patches, where they raised food to supplement provisions raised in the main fields. In the plantation world of Simon Brown, a slave in Virginia in the mid–nineteenth century, slaves grew "pinders" or peanuts and maize along with tubers such as sweet potatoes in their gardens. Brown carried this knowledge with him to South Carolina after emancipation, where he took care of the fields of other black South Carolinians. As Frederick Douglass recalled about his grandmother Betsey, the Rev. William Faulkner recounted that Brown had special knowledge of nursing sweet potatoes. "They were the kind he planted in early spring in my mother's hot bed," Faulkner remembered. "The sprouts would be set out in rows later in her potato patch. When the crop was gathered in the fall, Simon would bank, or bury, the big potatoes in large dirt-covered mounds, safe from the frost. The little ones, the slips, he would cover in a smaller bank," a practice that had parallels in Central Africa.[64] Celestia Avery, a former Georgia slave, recalled that on her plantation, "cotton, corn, peas, potatoes, (etc.) were the main crops raised." Henry Brand and others on the plantation where he toiled raised "cotton, corn, cane, vegetables, and livestock." He added, "More cotton was grown than anything else." Rachel Adams, who survived slavery in Georgia, stated, "Of course they had a garden, and it had something of just about everything that we knew about in the way of garden sass growing in it." Just south in Tallahassee, the former slave Shack Thomas raised "corn, peanuts, a little bit of cotton and potatoes."[65] Black agriculturalists were called upon for their expertise into the postbellum period, as was the case with the former slave Byrl Anderson of Virginia. He revealed that when a Mrs. Goode moved nearby, "she got me as her personal advisor for her farm. I used to tell her what kind of things to plant in certain kinds of land and she always had good success with her crops."[66] Southern agricultural life in many ways relied not only on the physical labor of slaves like Anderson but also on their knowledge.

In the cotton state of Mississippi, slaves cultivated their own food from the rich soils, raising corn and intercropping them with peas. Louis Hughes recalled about plantations in Mississippi that "cabbage and yams, a large sweet potato, coarser than the kind generally used by the whites and not so delicate in flavor, were also raised in liberal quantities." Slave blacksmiths and carpenters, Hughes added, also made all of the plantation tools.[67] On and around the Louisiana bayou plantation owned by Edwin Epps, slaves raised sugarcane, cotton, and corn as the primary crops, but they also cultivated sweet potatoes and raised garden crops. Solomon Northrup, who toiled in this region, added that "the swamps are overrun with cattle."[68]

In the early nineteenth century, Louisiana still had a significant African labor force. Adding to the American-born population, slaves from Africa came directly through the Atlantic slave trade, with Haitian planters who fled from the island during the Haitian Revolution, and through other means. Furthermore, they arrived through the domestic slave trade from eastern seaboard states such as South Carolina, which imported over seventy thousand slaves from Africa in the first decade of the nineteenth century and had an approximately 20 percent African population around 1810.[69] This process explains the presence of Patsey, whose mother survived the Middle Passage and passed through Cuba before being carried to the Williamsburgh, South Carolina, plantation owned by James Buford. To set up his plantation, Edwin Epps of Louisiana bought Patsey along with eight other slaves, and she was among the most prized. Driven under the lash, Patsey split rails and drove work animals, and her knowledge of cotton cultivation and harvesting was so highly regarded that others deemed her "queen of the field."[70]

While after the Revolution the cotton boom crowded indigo out of the export markets, it continued on small scales in the antebellum period. Within the domestic economy of the antebellum South, slaves had a number of possibilities available for dyeing fabrics, but it appears that most chose *blue* textile dyes. To some, the color red conjured painful memories of their capture into slavery. For instance, Shack Thomas, who was held by Jim Campbell in Tallahassee, Florida, recalled that his father, Adam, had had an aversion toward red for that reason:

His father, he says, used to spend hours after the candles were out telling him and his brothers about his capture and subsequent slavery. Adam was a native of the West Coast of Africa, and when quite a young man was attracted one day to a large ship that had just come near his home. With many others he was attracted aboard by bright red handkerchiefs, shawls and other articles in the hands of the seamen. Shortly afterwards he was securely bound in the hold of the ship, to be later sold somewhere in America. Thomas does not know exactly where Adam landed, but knows that his father had been in Florida many years before his birth. "I guess that's why I can't stand red things now," he says; "my pa hated the sight of it."[71]

A considerable number of antebellum slaves, whose forebears planted indigo for mass consumption in the colonial period, continued the practice well into nineteenth century, in some cases in altered forms. Arrie Binns, a former slave from Georgia, recounted her mother's domestic labor. "Ma made our clothes and we had pretty dresses too. She dyed some blue and brown striped. We grew the indigo she used for the blue, right there on the plantation, and she used bark and leaves to make the tan and brown colors."[72] While in West Africa men dominated weaving practices, some women slaves performed that craft in the antebellum South. Revealing the transition in the gender division of labor in textile production during slavery, James Bolton recalled, "One slave woman did all the weaving in a separate room called the loom house. The cloth was dyed with home-made coloring. They used indigo for blue."[73] On the Georgia plantation where Rhodus Walton toiled as a slave, "indigo, found in the cotton patch, was the chief type of dye."[74] Referring to the upland soils in which indigo grows, Genia Woodberry of South Carolina recounted that "they made the blue cloth out of that thing that they raised right there on the plantation called indigo. There is some of that indigo that grows up there on the Sand Hills this day and time, but nobody ever worries about it anymore."[75] And Patience Campbell of Florida, who had learned to spin and weave when she was young, remembered that "the cloth and thread were dyed various colors," though she knew "only how blue was obtained by allowing the indigo plant to rot in the water and straining the result."[76] Through these small-scale practices and labors of love, slave women passed on agricultural and craft knowledge with deep African roots. And this memory flowed forward into the twentieth century, memorialized by Toni Morrison in *Beloved*, whose main character, Sethe, recalls her mother working in the rice fields and "working indigo."[77]

Paralleling their work in indigo cultivation and processing, slave women continued to carry out small-scale textile production into the nineteenth century. It was not unusual for them to produce "homespun cloth," which might even clothe their owners. In the opening decades of the century on the Virginia Tayloe family estate, women named Judy, Betsy, Else, Lizza, Nanny, Winney, Izzard, Sylva, Agga, Nancy, Grace, Phillis, and Patty turned cotton and wool into textiles.[78] These practices endured well into the century. Rachel Adams reported about her mother that her "job was to weave all the cloth for the white folks."[79] Celestia Avery recalled that her grandmother Sylvia Heard did the bulk of the spinning and weaving on her plantation.[80] And like kente cloth weavers from the Gold Coast, the former slave Clara Allen, who was a weaver, named the textile patterns that she wove. While she remained illiterate, she wrote her history on the textiles in her cabin.[81]

Slave artisans performed other kinds of work, alternating between different kinds of labor. James Bolton, in Georgia, remembered how slaves there "caught fish most generally with hook and line, but the carpenters of our plantation knew how to make basket traps that sure enough did lay in the fish"—a practice also employed by Africans along the rivers that led from the interior of the Gold Coast into the Atlantic.[82] Lindsey Moore was a blacksmith who had also learned tanning as a youth. He "used to watch carefully whenever a cow was skinned and its hide tanned to make shoes for the women and the 'folks in the big house.' Through his attention to the tanning operations he learned everything about tanning except one solution that he could not discover. It was not until years later that he learned the jealously-guarded ingredient was plain salt and water."[83] As slaves born in the South learned from their elders, some picked up the skill from slaves born in Africa. For instance, Henry Williams of Georgia used to "help Daddy Patty in his tanning yard over on the water by the cemetery. Patty was a shoemaker too and he used to make all kind of things out of hides and skins." Williams added that Patty and his wife were "both from Africa and as I remember they were Ibos. They were about middle height and heavy built. . . . Daddy Patty, he used to talk to the men in the tanning yard about where he came from. He didn't talk to me, but I heard him."[84]

Struggles between slaves and slaveholders could revolve around their skills. For example, during the Civil War, C. W. B. Gordon and his father, like the Africans in seventeenth-century Jamaica, fled from slavery in a dugout canoe. Gordon recalled, "We had to cross the river in a canoe to get to Plymouth. The old canoe was a dugout made from a tree by my father. This was a remarkable thing for him to do. He used a broad ax and add [adz]. You see, you would have to have a good amount of mechanical ideas to know how to do this."[85] In this instance, the knowledge transmitted over generations provided a means for this group of slaves to claim their freedom. And the epigraph to this chapter recounts the story of one enslaved African, Old Man Okra, who drew on African building skills to make himself a hut and then was forced to pull it down because "Master . . . didn't want an African hut on his place."[86]

African workers carried a reservoir of knowledge across the Atlantic that allowed them to make significant contributions to agricultural and nonagricultural production not only in the colonial period but in the antebellum period as well. And the impact of Africans on the American landscape had important political ramifications. The nineteenth-century black intellectual and political organizer Martin Delany realized the importance of African contributions to American slave plantations. Poring over both American history texts and travel writings of Englishmen who had explored West Africa in the nineteenth century, Delany argued that Africans had shaped North American plantation development. He wrote, "It is notorious, that in the planting States, the blacks themselves are the only skillful cultivators—the proprietor knowing little or nothing about the art, save that which he learns from the African husbandman, while his ignorant white overseer, who is merely there to see that the work is attended to, knows a great deal less." He continued, "Tobacco, cotton, rice, hemp, indigo, the improvement of Indian corn, and many other important products, are all the result of African skill and labor in this country." He added that African herdsmen had shaped the development of the American livestock industry.[87]

At the close of the Civil War, Delany addressed a gathering of hundreds of freedmen and women on St. Helena Island, South Carolina, and reaffirmed what they knew about the importance of their labor to the antebellum South. He stated, "You men and women, every one of you around me, made thousands and thousands of dollars. Only *you* were the means for your master to lead the idle and inglorious life, and to give his children the education which he denied you for fear you may awake to conscience." And he added that Africans had placed a distinct mark on the material life of the South. Delany continued, "If I look around me, I tell you, all the houses on this Island and in Beaufort, they are all familiar to the eye, they are the same structures which I have met with in Africa."[88]

Into the nineteenth century, Africans imported in the final years of the slave trade or smuggled into the United States continued to shape the material world of the South. With people such as Old Man Okra or Albert Carolina's grandparents in the antebellum South, Africans had an even broader influence in the colonial era. Certainly they learned skills from Indian and English workers, but they also drew upon pools of knowledge they had acquired in Africa before being taken captive. Africans and their descendants worked at spinning wheels and dyeing vats, in fishing waters and pottery workshops, in blacksmiths' forges and copper mines. In so doing, they placed a distinct imprint on the Anglo-American world, and in the process they underwent their own transformation.

6

Natural Worship

Slavery, the Environment, and Black Consciousness in the Antebellum South

First, we must realize that no such institution as the Negro church could rear itself without definite historical foundations. These foundations we can find if we remember that the social history of the Negro did not start in America. He was brought from a definite social environment,—the polygamous clan life under the headship of the chief and the potent influence of the priest. His religion was nature-worship, with profound belief in invisible surrounding influences, good and bad, and his worship was through incantation and sacrifice.

—W. E. B. Du Bois, *The Souls of Black Folk* (1903)

Working in the indigo and cotton fields, on the tobacco plantations and rice estates, in the fishing waters and cattle pastures, the majority of slaves spent most of their waking hours exposed to and grappling with the forces of nature. They daily witnessed the mysteries of seeds transforming into plants, newborn animals growing up, and rivers continuing to yield fish. They cleared forests to make way for staple crops, and they went into the forests that remained to beseech for deliverance. Under the surveillance of their masters or plantation overseers, slaves worked between the burning sun and the heavy soil, covered only at times by the shadows of the plants that they cultivated. And to cope with the pain that racked their bodies, they looked into the natural world for healing balms. Because through their work slaves spent the bulk of their time dealing with nature, it figures prominently in their artwork and in their ideas about life, power, and social relations. In their reflections on their experience and on more transcendent matters, natural metaphors abounded.

In this way, slaves were much like other people who worked in premodern societies or under forced labor conditions. One example in another context is Hilda Vitzthum, a survivor of the Soviet gulags. Like Africans who experienced unthinkable losses in the Middle Passage or their descendants in the antebellum South who lived under the constant shadow of the domestic slave trade, Vitzthum survived the Stalinist era, when she lost her husband and children during her imprisonment in the gulags. She faced the harshest elements of nature, yet she also saw in it glimpses of the sublime. When she was young, her father took her on hikes into the forests and mountains to catch the sunset, and this sensibility helped her survive the bitter elements of nature. After making a five-day trek on foot from Asinovka, she "could not resist the magic of the wintry landscape." She added, "When we reached a clearing and I saw the tall, snow-covered trees glittering in the noon sunshine, I was overwhelmed."[1] Months later and after having been displaced several times, she was transported to Volosnitsa, where she continued to feel moments of inspiration in the midst of deep suffering. After looking around her, observing the desolation and falling into despair, she "noticed a little daisy that sprouted from this scarred and trampled earth." She went on to ask, "Had this plain little flower, which had grown despite the thousands of footsteps that daily tramped by, become a symbol for me?"[2] For Vitzthum, the daisy represented a potential that was not crushed by the Soviet forced labor system.

Like Vitzthum, slaves in the antebellum South looked to the natural world as a source of power and inspiration, even though they confronted its sharpest edge. Their autobiographies, folklore, music, and oral histories are filled with ideas about the natural world. Surviving sources tell us that slaves marked time through nature, worshipped within the context of nature, found momentary refuge in nature as a means to escape punishment, and extracted healing energies from nature. Building on the previous chapters that looked at the ways that slaves extracted material goods from nature through work practices inherited from Africa, this chapter will explore the ways that slaves in the antebellum South spun political, social, and religious ideas out of the natural world. In so doing, they created what anthropologist Eric Wolf terms an alternative ideology, which would "sound a systematic counterpoint to the mainstream of communication."[3] For instance, slaves contested the mainstream idea of planter paternalism that portrayed slave society as a big family in which slaveholders were the parents and slaves their dependent children. For slaves in the Old South, different visions emerged; nature spoke, revealing mysteries and telling stories, recounting memories and portending the future, ushering in change and offering rootedness in a troubled world.

Slaves spoke about that troubled world in a language laden with metaphors from the natural realm. Slaves read patterns in nature as allegories of the story of slavery, and in some contexts nature was the site of historical memory. For people who had little access to written means of recording their history, the natural world yielded mnemonic devices for slaves.[4] Mnemonic devices are deployed within specific historical contexts and through ongoing dialogues between memory bearers and their audiences, a process that enables people to access and transmit historical knowledge. Such was the case in the Lowcountry creeks and swamps of Georgia and South Carolina, which contained the voices and memories of the slaves' African ancestors, haunting the people who entered. For example, the father of Paul Singleton, who was a slave near Darien, Georgia, heard the sound of ghosts that lurked in the creeks and spoke of the illegal slave trade. "Lots of times, he told me another story about a slave ship that was about to be caught by a revenue boat. The slave ship slipped through the back of a river into a creek. There were about fifty slaves onboard. The slave runners tied rocks around the slaves' necks and threw them overboard to drown." Singleton continued, "They say you can hear them moaning and groaning in the creek if you go near there today."[5] In this way, the rivers of coastal Georgia contained the memories of the ancestral passage through the Atlantic slave trade.

Slaves and their descendants also deployed mnemonic devices from nature to recount the story of the domestic slave trade, as in the legend of Boggy Gut swamp in South Carolina, where the slave trader Ole Man Rogan bought and sold slaves. Through a dialogue between "Old Bill" and his audience, a historical picture of the domestic slave trade and its impact on black and white southerners emerged. Ole Man Rogan parted families during his slave trading, and he was said to have "always looked satisfied when he saw tears running down the face of a woman when she was weeping for her child." He paid a price for slave trading, because after he died, "his spirit wandered and wandered from Boggy Gut to the river and wandered across the big swamps to Congaree." For black people in South Carolina, Boggy Gut not only contained the restless spirit of Ole Man Rogan but also echoed with the memories of slavery. As Old Bill recalled,

Some time in the night if you sit on Boggy Gut, you'll hear the rattle of the chains, you'll hear a baby crying every which a way, and you'll hear a mother calling for her child in the dark night on Boggy Gut. And you can sit on the edge of Boggy Gut and you'll see men in chains bent over with their heads in their hands—the sign of distress. While you sit, you can see the spirit of Ole Man Rogan coming across the big swamps. You can see him look at the women and men and children, and you see him laugh—laugh at the distress and tears on Boggy Gut, and he laughs like he is satisfied, but he's had no rest.[6]

The creeks in the Chesapeake had similar stories to tell. On the estate of Edward Lloyd in Talbot County on Maryland's Eastern Shore, a slave Demby ran into a creek to prevent further punishment from the plantation overseer, who gave Demby to the count of three to come out. When Demby resisted, the overseer Mr. Gore took aim and fired his musket at Demby, and the creek soon became his grave. Creeks contained the voices of the dead, heard by those who knew the stories of American slavery and the Atlantic slave trade and their horrors.[7]

Demby had sought a temporary refuge in the waters, looking for protection from his overseer who hovered over him like the boiling sun. Overseers' presence continued to haunt slaves. Frances Kimbrough of Georgia recalled that after Jessie Kimbrough, the "young marster" of the plantation, died she could see "his ghost leaning against a pine tree, watching his former slaves working the field."[8] Plantation overseers such as Mr. Gore and Jessie Kimbrough enforced a labor regime with a social and political order defined in part by one's relationship to the sun. As the American folk music scholar Alan Lomax writes, "From the beginning, it was the white man standing in the shade, shouting orders with a club or whip or gun in his hand—while out in the sun the blacks sweated with the raw stuff of wealth, cursing under their breath, but singing at the tops of their voices."[9] Those songs resonated into the slave quarters, where slave artisans were at work. Talking about his mother who worked textiles, George White stated, "When mama was going around seeing if the other slaves had done their carding, she would sing: 'Keep your eye on the sun / See how she runs / Don't let her catch you with your work undone / I'm trouble, I'm trouble."[10] Even slave children, who were generally spared the most arduous tasks, spoke about plantation power dynamics by referring to the sun. As Charlie Hudson recalled, "When work got tight and hot in crop time, I helped the other children tote water to the hands."[11]

And Henry Box Brown recalled how, at a young age, "as the hot sun sent forth its scorching rays upon my tender head, did I look forward with dismay, to the time, when I, like my fellow slaves, should be driven by the task-master's cruel lash, to the performance of unrequited toil upon the plantation of my master."[12] He had good reason to be dismayed.

When slaves stood away from the earshot of their owners and overseers, the pain of toiling under the sun entered their conversations, shaped their memories, influenced their imagination, and informed their worship. After Henry Box Brown's family was sold into slavery in South Carolina, he imagined working under the sun as a sign of their distress. "Far, far away in Carolina's swamps are they now, toiling beneath the scorching rays of the hot sun."[13] The intensity would have been like that which Solomon Northrup endured on the Louisiana plantation of John Tibeats. "As the sun approached the meridian that day it became insufferably warm. Its hot rays scorched the ground. The earth almost blistered the foot that stood upon it. I was without coat or hat, standing bareheaded, exposed to its burning blaze. Great drops of perspiration rolled down my face, drenching the scanty apparel wherewith I was clothed." In that moment, his call for relief went unheard. He added, "Over the fence, a very little way off, the peach trees cast their cool, delicious shadows on the grass. I would gladly have given a long year of service to have been enabled to exchange the heated oven, as it were, wherein I stood, for a seat beneath their branches."[14] That spot was reserved for plantation overseers, as Northrup and former slaves such as Benjamin Johnson understood; he recalled that "the overseer would be sitting down under a tree and he would holler 'keep going.' The sweat would be just running off of you."[15]

The sun was seared into the memories even of slaves who weren't involved in field work. William Wells Brown wrote that when he had been a slave in Missouri, "the plantation being four miles away from the city, I had to drive the family to church. I always dreaded the approach of the Sabbath; for, during service, I was obliged to stand by the horses in the hot broiling sun, or in the rain, just as it happened."[16] Slaves carried this sensibility into their religious life and practices. During a prayer meeting in Virginia, one slave minister beseeched, "Please, Lord, the load of slavery is so heavy it's about to destroy us all. The grass in the cotton field is so high. The sun is so hot. We almost perish in the middle of the day. Do, Master, have mercy and help us please."[17] The refrain of enslaved field workers was that they worked under the scorching rays of the sun, both a literal and figurative statement about slave labor and plantation power dynamics.

During the antebellum period, the presence of the domestic slave trade bore down on the enslaved much like the burning rays of the sun under which they worked. From 1820 to 1860, southerners entered into two million slave sale transactions, with one-third of the sales carrying slaves over state lines.[18] The threat and recollection of the auction block, the presence of speculators creeping through the Upper South looking to buy slaves, and the separation of families wore on slaves, and they used natural metaphors to discuss the process through which they journeyed. For example, the mother of Henry Box Brown pointed to nature to teach him lessons about the domestic slave trade before his own family was threatened with breakup. Brown recalled that his mother, "pointing to the forest trees adjacent, now being stripped of their thick foliage by autumnal winds, would say to me, 'my son, as yonder leaves are stripped from off the trees of the forest, so are the children of slaves swept away from them by the hands of cruel tyrants.'"[19] While slaves harvested crops, speculators and planters harvested slaves.

Working under the sun added intensity to an already grueling forced labor routine, which reached its extreme in the marshes and swamps of Louisiana and the South Carolina, Georgia, and Florida Lowcountry. In his political opposition to slavery, Henry Box Brown invoked the image of "Carolina's pestilential swamps," and slaves who had family sold during the domestic slave trade to the Carolinas sang, "Gone,—gone,—sold and gone, to the rice swamp dank and lone!"[20] The swamps were a haunting presence to black people and affected the artwork of Thaddeus Goodson of Columbia, South Carolina. Though he was born after the Civil War, his sense of the swamps reverberated from the antebellum period. As mentioned before, the swamps of Boggy Gut were haunted by Ole Man Rogan's wandering spirit and the voices of the people he had sold. The master storyteller and poet informed his audience, "I've been down in the big swamps of the Congaree." Someone responded, "Tell us, brother?" Goodson went on, "I've been down to the Congaree in the swamps . . . where owles on a dead limb talk of the dead and laugh like the dead, way down in the big swamps of the Congaree."[21]

Like a Central African shaman, Goodson prophesied from the sounds of birds that death was impending. Duarte Lopez, who was on the Central African coast during the years of the slave trade, wrote that people there "are greatly given to *Divination* by birdes" and that if a bird cried in a particular way it was a foreboding sign.[22] This belief resonated through the period of slavery. For instance, Dye Williams of Georgia recounted that she knew that her son was going to die soon when she heard an owl hoot-ing.[23] Goodson also realized that the world of slavery in the antebellum Lowcountry's marshes *was* a world of the dead, where malnutrition, in-fant mortality, malaria, and other tropical diseases led to alarmingly high mortality rates. For instance, over a fifteen-year period (1819–34) on the Butler Island plantation of Georgia, over 16 percent of slave children born alive died within the first two weeks of birth.[24]

This grim reality figured into Goodson's portrait of the swamps, where he saw "trees sweat like a man." His poetry reminded his audience of the physiological toll of slave labor, and while Central African ideas shaped his poetry, it was forged through the experience of American slavery. For example, he refashioned the claim that cotton was king in the South and pointed out the irony of the national anthem's lines about America being the land of the free and the home of the brave by calling the Congaree swamps "the land of poison, where the yellow-fly stings, in the home of the fever and where death is king." In a sobering conclusion to his poem of entering into the land of the dead, Goodson ends, "That's where I've been, down in the big swamps. Down in the land of mosquitoes, way down in the big swamps on the Congaree."[25]

The swamps were so nightmarish that they drove some to seek a spiri-tual return to Africa. In the 1780s, a group of slaves were brought to the swamps of coastal North Carolina to dig a canal from the Scuppernong Lake to the Scuppernong River, and many succumbed to the brutal work routine. The plantation overseer recounted, "They were kept at night in cabins on the shore of the lake. At night they would begin to sing their native songs, and in a short while would become so wrought up that, ut-terly oblivious to the danger involved, they would grasp their bundles of personal effects, swing them over their shoulders, and setting their faces towards Africa, would march down into the water singing as they marched till recalled to their senses only by the drowning of some of the party."[26] One wonders whether, as in the creeks of coastal Georgia that contained the voices of the dead, one could hear the sound of ghosts near the Scuppernong Lake.

The enslaved expressed their grief through natural metaphor, particu-larly comparing slavery to clouds hanging overhead. On remembering the eve of being sold from William Ford to John Tibeats, who proved to be more cruel in his punishments, Solomon Northrup wrote, "Clouds were gathering in the horizon—forerunners of a pitiless storm that was soon to break over me."[27] Henry Box Brown invoked similar imagery to mobilize

opposition to slavery: "Imagine, reader, a fearful cloud, gathering blackness as it advances towards you, and increasing in size constantly; hover-
ing in the deep blue vault of the firmament above you, which cloud seems
loaded with the elements of destruction, and from the contents of which
you are certain you cannot escape."[28] And black people in South Carolina spoke about clouds to give voice to their pain. On visiting a Carolina plantation, William Wells Brown observed, "The night was dark, the
rain descended in torrents from the black and overhanging clouds, and
the thunder, accompanied with vivid flashes of lightning, resounded fear-
fully." Brown witnessed a prayer meeting, led by an elder who poured
forth "such a prayer as but few outside of this injured race could have
given." The people gathered then followed another slave in song, who intoned, "Oh! breth-er-en, my way, my way's cloudy, my way, go send them
angels down. Oh! breth-er-en, my way, my way's cloudy, my way, Go send
them angels down."[29] With both the rays of the sun and the clouds in the
sky representing a menacing planter class, the "signs" from nature meant
that the possibilities for escape seemed closed.

Many slaves spoke about the power struggle between masters and
slaves indirectly, pointing to forms of nature to give voice to their own
discontent. One slave song summed up the exploitative labor dynamics of
antebellum plantations in the lines, "The Old bee makes the honey comb,
the young bee makes the honey. The niggers make the cotton and corn,
and the white folks get the money."[30] William Wells Brown recorded a
similar song from a slave named Cato, who intoned, "The big bee flies
high, the little bee makes the honey, the black man raises the cotton, and
the white man gets the money."[31] This sentiment paralleled the more well-
known work song with which Frederick Douglass grew up on the Eastern
Shore of Maryland that went, "We raise the wheat, they give us the corn;
We bake the bread they give us the crust; We sift the meal; They give us
the husk; We peel the meat, They give us the skin."[32]

Slaves could invoke the impersonal world of nature to talk about the
exploitative and demeaning system of slave labor. In fundamental ways,
planters set the tone for the conversation, having legally defined slaves as
chattel in the seventeenth century. Yet slaves adopted and transformed
this language, turning the tables ideologically to create a vision that challenged the claims of white planters to superiority and their sense of man-
hood. For instance, Simon Brown, born in Virginia, said about the owners of a woman that he was courting, "Like many white men all over the
South, they appeared to me—and to all the slaves mostly—to be lower

than the beasts of the woods. We had no real respect for them. A wolf or a tiger would fight to defend his young. He would never forsake his children. But a white man would force a slave woman to have children by him and then hold his own blood offspring in slavery."³³ Through this critique, Simon Brown revealed a strain of thought that held slaveholding to be simultaneously unmanly and unnatural. And in doing so, he challenged the paternalistic claims of slave owners.

Slaves also created an ideology that opposed the institution of slavery by comparing their own status to that of animals. They drew parallels between their work in the fields and the horrors of the auction block to the lives of beasts. Brown told a young William J. Faulkner, who sat at the feet of the elder Brown as he recalled stories about slavery, "You see, in slavery days, black people weren't treated like human beings, but like work animals."³⁴ And in the words of Fountain Hewes, who was born in Charlottesville, Virginia, and whose grandfather was owned by Thomas Jefferson, "We were slaves, we belonged to people. They'd sell us like they sell horses, and cows, and hogs and all like that, and have an auction bench, and they put you up on the bench and bid on you the same way that you'd bid on cattle." He added, "If my master wanted to send me, he never said you could get on a horse and ride. You'd walk. You'd be barefooted and cold, and it didn't make any difference. You weren't much more to some of them than a dog in those days, you wouldn't be treated as good as you treat dogs now."³⁵ And looking back at the days before his sale down the Ohio River, Henry Bibb said that his fate was for him "to be sold like an ox, into hopeless bondage, and to be worked under the flesh-devouring lash during life, without wages."³⁶ Being bought and sold and working without wages, slaves and their descendants compared their lot in the antebellum South to that of animals.

The writings of many slaves repeated a refrain that slaveholders, by labeling and treating slaves as chattel, themselves became like animals. Likening her owner Dr. Flint to a snake, Harriet Jacobs labeled him a "venomous old reprobate."³⁷ Henry Box Brown asserted about planters "that all who drank of this hateful cup were transformed into some vile animal" and that his owner "so became a perfect brute in his treatment of slaves"; he also referred to the planter class as "the bloodhounds of the South."³⁸ Simon Brown opined, "You know that folks in a heap of ways are like the creatures in the Deep Woods. They act as if they're not any better than the animals that kill and eat one another."³⁹ Henry Bibb, recollecting his family's escape from his plantation into the swamps of Louisiana, found himself surrounded by a pack of wolves. He added that "my chance was far better among the howling wolves in the Red River Swamp, than before Deacon Whitfield, on the cotton plantation."[40] Through these analogies, blacks unmasked the genteel, "paternalistic" veneer of slavery of Old South legend and peered into its violent core.

At its core, slavery was a system that gave slave owners property rights in people who could be put to work in places and at times that they would not willingly be.[41] Slaves were painfully aware of these property rights, as Fountain Hewes and Simon Brown pointed out, and they were clear about what they meant in terms of the impact of the elements on their bodies. For example, Armici Adams, a former slave from Virginia, recalled, "When it snowed, the work was very hard. I can remember carrying milk in the snow when it was snowing so hard that you couldn't see a foot ahead of yourself. When I got back I was so cold I couldn't get my hand off the bucket handle. They had to pry it off. My feet would freeze too. Missis used to thaw my hands and feet out every winter morning."[42] On top of the already rigorous labor they required of their slaves, slaveholders used the forces of nature as a way to control their slaves. For example, planters exposed slaves to the elements as a punishment. The North Carolina fugitive slave Harriet Jacobs recalled an instance in her childhood that illustrates this slaveholding tactic. Jacobs was wearing a new pair of shoes her grandmother had bought her to protect her from the snow. When Jacobs walked through the room of her mistress, the shoes made too much noise, and her mistress ordered her to "Take them off . . . and if you put them on again, I'll throw them into the fire." The mistress then sent Jacobs on an errand barefoot.[43]

Even when slaves resisted, the natural world seemed to place constraints on them and provide a tool for planter domination. For Harriet Jacobs, snakes and mosquitoes in the swamps of eastern North Carolina stood as obstacles to her escape. During her flight, the only refuge her uncle Phillip could find for her was in the swamps, where both of them "were covered with hundreds of mosquitos. In an hour's time they had so poisoned my flesh that I was a pitiful sight to behold. As the light increased, I saw snake after snake crawling round us." With no regrets, she added that "even those large, venomous snakes were less dreadful to my imagination" than the planters who claimed to be civilized.[44] And during her seven years in the garret of her grandmother's house before her ultimate escape from slavery, rats and mice were her companions. Others who sought to escape conjured frightful images about their "natural" surroundings.

Frederick Douglass plumbed the minds of slaves, which were tortured by images of attack. Speaking for himself and others who contemplated escape, he felt that they would be "stung by scorpions—chased by wild beasts—bitten by snakes; and worst of all, having succeeded in swimming rivers—encountering wild beasts—sleeping in the woods—suffering hunger, cold, heat and nakedness—we supposed ourselves to be overtaken by hired kidnappers."[45] So Douglass and others saw nature as a line of defense for slaveholders to hem in their enslaved population.

In their poetry and autobiographies, in their work songs and folklore, which reveal the political ideologies of slaves, nature was prominent. For slaves, nature was by no means always a benign force but had a malignant potential. Their daily exposures to the rays of the sun, the pestilence of the swamps, and the harshness of winters served as sobering reminders of their status as slaves. Nature also carried memories, of lakes that people waded into while struck with visions of a return to Africa, or fields where previous generations had toiled. In these ways, slaves' perceptions of the natural world paralleled those of people along West Africa's Gold Coast and its interior, who in particular believed that Nyame, the creator of the universe, had infused it with power, or *tumi*. As explained by Emmanuel Akyeampong and Pashington Obeng, "The Asante universe contained numerous participants—spirits, humans, animals, and plants. It was a universe of experience in which some of the participants were invisible." Furthermore, "the Asante universe was suffused with power," and "access to power (Twi: *tumi*: 'the ability to bring about change') was available to anyone who knew how to make use of *Onyame's* powerful universe for good or evil."[46]

In Asante, gaining access to and exercising *tumi* became the basis of social and political conflict as Asante political authorities attempted to impose violent control over their subjects by deploying *tumi* malevolently. However, they never held a monopoly on power. Simultaneously with these efforts at domination and often in response to them, people on the political margins sought to access *tumi* in ways that posed a challenge to the hegemony of Asante political elites and had the potential to spark social change. A parallel struggle emerged on North American slave plantations. Where white southern planters attempted to deploy the forces of nature toward their own ends, slaves developed systems of knowledge and strategies to tap into these forces to empower themselves.

Perhaps the most radical example of a slave whose dialogue with nature informed his resistance to slavery was "Prophet" Nat Turner. Struggling against the imposition of an overseer, Turner ran into the woods, where he remained for thirty days before returning to his plantation. He revealed that in the woods "the Spirit appeared to me and said, I had my wishes directed to things of this world, and not to the kingdom of heaven, and that I should return to the service of my earthly master." Soon after, he had a vision in which "the sun was darkened, the thunders rolled in the heavens, and blood flowed in the streams." Later, Turner withdrew from that world to contemplate "the Spirit" through observing the rhythms of the natural world. In his quest, he sought for it to "reveal to me the knowledge of the elements, the revolution of the planets, the operation of the tides, and changes of the seasons." Turner continued to avail himself of signs from nature, which extended in part from his labor. "While working in the field," Turner recalled, "I discovered drops of blood on the corn."[47]

Turner's vision resonated with other political claims, spoken in naturalistic terms, by black people elsewhere. For example, during the early nineteenth-century debate over the American Colonization Society's effort to return blacks to Africa, black political and religious figures such as Richard Allen and Absolom Jones argued that because "our ancestors (not of choice) were the first successful cultivators of the wilds of America, we their descendants feel ourselves entitled to participate in the blessings of her luxuriant soil, which their blood and sweat manured."[48] Given how other black people stressed how slaves and their ancestors had poured their blood into the soil, it was no great leap for Turner to see drops of it on the corn.

While organizing his insurrection, Turner also looked to the forests and the skies for knowledge, tapping into their *tumi*. He "found on the leaves in the woods hieroglyphic characters, and numbers, with the forms of men in different attitudes." And he timed his decision to inform a small band of confidantes of his planned rebellion by signs from nature, which took the form of a solar eclipse in February of 1831.[49] Turner, like other slaves in the antebellum South, saw in nature's signs a call to change. And in the process of reading its signs, slaves at times blurred the line between nature and the human experience, bringing the information they garnered from nature into their artwork, education of young people, labor struggles, and political perspectives.

Even the slightest hint from nature pushed slaves forward. While Nat Turner acted along dramatic, violent lines for slave liberation, other slaves, realizing the overwhelming armed might of the planter class, believed stoically that change would happen over a longer time. George White, who was born into slavery in Virginia in 1847, recalled that his mother had inspired him with the song "Keep inching along, Keep inching along, Inching like a two inch worm, You'll get there by an' by."[50] Other slaves expressed envy when looking at nature, seeing its creatures as privileged with a kind of freedom denied to slaves. Solomon Northrup, who was lured to Washington, D.C., kidnapped, taken to Richmond, and sold to the Deep South, recalled that during his captivity on the steamboat that took him south, "the sun shone out warmly; the birds were singing in the trees. The happy birds—I envied them. I wished for wings like them, that I might cleave the air to where my birdlings waited vainly for their father's coming, in the cooler region of the North." And like George White's grandmother, Northrup found inspiration in the seemingly smallest of creatures. Speaking proverbially, he remarked, "Life is dear to every living thing; the worm that crawls upon the ground will struggle for it."[51] This sensibility resonated in work songs and the heart of the blues, as in the words of the blues singer who hollered, "I'd rather be a catfish swimming in that deep blue sea, than to stay in Texas, treated like they wanted to do poor me."[52]

Through metaphors of flight and an identification with birds, slaves developed counterideologies that challenged planter domination. For example, black people in coastal Georgia made repeated claims that Africans had the power to fly back to Africa. After one overseer tried to punish a group of Africans, they were said to "rise up in the sky and turn themselves into buzzards and fly right back to Africa."[53] Harriet Tubman had a similar identification with birds and flight. She recalled that during her days as a slave in Maryland, "she used to dream of flying over fields and towns, and rivers and mountains, looking down upon them 'like a bird,' and reaching at last a great fence, or sometimes a river, over which she would fly."[54] Behind the identification with the fish that swam the seas, the birds flying aloft, and the inchworm that snuck by generally unnoticed, slaves simultaneously protested the exploitative dynamics of antebellum forced labor camps and saw a vision of different life possibilities.

Slaves grappled with that tension, between the painful and creative potentialities of nature, in the swamplands. As already noted, slaves found the swamps to be "lands of poison." Yet conversely many sought refuge from slavery in the lowland marshes, such as the Dismal Swamp of North Carolina and Virginia and the swamps of Louisiana. For instance, Henry Bibb and his family fled into the swamps near the Red River in Louisiana, hoping to find their way to freedom. Yet the swamp creatures seemed to parallel the violence of the plantation world. Bibb recalled, "About the dead hour of the night I was roused by the awful howling of a gang of blood-thirsty wolves, which had found us out and surrounded us as their prey, there in the dark wilderness many miles from any house or settlement."[55] While Bibb's flight into the swamps failed, other slaves found the liberation Bibb and his family sought. Simon Brown recounted the story of "Big Tom," who fled into the Dismal Swamp of Virginia, fended off bloodhounds sent after him, and successfully escaped to an Indian village.[56] Omar, the grandfather of jazz artist Sidney Bechet, roamed the bayous of the Lower Mississippi Valley and was said to live like a "free slave long before Emancipation."[57]

Furthermore, some saw in the swamps a sacred dimension. The anthropologist and novelist Zora Neale Hurston pointed out that the swamps offered a context for black conversion experiences and religious visions. She wrote, "The vision is a very definite part of Negro religion. . . . The cemetery, to a people who fear the dead, is a most suggestive place to gain visions. The dense swamp with the possibility of bodily mishaps is another."[58] Such a vision was revealed to Solomon Northrup in the swamps of Louisiana. In spite of the "dreariness" of the marshes, he saw within them a pulsation of life. "Not by human dwellings—not in crowded cities alone, are the sights and sounds of life. The wildest places of the earth are full of them. Even in the heart of that dismal swamp, God has provided a refuge and a dwelling place for millions of living things."[59] Upon entering this refuge for other forms of life, Northrup realized the possibility for a refuge for himself, which he would eventually find.

Slaves also transformed "the woods" into a refuge; the forests had a kind of *tumi* that allowed them to effect change in their lives. Liza Brown, who was a slave in Virginia, vividly remembers that slaves fled to the woods for protection. She recalled, "Yes, the slaves used to run away from our flock and stay in the woods." Cornelia Carter had an even more intimate memory. She remembered about slavery that "Father got beat up so much that after a while he ran away and lived in the woods." Horace Tonsler was inspired by a slave Berkeley Bulluck, who told him how he had made an escape from slavery. "One day we were driving up the road and he showed me the very road he used when he first escaped. This road led to Bath County. He said he traveled at night by the moonshine. Said he would feel around the trees and whichever way the moss grew on, he knew that was the north direction."[60] In this way, the trees of the Old Dominion served as compasses and contained the history of slave flight.

While some slaves found in these temporary refuges a springboard for their ultimate escape, other slaves found their escape to be more fleeting. During instances of *petit marronage*, slaves fled into the forests and elsewhere for short periods, only to return back to their plantations.[61] The woods provided some personal and spiritual relief from the larger "cotton fever" sweeping the antebellum South, as one slave termed the cotton boom and the demand for slaves in the Deep South. With the pressures of the domestic slave trade, some slaves fled to the woods so that they could remain close to their families, and in some cases the response worked. One person who had been sold to a slave trader fled to the woods, which became his home for a year, until "Miss Sarah Ann bought him and united him with the rest of his family—his wife and three children." Lorenzo L. Ivy of Chatham, Virginia, exclaimed, "Runaways! Lord, yes, they had plenty of runaways." He added, "Sometimes slaves just ran away to the woods for a week or two to get a rest from the field, and then they would come on back. They never came back till they got the word, though. . . . My grandmother, named Sallie Douchard, stayed in the woods for three or four weeks." Douchard eventually returned and was spared the violence that led her to flee in the first place. However, many other slaves who fled temporarily into the woods faced severe consequences. Further torture or sale to the Deep South might face those who were caught in the woods or returned to their plantations.[62]

Slaves drew upon the woods not only for personal refuge but also for resources that they intended to use for protection on their plantations. As on the Gold Coast, in other parts of West Africa, and in Central Africa, a group of experts formed in the antebellum South who accessed the powers of the natural and spiritual world to protect their clients. On the Gold Coast and in its interior, for instance, a group of Sufi healers made protective amulets to protect their clients; and in Central Africa diviners gave their clients charms, or *nkisi*, to save them from harm. *Nkisi* contained elements from nature, such as herbs and roots.[63] The tie between Frederick Douglass and the conjurer Sandy demonstrates the ways slaves accessed power through their knowledge of the natural world. After being threatened by his overseer Covey, Douglass fled into the woods, where he "was buried in its somber gloom, and hushed in its solemn silence; hid from all human eyes; shut in with nature and nature's God, and absent from all human contrivances."[64] There he met Sandy, a conjurer who aided Douglass's resistance to the ceaseless violence he faced at the hands of Covey. Douglass poured his story out to Sandy and his wife, and Sandy offered his aid. According to Douglass, Sandy "was a genuine African, and had inherited some of the so called magical powers, said to be possessed by African and eastern nations. He told me he could help me; that, in those very woods, there was an herb, which in the morning might be found, possessing all the powers required for my protection." Though Douglass was first incredulous, he obeyed Sandy's order and ended up beating back Covey's attacks.[65] While diviners such as Sandy were concentrated in the eastern slave states, some carried the knowledge to the western states through the domestic slave trade. William Wells Brown recalls a Missouri slave named Dinkie, who "roamed through the woods" whenever he decided to and declared that he "got de power" and could know things "seen and unseen."[66] And as Douglass tapped into such knowledge to fend off the beating from Covey, Dinkie used his knowledge of the natural world and as a diviner to spare himself from an impending beating.

Like West and West Central Africans, southern slaves saw a tension between the forest and the village or plantation and moved back and forth between these two areas to create change in their lives. In West Central Africa, this tension reflected a larger cosmology that "deploys a series of complementary oppositions between the visible and the invisible, life and death, above and below, day and night, village and forest. This universe is organized in time as well as in space, in such a way that the other world is both the past and the future, and the movement of human life matches that of the sun. The same cosmology is general in forest West Africa."[67] Slaves such as William Wells Brown and Dinkie viewed the universe according to a similar set of dual, opposing forms.

In the antebellum South, black people turned the woods into sanctuaries. For example, Harriet Jacobs entered into the woods for contemplation, in her case to visit the burial grounds of her parents. Just before her flight from her owner to her grandmother's garret, where she stayed for seven years before making it to the North, she visited the gravesites of her parents in the woods, where slaves often buried their dead. Ryer Emmanuel of South Carolina had witnessed such burials when she was young. "When they were about to bury them, I used to see the lights many times and hear the people going along singing out yonder in the woods. All about in these woods, you can find plenty of those slavery graves." Emmanuel added, "Right over there across the creek in those big cedar trees, there is another slavery graveyard. People going by there could often hear talking and couldn't see anything, they tell me . . . and would hear babies crying all about there too." So when Harriet Jacobs went into the woods to visit her parents' gravesite, she entered a world where the ancestors spoke to the living. She wrote, "The graveyard was in the woods, and twilight was coming on. Nothing broke the death-like stillness except the occasional twitter of a bird." In this stillness, she knelt before their graves and "poured forth a prayer to God for guidance." She received an answer on her way from the gravesite when she heard what sounded like her father's voice, "bidding me not to tarry till I reached freedom or the grave."[68]

The movement of the sun was also central to slave philosophy, artwork, and cultural and religious practices. The sun not only scorched enslaved workers who toiled under its rays but represented by its movement the possibilities for transformation and the cyclical nature of the human experience. In particular, black people in the antebellum South inherited the Central African belief that human life passes like the sun's cycle through four phases—birth, maturity, death, and ancestry. They represented this cyclical movement by a circle with a cross overlapping it and by the ring shout, a counterclockwise dance that represented these phases. Through these beliefs and practices, African descendants tapped into ancestral knowledge.[69] After sunset, though exhausted from their plantation work regimen, slaves gained access to this ancestral knowledge, going into the woods or elsewhere to shout, and they gave reverence to the sun as it rose. Rosa Grant of coastal Georgia recounted how her grandmother, who was from Africa, had told "her about the harvest time when the folks stayed up all night to shout. At sunup, they sang and prayed and said that they will live better and be more thankful the next year." And George Smith "remembered hearing the older Negroes tell of having watches on certain occasions when they sat up all night waiting for sunrise. When the sun at last appeared over the horizon, they would start a slow-dance and bow to the sun."[70]

Yet as the sun rose it marked the beginning of another day's work, as it did for a gang of slaves hired out to work on a Virginia railroad that was to pass through Appomattox. Painting a vivid image of the morning sun that accompanied workers who cleared forests from the tracks, Fannie Berry recalled that "they all started coming from all directions with their axes on their shoulders, and the mist and fog was hanging over the pines, and the sun was just breaking across the fields."[71] If it rained, they might sing a verse like the "John Brown's Hammer" song, which went, "Everywhere I look this morning, look like rain, baby, look like rain. I got a rainbow tied around my shoulder, ain't gonna rain, baby, ain't gonna rain."[72] Though the sun bore down on them intensely during their field labor, and though many were afraid that as the day passed and the sun set they would be caught "with their work undone," slaves still revered the *movement* and cycles of the sun. The movement of the sun perhaps reminded them that "trouble don't last always." It was as if through their voices slaves channeled the powers of nature, which, whether in the form of a rainbow or the fields, offered them strength and bodily protection.

While slaves had little access to the fruits of the plantation fields, those fields teemed with energy, and slaves drew upon this to make it through their days of labor. In particular, they transmuted the power of the fields and the skies surrounding them into songs that sustained them as they worked. Simon Brown invoked this sense when he recounted that among slaves in Virginia, "Many times, in the field, black voices would sing, 'Over my head, there's music in the air; There must be God somewhere.'" Brown added that this allowed them to make it through periods of fatigue. Under some cases, when some slaves suffered from exhaustion and became vulnerable to punishment, their leader would exhort them to "'to reach inside your hearts and bring out a song, a song of salvation, of freedom. You've got a lot of songs of salvation in your hearts.' With that, the slaves began to sing, and they were refreshed."[73] Like people on the Gold Coast, slaves in Louisiana used the power of speech and song to access power in nature. The New Orleans jazz musician Sidney Bechet theorized that "the only thing they had that couldn't be taken from them was their music. Their song, it was coming right up from the fields, settling itself in their feet and working right up, right up into their stomachs, their spirit, into their fear, into their longing."[74] And those songs resonated beyond the immediate fields. As Marrinda Jane Singleton recalled about slave religious meetings, "Here we would pray and sing in our own feelings and expressions singing in long and common meters sounding high over the hills."[75] Through their song, they developed a deeper connection to the fields, where in some places generations of slaves had poured out their labor.

As they worked in the fields and forests, they connected to the land while simultaneously knowing their fragile connection to it. Slaves in Virginia, as they cleared forests, would create songs that acknowledged the possibility of their being sold on the slave market. Fannie Berry remembered slaves felling pine trees and singing a "sorrowful song" that went, "This time tomorrow night, Where will I be? I'll be gone, gone, gone, Down to Tennessee." She recalled the woods would just "ring with this song."[76]

Within the context of the unimaginable pressures that the domestic slave trade placed on slaves in the antebellum South and the fragility of the ties between people within the slave community, many slaves become lovers of the natural world and saw transformative power in it. Much as Hilda Vitzthum saw in a small daisy that grew in the desolation of the Soviet gulags an image of her own survival, some slaves saw in the flowering of nature possibilities for their own transformation. Even the gardens of their owners delighted slaves. Solomon Northrup said of the Ford plantation in Louisiana, "I strolled into the madam's garden. Though it was a season of the year when the voices of the birds are silent, and the trees are stripped of their summer glories in more frigid climes, yet the whole variety of roses were then blooming there, and the long, luxuriant vines creeping over the frames."[77] The former slave Clara Allen remembered being sent to a plantation in Monroe County that had "gardens and a big lake just outside the yard. Every kind of flower that ever grew."[78] Louis Hughes said about the ironic beauty of the southern landscape, "Flowers grew in profusion everywhere through the south, and it has, properly, been called the land of flowers."[79] And Harriet Jacobs recalled that after the winter passed in coastal North Carolina, "The beautiful spring came; and when Nature resumes her loveliness, the human soul is apt to revive also. My drooping hopes came to life again with the flowers."[80]

The spontaneous growth of plants in the rural South gave way in some places to slave horticultural practices, enabling slaves to have a more reliable source of inspiration in a world of family separation and uncertainty. Nathaniel John Lewis of Georgia claimed that the plants in his garden provided him with protection. On the path leading to his house in coastal Georgia, Charles Hunter had a garden of "brightly colored flowers."[81] And on the property of the North Carolinian Priscilla Joiner, "the garden was immaculately kept. Rose bushes climbed the houseside. The late fall breeze wafted dying pink petals over the whole garden; magnolias, petunias, tulips were in bloom. As she led us from bush to bush, Priscilla Joiner fondled occasional flowers and seemed to take on strength from them." Joiner, who lived alone and had little contact with her children, drew comfort from her garden. "I have my own place here and my flowers. What more could an old woman want?"[82]

In tending to the natural world, black people simultaneously tended to their own selves. For instance, Mildred Heard recalled, "Once a little red bird got hurt and I caught it and nursed it back to health and this bird began to act just like a pet. When I saw the bird was well enough to leave I tied a red string around its leg so that I would know it if I saw it again. After that for three years my little bird used to fly back and sit on the steps until I would feed him and then he would fly away."[83] Given the deep significance that slaves gave to flight, as in their stories about Africans flying back to Africa, Heard's practice of nursing this bird back to health must have offered her a great deal of succor in the midst of the pressures of black life in the rural South.

Other slaves captured a sense of the sublime under the stars. The meteor storm of 1833 was emblazoned in the psyche of many slaves for decades. Some former slaves such as Rastus Jones and Baily Cunningham had early memories of it. Cunningham claimed to have been eight years old when the meteors "began to fall about sundown and fall all night. They fell like rain. They looked like little balls about as big as marbles with a long streak of fire to them. They fell everywhere but you couldn't hear them. They did not hit the ground or the house. We were all scared and did not go out of the house but could see them everywhere."[84] Black people in Georgia also invoked the memory of the meteor shower. Edie Dennis remembered "the wonderful manner in which the stars shot across the heavens by the thousands, when every sign seemed to point to the destruction of the earth."[85] For the slaves who witnessed it and passed knowledge of it to succeeding generations, the meteor shower called forth awe and fear that momentarily equalized everyone under its domain. It served as a marker of time, influenced their artwork, and gave slaves a language to understand the Civil War, which for some replicated this natural event. As Charles Grandy stated, "Did you ever see stars a-shootin? Well they were shooting one right after the other—fast! Then a great big star over in the east came right down almost to the earth. I saw it myself. It was a sign of the war, alright."[86] And the meteor showers inspired the black artist Harriet Powers, who had been born a slave in Georgia in 1837 and who depicted it over sixty years later in a quilt she made in 1898.[87]

Most spectacularly displayed during meteor showers, the night sky held for slaves a deep political, social, and spiritual significance. Under the cover of darkness, fugitive slaves made their escape from southern slave labor camps. After sunset, slaves reenergized themselves from exhausting field work through the social life of the slave quarters and in the woods. Ellen Lindsey remembered that her father "used to lay flat on his back and tell time by the stars."[88] Some simply gazed at the stars in wonder. Even in the midst of the nightmarish experience of slavery in the coastal swamps, slaves revered the beauty of the night sky. For instance, Daphney Wright, who was a slave in the South Carolina Lowcountry, recalled, "When the stars would come out there over the water it was a beautiful sight!"[89] Perhaps for this reason, slaves in Virginia intoned, "I've been in the valley praying all night, All night—all night, All night—All night. Give me a little more time to pray. I've been in the valley mourning all night, I've been in the valley mourning all night, I've been in the valley mourning all night."[90]

For slaves, nature possessed its own wonders; however, the contexts of slavery and freedom sharpened their sense of its meaning. When Harriet Tubman passed into northern lands from slavery in Maryland, she saw that "there was such glory over everything, the sun came like gold through the trees, and over the fields, and I felt like I was in heaven."[91] Upon being captured during an attempted escape from slavery, Henry Bibb seemed to have been awakened to natural beauty. He recalled that, "while I was permitted to gaze on the beauties of nature, on free soil, as I passed down the river, things looked to me uncommonly pleasant: The green trees and wild flowers of the forest; the ripening harvest fields waving with their gentle breezes of Heaven; and the honest farmers tilling their soil and living by their own toil." And when he made his final escape, the new political context shaped his sense of the natural world. Bibb recounted that as he passed up the Ohio River toward his freedom, "notwithstanding I was deeply interested while standing on the deck of the steamer looking at the beauties of nature on either side of the river, as she pressed her way up the stream, my very soul was pained to look upon the slaves in the fields of Kentucky, still toiling under their task-masters without pay."[92]

In a world where planters tried to bind slaves to particular pieces of land, the movement and flow of rivers took on political and spiritual meanings. And for many slaves, the waters became the medium for Christian conversion. Slaves conducted their baptismal ceremonies in ponds, and others took slaves to the rivers for this rite of passage. "There weren't any pools in the churches to baptize folks in then, so they took them down to the creek," Elisha Doc Garey recounted. She added, "First a deacon went in and measured the water with a stick to find a safe and suitable place—then they were ready for the preacher and the candidates. Everybody else stood on the banks of the creek and joined in the singing. Some of the songs were: 'Lead Me to the Water to be Baptized.'"[93] Similarly, Callie Elder recalled, "All I know about baptizing is they just took them to the river and plunged them in. They sung something about: 'Going to the River to be Baptized.'"[94] And though Carrie Hudson didn't participate in the ritual, she witnessed other slaves pass through the baptismal waters. She stated, "I can see them folks now, marching down to the creek, back of the church, and all the candidates dressed in the whitest of white clothes, that was the style then. Everybody joined in the singing, and the words were like this: 'Marching for the water, for to be baptized.'[95] Understanding baptism as simultaneously an act of purification and a means of accessing spiritual power, slaves marched to the rivers when they were at ebb "so the sins would be washed away." When they got there, the preacher took the candidates one by one into the river and dipped them in the water. "Then he made a prayer for the river to wash away the sins."[96] Marching to the rivers and through baptism, slaves, though they could not wash away slavery, could become transformed in other ways.

The agricultural fields, where slaves transmuted seeds into crops, offered another site for slave spiritual transformation and conversion to Christianity. Like Nat Turner, who had visions when he was in the fields of Southampton County, Virginia, many slaves captured sublime messages in the midst of field labor. One slave remembered, "One day while in the field plowing I heard a voice." Another slave told of her conversion experience: "One day, a year later, I was out chopping in the field. The corn was high and the weather was hot. I was feeling joyous and glad for I wanted to eat and I was thinking of coming to the dance and the good time I was going to have. Suddenly I heard a voice. It called 'Mary! Mary!'" One slave recalled, "One Thursday morning, the sun was shining bright, I was chopping corn in the garden, when a voice 'hollered' and said, 'Oh, Nancy, you got to die and can't live.'"[97]

Through their daily labor, work songs, and conversion experiences, slaves developed a deep connection to the cultivated soil; however, it was more often the outskirts of the primary work fields that offered slaves their refuge. Slaves went into thickets and forests for contemplation and religious camp meetings, where they created a world beyond the control of planters. This connection to the natural world salved the wounds of separation brought about by the slave trade. One slave recalled that after being sold to a planter in Louisiana, "I started to praying and calling on God and let what come that might. I somehow found time and a chance to slip to the bushes and ask God to have mercy on me and save my soul." The woods also provided cover for collective meetings of slaves, who connected simultaneously with nature and with their ancestors through "the shout." One person recalled that "the old folks used to slip out in the fields and thickets to have prayer meetings and my mother always took me along for fear something would happen to me if left behind. They would all get around a kettle on their hands and knees and sing and pray and shout and cry." The meetings made a deep impression on the youths, one of whom stated, "I will never forget some of the meetings in the fields and thickets where the old folks got together in the quiet hours of the night and lifted their voices to glory." Another slave recalled, "God first spoke to me when I was eight years old. I was down in the thicket getting some brush to kindle a fire."[98] Thus nature became a means for the conversion process.

Because of the domestic slave trade, the prospect of being uprooted shadowed slave life in the antebellum South. Given such uncertainty, the rooted nature of trees and forests spoke to slaves in significant ways. Some went in solitude and sought to recreate practices carried from Africa through the Atlantic slave trade. According to the former slave Julia Henderson, "I can remember my father's father, Horace his name was, going to that pine tree. Miss, it would be just like that yard, it was clean because he prayed there so much. I didn't know if he prayed like we did, but he got down on his knees and spoke an African prayer."[99] As slaves formed religious communities, they often noted more about the natural context of worship than about the sermons themselves, and the songs that slaves sang were often laden with natural metaphors. For instance, the brush harbors where many slaves in the antebellum period went for worship stayed in the memory of former slaves. As Simon Brown describes black worship in Virginia, slaves worshipped in brush harbors or under trees, and they sang "natural" songs upon returning, such as "Go Down to the River Jordan," "Wade in the water, children; O, wade in the water, children; Wade in the water, children; God's going to trouble the water," or "Oh, my soul got happy When I come out the wilderness, Come out the wilderness; Oh my soul got happy When I come out the wilderness; I'm a-leaning on the Lord."[100]

From working under the burning sun to holding camp meetings under the cover of the night sky, slaves drew upon the natural world for symbolic and political resources. The compelling beauty of the foliage and flowering of the South simultaneously inspired awe in slaves and served as a cruel reminder that the full blossoming of most slaves would not be actualized. The forests, swamps, and rivers spoke with the voices of the dead, and the soil was soaked with the blood and sweat of the living. The woods were simultaneously a natural barrier to slaves' escape, a refuge for fugitives, and a sanctuary for religious devotees. The sun beating down on slaves during the daytime in many ways defined their status as unfree labor, while the night sky, periodically revealing the marvels of shooting stars, inspired visions of freedom.

Notes

INTRODUCTION

1. David Eltis, "Free and Coerced Transatlantic Migrations: Some Comparisons," *American Historical Review* 88 (April 1983): 252; Robin Blackburn, *The Making of New World Slavery: From the Baroque to the Modern, 1492–1800* (New York: Verso, 1997).

2. Edmund Morgan, *American Slavery, American Freedom: The Ordeal of Colonial Virginia* (New York: W. W. Norton, 1975); Philip D. Morgan, *Slave Counterpoint: Black Culture in the Eighteenth-Century Chesapeake and Lowcountry* (Chapel Hill: University of North Carolina Press, 1998); Gary A. Puckrein, *Little England: Plantation Society and Anglo-Barbadian Politics, 1627–1700* (New York: New York University Press, 1984); Betty Wood, *The Origins of American Slavery: Freedom and Bondage in the American Colonies* (New York: Hill and Wang, 1997), 40–67.

3. Elizabeth Donnan, ed., *Documents Illustrative of the Slave Trade to America*, vol. 1, *1441–1700* (1930–35; repr., New York: Octagon Books, 1965), 156.

4. Ronald Bailey, "The Slave(ry) Trade and the Development of Capitalism in the United States: The Textile Industry in New England," *Social Science History* 14 (Autumn 1990): 373–414.

5. Eltis, "Free and Coerced Transatlantic Migrations," 252; Jack Greene, "The American Revolution," *American Historical Review* 105 (February 2000): 93–102; Gordon Wood, *The Radicalism of the American Revolution* (New York: Alfred A. Knopf, 1992); Puckrein, *Little England*.

6. Based on a query of David Eltis et al.'s online database, Voyages: The Trans-Atlantic Slave Trade Database, www.slavevoyages.org/tast/database/index.faces.

7. Robert Harms, *The Diligent: A Voyage through the Worlds of the Slave Trade* (New York: Basic Books, 2002), 300.

8. Patricia A. Molen, "Population and Social Patterns in Barbados in the Early Eighteenth Century," *William and Mary Quarterly*, 3rd ser., 28 (April 1971): 289.

9. Donnan, *Documents Illustrative*, 2:148.

10. Trevor Burnard, "European Migration to Jamaica, 1655–1780," *William and Mary Quarterly*, 3rd ser., 53 (October 1996): 772; Donnan, *Documents Illustrative*, 1:174.

11. Michael Craton, *Searching for the Invisible Man: Slaves and Plantation Life in Jamaica* (Cambridge, MA: Harvard University Press, 1978), 53–54.

12. Aaron S. Fogleman, "From Slaves, Convicts, and Servants to Free Passengers: The Transformation of Immigration in the Era of the American Revolution," *American Historical Review* 85 (June 1998): 43–76.

13. Peter H. Wood, *Black Majority: Negroes in Colonial South Carolina from 1670 through the Stono Rebellion* (New York: W. W. Norton, 1974), ch. 5; Jennifer Morgan, *Laboring Women: Reproduction and Gender in New World Slavery* (Philadelphia: University of Pennsylvania Press, 2004), 128–43.

14. P. Morgan, *Slave Counterpoint*, 59–61.

15. E. Morgan, *American Slavery, American Freedom*, chs. 13 and 15.

16. U.S. Department of Commerce, *Historical Statistics of the United States*, pt. 2, *Colonial Times to 1970* (Washington, DC: U.S. Department of Commerce, 1975), 1168; P. Morgan, *Slave Counterpoint*, 61.

17. Eltis et al., Voyages database.

18. Michael Gomez, *Exchanging Our Country Marks: The Transformation of African Identities in the Colonial and Antebellum South* (Chapel Hill: University of North Carolina Press, 1998), 17–37.

19. Michael Tadman, "The Demographic Costs of Sugar: Debates on Slave Societies and Natural Increase in the Americas," *American Historical Review* 105 (October 2000): 1534–64; P. Wood, *Black Majority*, 63–91; P. Morgan, *Slave Counterpoint*; Ira Berlin, *Many Thousands Gone: The First Two Centuries of Slavery in North America* (Cambridge, MA: Harvard University Press, 1998); Ira Berlin and Philip Morgan, eds., *Cultivation and Culture: Labor and the Shaping of Slave Life in America* (Charlottesville: University Press of Virginia, 1993).

20. Joyce Chaplin, *An Anxious Pursuit: Agricultural Innovation and Modernity in the Lower South, 1730–1815* (Chapel Hill: University of North Carolina Press, 1993), 190–220; P. Morgan, *Slave Counterpoint*, 361, 368; David Eltis, "New Estimates of Exports from Barbados and Jamaica," *William and Mary Quarterly*, 3rd ser., 52 (October 1995): 631–48; Puckrein, *Little England*, 40–72.

21. Donnan, *Documents Illustrative*, 1:379.

22. South Carolina Historical Society, *Collections of the South Carolina Historical Society*, vol. 5 (Charleston: South Carolina Historical Society, 1897), 125.

23. P. Wood, *Black Majority*, 20–28; J. Morgan, *Laboring Women*, 123–28.

24. April Hatfield, *Atlantic Virginia: Intercolonial Relations in the Seventeenth Century* (Philadelphia: University of Pennsylvania Press, 2004), 143–50; Russell R. Menard, "The Maryland Slave Population, 1658 to 1730: A Demographic Profile of Blacks in Four Counties," *William and Mary Quarterly*, 3rd ser., 32 (January 1975): 31.

25. P. Wood, *Black Majority*, 32; Hatfield, *Atlantic Virginia*, 52–53, 154–55.

26. Berlin, *Many Thousands Gone*; P. Morgan, *Slave Counterpoint*; Berlin and Morgan, *Cultivation and Culture*.

27. Martin Delany, *The Condition, Elevation, Emigration, and Destiny of the Colored People of the United States* (1852; repr., Baltimore: Black Classics Press, 1993); P. Wood, *Black Majority*, 35–62; Daniel C. Littlefield, *Rice and Slaves: Ethnicity and the Slave Trade in Colonial South Carolina* (1981; repr., Urbana: University of Illinois Press, 1991), 74–114; Gwendolyn Midlo Hall, *Africans in Colonial Louisiana: The Development of Afro-Creole Culture in the Eighteenth Century* (Baton Rouge: Louisiana State University Press, 1992), 120–42.

28. Judith Carney, *Black Rice: The African Origins of Rice Cultivation in the Americas* (Cambridge, MA: Harvard University Press, 2001).

29. Anthony S. Parent, *Foul Means: The Formation of a Slave Society in Virginia, 1660–1740* (Chapel Hill: University of North Carolina Press, 2003), 60–66; Lorena S. Walsh, *From Calabar to Carter's Grove: The History of a Virginia Slave Community* (Charlottesville: University Press of Virginia, 1997), 61–65.

30. Gwendolyn Midlo Hall, *Slavery and African Ethnicities in the Americas: Restoring the Links* (Chapel Hill: University of North Carolina Press, 2005), 122 and passim; Peter H. Wood, "'It Was a Negro Taught Them': A New Look at African Labor in Early South Carolina," *Journal of Asian and African Studies* 9:3–4 (1974): 160–79; Kevin Dawson, "Enslaved Swimmers and Divers in the Atlantic World," *Journal of American History* 92 (March 2006): 1327–55; John K. Thornton, *Africa and Africans in the Making of the Atlantic World, 1400–1800*, 2nd ed. (New York: Cambridge University Press, 1998), 135.

31. David Eltis, Philip Morgan, and David Richardson, "Agency and Diaspora in Atlantic History: Reassessing the African Contributions to Rice Cultivation in the Americas," *American Historical Review* 112 (December 2007): 1329–58.

32. I have listened to the advice of Ghanaian archeologist James Anquandah, who during my year of research at the University of Ghana insisted that the study of precolonial West African history requires an interdisciplinary approach.

33. In response to feedback on an earlier draft of this book, I have "translated" the interviews and folklore used in chapters 5 and 6 into Standard English.

34. Jane I. Guyer and Samuel M. Eno Belinga, "Wealth in People as Wealth in Knowledge: Accumulation and Composition in Equatorial Africa," *Journal of African History* 36 (1995): 91–120.

35. Leland Ferguson, *Uncommon Ground: Archeology and Early Afro-American Life* (Washington, DC: Smithsonian Institution Press, 1992); Gomez, *Exchanging Our Country Marks*; Rachel Harding, *A Refuge in Thunder: Candomble and Alternative Spaces of Blackness* (Bloomington: Indiana University Press, 2000); Sterling Stuckey, *Slave Culture: Nationalist Theory and the Foundations of Black America* (New York: Oxford University Press, 1987); James Sweet, *Recreating Africa: Culture, Kinship, and Religion in the African Portuguese World, 1441–1730* (Chapel Hill: University of North Carolina Press, 2003); Robert Farris Thompson, *Flash of the Spirit: African and Afro-American Art and Philosophy* (New York: Random House, 1983); Thornton, *Africa and Africans.*

CHAPTER 1

1. Fernand Braudel, *Civilization and Capitalism, 15th–18th Century,* vol. 1, *The Structures of Everyday Life,* trans. Sian Reynolds (New York: Harper and Row, 1981); the quotation is from Braudel's *Afterthoughts on Material Civilization and Capitalism,* trans. Patricia M. Ranum (Baltimore: Johns Hopkins University Press, 1977), 8.

2. Stephanie Smallwood, *Saltwater Slavery: A Middle Passage from Africa to American Diaspora* (Cambridge, MA: Harvard University Press, 2007); Cedric Robinson, *Black Marxism: The Making of the Black Radical Tradition* (1983; repr., Chapel Hill: University of North Carolina Press, 2000), 111–20.

3. Paul E . Lovejoy, "The Internal Trade of West Africa to 1800," in *History of West Africa,* 3rd ed., ed. J. F. E. Ajayi and Michael Crowder (London: Longman, 1985), 1:667–87; Ivor Wilks, *Forests of Gold: Essays on the Akan and the Kingdom of Asante* (Athens: Ohio University Press, 1993), 2–28.

4. Elliott P. Skinner, "West African Economic Systems," in *Economic Transition in Africa,* ed. Melville Herskovits and Mitchell Harwitz (Evanston: Northwestern University Press, 1964), 85–86. I am indebted to Professor George Hagan, Institute of African Studies, Legon, Ghana, for the notion that markets were sites of exchange of "cultural goods," stated during his feedback on a presentation I gave in his African Social Systems course in spring 1997.

5. Pieter de Marees, *Description and Historical Account of the Gold Kingdom of Guinea* (1602), ed. and trans. Albert Van Dantzig and Adam Jones (New York: Oxford University Press, 1987), 63. "Millie" was millet, and "Bachovens" were a kind of banana (110–12, 161 n. 1).

6. For a general discussion of West African gold, kola, and salt production, see Lovejoy, "Internal Trade," 653–63; Paul Lovejoy, *Caravans of Kola: The Hausa Kola Trade, 1700–1900* (Zaria, Nigeria: Ahmadu Bello University, 1980); and Timothy F. Garrard, *Akan Weights and the Gold Trade* (New York: Longman, 1980). On the Wangara, see Wilks, *Forests of Gold,* ch. 1.

7. Skinner, "West African Economic Systems," 85; Jan Hogendorn and Marion Johnson, *The Shell Money of the Slave Trade* (Cambridge: Cambridge University Press, 1986), 58–62.

8. The concept of a web of trading relations is drawn from historical anthropologist Eric Wolf, who notes, "Africa south of the Sahara was not the isolated, backward area of European imagination, but an integral part of a web of relations that connected forest cultivators and miners with savanna and desert traders and with the merchants and rulers of the North African settled belt." Eric R. Wolf, *Europe and the People without History* (Berkeley: University of California Press, 1982), 40.

9. African patrons' habits of material acquisition and conspicuous consumption plunged many of them into debt, which they covered by capturing

outsiders and selling them to European merchants. Joseph C. Miller, *Way of Death: Merchant Capitalism and the Angolan Slave Trade, 1730–1830* (Madison: University of Wisconsin Press, 1988). The tragedy of modern consumption is explored by Herbert Marcuse in *One-Dimensional Man: Studies in the Ideology of Advanced Industrial Society* (Boston: Beacon Press, 1964).

10. David Birmingham, "Early African Trade in Angola and Its Hinterland," in *Pre-colonial African Trade,* ed. Richard Gray and David Birmingham (New York: Oxford University Press, 1970), 163–73; J. Miller, *Way of Death,* 54–62; Jan Vansina, "Peoples of the Forest," in *History of Central Africa,* ed. David Birmingham and Phyllis M. Martin (New York: Longman, 1983), 1:87.

11. Jan Vansina, *The Children of Woot: A History of the Kuba Peoples* (Madison: University of Wisconsin Press, 1978), 186–96; Vansina, "Peoples of the Forest," 87; John K. Thornton, *The Kingdom of Kongo: Civil War and Transition, 1641–1718* (Madison: University of Wisconsin Press, 1983), 32–33; Anne Hilton, *The Kingdom of Kongo* (New York: Oxford University Press, 1985), 7; quote is from Georges Balandier, *Daily Life in the Kingdom of Kongo: From the Sixteenth to the Eighteenth Century,* trans. Helen Weaver (London: George Allen and Unwin, 1968), 133.

12. For an extended discussion of this process, see J. Miller, *Way of Death,* chs. 1 and 2.

13. J. D. Fage, "The Effect of the Export Slave Trade on African Populations," in *The Population Factor in African Studies,* ed. R. P. Moss and R. J. A. R. Rathbone (London: University of London Press, 1975), 18.

14. Richard Hull, *African Cities and Towns before the European Conquest* (New York: W. W. Norton, 1976); Peter Garlake, *The Kingdoms of Africa* (Oxford: Elsevier-Phaidon, 1978).

15. Akin L. Mabogunje and Paul Richards, "Land and People: Models of Spatial and Ecological Processes in West African History," in Ajayi and Crowder, *History of West Africa,* 1:6–12; Timothy Insoll, "Iron-Age Gao: An Archaeological Contribution," *Journal of African History* 38:1 (1997): 1–30; Graham Connah, *African Civilizations: An Archaeological Perspective* (New York: Cambridge University Press, 2001), ch. 4. The West African savannah and forest zones will be defined more clearly in chapter 2.

16. Ivor Wilks, *Asante in the Nineteenth Century: The Structure and Evolution of a Political Order* (London: Cambridge University Press, 1975), 178–79; Lovejoy, "Internal Trade," 677; Akin L. Mabogunje, *Urbanization in Nigeria* (New York: Africana, 1968), 54–55.

17. A. W. Lawrence, *Fortified Trade-Posts: The English in West Africa, 1645–1822* (London: Jonathan Cape, 1963), 164; Jean Barbot, *Barbot on Guinea: The Writings of Jean Barbot on West Africa, 1678–1712,* ed. P. E. H. Hair, Adam Jones, and Robin Law (London: Hakluyt Society, 1992), 2:547; Ray Kea, *Settlements, Trade, and Polities in the Seventeenth-Century Gold Coast* (Baltimore: Johns Hopkins University Press, 1982), 38.

18. Mabogunje, *Urbanization in Nigeria,* 64, 91.

19. John K. Thornton, "Mbanza Kongo/Sao Salvador: Kongo's Holy City," in *Africa's Urban Past,* ed. David M. Anderson and Richard Rathbone (Portsmouth, NH: Heinemann, 2000), 67–68 and n. 6.

20. Thornton, *Kingdom of Kongo,* 38–39; J. Miller, *Way of Death,* 9.

21. Thornton, "Mbanza Kongo/Sao Salvador," 67.

22. Merrick Posnansky, "Early Agricultural Societies in Ghana," in *From Hunters to Farmers: The Causes and Consequences of Food Production in Africa,* ed. J. Desmond Clark and Steven A. Brandt (Berkeley: University of California Press, 1984), 150–51.

23. Hull, *African Cities and Towns,* 33–41; Graham Connah, "African City Walls: A Neglected Source?" in Anderson and Rathbone, *Africa's Urban Past,* 39–45; Thornton, "Mbanza Kongo/Sao Salvador," 67–68.

24. Thornton, "Mbanza Kongo/Sao Salvador," 68.

25. Quoted in Balandier, *Daily Life,* 150.

26. Graham Connah, *The Archeology of Benin: Excavations and Other Researches in and around Benin City, Nigeria* (Oxford: Clarendon Press, 1975), 98–106; P. Amory Talbot, *The Peoples of Southern Nigeria: A Sketch of Their History, Ethnology and Languages, with an Abstract of the 1921 Census,* vol. 3, *Ethnology* (London: Oxford University Press, 1926), 903–46.

27. Skinner, "West African Economic Systems," 83–84.

28. J. Miller, *Way of Death,* 110–11; Hilton, *Kingdom of Kongo,* 108.

29. John Thornton has asserted that political consolidation, economic exchange, and multilingualism forged West Africa into two major sociocultural units—Upper Guinea, from Senegal to just south of Cape Mount in modern Liberia; and Lower Guinea, from western Côte D'Ivoire to Nigeria. Thornton, *Africa and Africans,* 183–90.

30. A. Hampate Ba, "The Living Tradition," in *General History of Africa,* vol. 1, *Methodology and Prehistory,* ed. J. Ki-Zerbo (Berkeley: University of California Press, 1981), 185–87; Tal Tamari, "The Development of Caste Systems in West Africa," *Journal of African History* 32:2 (1991): 221–50.

31. Major Denham, F. R. S., Captain Clapperton, and the Late Doctor Oudney, *Narrative of Travels and Discoveries in Northern and Central Africa in the Years 1822, 1823, and 1824* (1826; repr., London: Darf, 1985), 2:402.

32. Skinner, "West African Economic Systems," 82.

33. Kea, *Settlements, Trade, and Polities,* 105–6, 199–201.

34. Ann Stahl and Maria Das Dores Cruz, "Men and Women in a Market Economy: Gender and Craft Production in West Central Africa ca. 1775–1995," in *Gender in African Prehistory,* ed. Susan Kent (Walnut Creek, CA: AltaMira Press, 1998), 39–67.

35. A. A. Boahen, "The States and Cultures of the Lower Guinea Coast," in *General History of Africa,* vol. 5, *Africa from the Sixteenth to the Eighteenth*

Centuries, ed. B. A. Ogot (Berkeley: University of California Press, 1992), 417–24; J. K. Fynn, *Asante and Its Neighbours, 1700–1807* (Evanston: Northwestern University Press, 1971); Wilks, *Asante,* 64–71, 305–6.

36. Philip de Barros, "Bassar: A Quantified, Chronologically Controlled, Regional Approach to a Traditional Iron Production Centre in West Africa," *Africa* 56:2 (1986): 153.

37. Candace L. Goucher and Eugenia Herbert, "The Blooms of Banjeli: Technology and Gender in West African Iron Making," in *The Culture and Technology of African Iron Production,* ed. Peter R. Schmidt (Gainesville: University Press of Florida, 1996), 40–57.

38. De Barros, "Bassar," 171.

39. For research on a comparable site in Central Africa, see Jean-Pierre Warnier and Ian Fowler, "A Ruhr in Central Africa," *Africa: Journal of the International African Institute* 49:4 (1979): 329–51.

40. William Bosman, *A New and Accurate Description of the Coast of Guinea,* ed. John Ralph Willis, J. D. Fage, and R. E. Bradbury (1705; repr., London: Cass, 1967), 43; Jean Barbot, *A Description of the Coasts of North and South-Guinea* (London, 1732), 156, 261; de Marees, *Description,* 63–64, 121–24; Sir Dalby Thomas, Cape Coast Castle, to the Board of Trade and Plantations, Royal African Company, November 26, 1709, Furley Collections, Balme Library, University of Ghana, N38.

41. De Marees, *Description,* 26–27.

42. Geographer F. R. Irvine has found that oral traditions in Accra had over one thousand words for fish. F. R. Irvine, *The Fish and Fisheries of the Gold Coast* (London: Crown Agents for the Colonies, 1947), xiv.

43. Richard Austin Freeman, *Travels and Life in Ashanti and Jaman* (1898; repr., London: Frank Cass, 1967), 288.

44. Michel Adanson, *A Voyage to Senegal, the Isle of Goree, and the River Gambia* (London: J. Nourse and W. Johnston, 1759), 251.

45. As the religious studies scholar Dominique Zahan notes in relation to African spirituality, "Things and beings are not obstacles to the knowledge of God; rather they constitute signifiers and indices which reveal the divine being." Dominique Zahan, "Some Reflections on African Spirituality," in *African Spirituality: Forms, Meanings, and Expressions,* ed. Jacob K. Olupona (New York: Crossroad, 2000), 5.

46. R. Addo-Fenning, "The Gyadam Episode, 1824–70: An Aspect of Akyem Abuakwa History," *Universitas: An Interfaculty Journal* (University of Ghana), n.s., 6 (May 1997): 182.

47. Barbot, *Description,* 152, 261, 266.

48. De Marees, *Description,* 118–19; Richard B. Nunoo, "Canoe Decoration in Ghana," *African Arts* 7 (Spring 1974): 32–35.

49. Pieter Van Den Broecke, *Journal of Voyages to Cape Verde, Guinea, and Angola (1605–1612),* ed. and trans. J. D. La Fleur (London: Hakluyt Society, 2000), 60.

50. J. Miller, *Way of Death*, 54, 100.

51. Birmingham, "Early African Trade," 164–65; quote from Vansina, *Children of Woot*, 174; Thornton, *Kingdom of Kongo*, 34; Balandier, *Daily Life*, 159; J. Miller, *Way of Death*, 57.

52. Jan Vansina, *How Societies Are Born: Governance in West Central Africa before 1600* (Charlottesville: University of Virginia Press, 2004), 220, 221 n. 43.

53. Vansina, *Children of Woot*, 183.

54. Van Den Broecke, *Journal of Voyages*, 100.

55. Thornton, *Kingdom of Kongo*, 34; J. Miller, *Way of Death*, 54; quote from Balandier, *Daily Life*, 105.

56. For the early history of metallurgy in Central Africa, see Vansina, *How Societies Are Born*.

57. Balandier, *Daily Life*, 108; J. Miller, *Way of Death*, 55, 181; Thornton, *Kingdom of Kongo*, 33.

58. Van Den Broecke, *Journal of Voyages*, 100.

59. Eugenia Herbert, *The Red Gold of Africa: Copper in Precolonial History and Culture* (Madison: University of Wisconsin Press, 1984), 19–21, 42–44; J. Miller, *Way of Death*, 181.

60. Camara Laye, *The Dark Child: The Autobiography of an African Boy* (New York: Farrar, Straus and Giroux, 1954), 31–41.

61. Guyer and Belinga, "Wealth in People," 93.

CHAPTER 2

1. *A Perfect Description of Virginia; Being a Full and True Relation of the Present State of the Plantation, their Health, Peace, and Plenty, the Number of People, with the Abundance of Cattell, Fowl, Fish, etc.* (London, 1649), 14.

2. P. Wood, *Black Majority*, ch. 2; Littlefield, *Rice and Slaves*, 74–114; Parent, *Foul Means*, 60–66; Walsh, *From Calabar*, 61–65; Hall, *Africans in Colonial Louisiana*, 120–42; Carney, *Black Rice*.

3. As an extensive literature demonstrates, West African agriculture dates back millennia. For example, see Ann Brower Stahl, "A History and Critique of Investigations into Early African Agriculture," in Clark and Brandt, *From Hunters to Farmers*, 9–21; C. Ehret, "Historical/Linguistic Evidence for Early African Food Production," in Clark and Brandt, *From Hunters to Farmers*, 29–30, 36; Jack R. Harlan, "The Origins of Indigenous African Agriculture," in *The Cambridge History of Africa*, ed. J. D. Fage and Roland Oliver, vol. 1, *From Earliest Times to c. 500 B.C.*, ed. J. Desmond Clark (New York: Cambridge University Press, 1982), 635–39; C. T. Shaw, "The Prehistory of West Africa," in Ki-Zerbo, *General History of Africa*, vol. 1, *Methodology and African Prehistory*, 627.

4. James Giblin, "Trypanosomiasis Control in African History: An Evaded Issue?" *Journal of African History* 31:1 (1990): 63; W. B. Morgan and J. C. Pugh, *West Africa* (London: Methuen, 1969), 66, 69, 206–8.

5. W. Morgan and Pugh, *West Africa*, ch. 5; S. Diarra, "Historical Geography: Physical Aspects," in Ki-Zerbo, *General History of Africa*, vol. 1, *Methodology and Prehistory*, 324–26.

6. W. Morgan and Pugh, *West Africa*, 208–10, 213–15; Diarra, "Historical Geography," 330.

7. Diarra, "Historical Geography," 329; Akin L. Mabogunje, "Historical Geography: Economic Aspects," in Ki-Zerbo, *General History of Africa*, vol. 1, *Methodology and Prehistory*, 345.

8. Diarra, "Historical Geography," 325; Jan Vansina, *Paths in the Rainforest: Toward a History of Political Tradition in Equatorial Africa* (Madison: University of Wisconsin Press, 1990), 38–41; David Birmingham, "Society and Economy before A.D. 1400," in Birmingham and Martin, *History of Central Africa*, 1:3.

9. J. Miller, *Way of Death*, 14; Thornton, *Kingdom of Kongo*, 7; Hilton, *Kingdom of Kongo*, 1; Vansina, *Children of Woot*, 172–73; Robert W. Harms, *River of Wealth, River of Sorrow: The Central Zaire Basin in the Era of the Slave and Ivory Trade, 1500–1891* (New Haven: Yale University Press, 1981), 15–16.

10. Vansina, *Paths in the Rainforest*, 38; Robert Harms, *Games against Nature: An Eco-Cultural History of the Nunu of Equatorial Africa* (New York: Cambridge University Press, 1987), 30–31.

11. Vansina, *How Societies Are Born*, 101.

12. W. Morgan and Pugh, *West Africa*, 184, 191; Eric R. Wolf, *Peasants* (Englewood Cliffs, NJ: Prentice Hall, 1966); Joseph C. Miller, "The Paradoxes of Impoverishment in the Atlantic Zone," in Birmingham and Miller, *History of Central Africa*, 1:119.

13. Sophia D. Lokko, "Hunger Hooting Festival in Ghana," *Drama Review* 25 (Winter 1981): 43–50.

14. Paul Richards, *Indigenous Agricultural Revolution: Ecology and Food Production in Africa* (Boulder, CO: Westview Press, 1985).

15. W. Morgan and Pugh, West Africa, 98; Joseph C. Miller, "The Significance of Drought, Disease and Famine in the Agriculturally Marginal Zones of West-Central Africa," *Journal of African History* 23:1 (1982): 31.

16. James D. McCann, *Maize and Grace: Africa's Encounter with a New World Crop* (Cambridge, MA: Harvard University Press, 2005), chs. 2 and 3; David R. Harris, "Traditional Systems of Plant Food Production and the Origins of Agriculture in West Africa," in *Origins of African Plant Domestication*, ed. Jack R. Harlan, Jan M. J. de Wet, and Ann B. L. Stemler (The Hague: Mouton, 1976), 329; William O. Jones, *Manioc in Africa* (Stanford: Stanford University Press, 1959), 60–80; Marvin P. Miracle, *Maize in Tropical Africa* (Madison: University

of Wisconsin Press, 1966), 87–93; J. Miller, *Way of Death*, 18–21; Vansina, *Paths in the Rainforest*, 86. Most sources assert that Europeans brought maize to West Africa in the sixteenth or seventeenth century. Others open the possibility that a pre-Columbian exchange between West Africa and Europe brought maize to West Africa as early as the fourteenth century. See David H. Kelley, "An Essay on Pre-Columbian Contacts between the Americas and Other Areas, with Special Reference to the Work of Ivan Van Sertima," in *Race, Discourse, and the Origin of the Americas: A New World View*, ed. Vera Lawrence Hyatt and Rex Nettleford (Washington, DC: Smithsonian Institution Press, 1995), 117–18.

17. W. Morgan and Pugh, *West Africa*, 105; J. Miller, *Way of Death*, 19–20.

18. G. R. Crone, ed., *The Voyages of Cadamosto and Other Documents on Western Africa*, 2nd ser., no. 80 (London: Hakluyt Society, 1937), 30, 42.

19. Nicolas Villault, *A Relation of the Coasts of Africk called Guinee; With a Description of the Countreys, Manners and Customs of the Inhabitants; of the Productions of the Earth, and the Merchandise and Commodities it Affords; with Some Historical Observations upon the Coasts* (London: John Starkey, 1670), 46–47, 276.

20. Carney, *Black Rice*, 58–68; the Akan proverb is from Adam Jones in de Marees, *Description*, 159 n. 4.

21. William Finch, "Observations of William Finch, Merchant, Taken out of his large Journall" (August 1607), in Samuel Purchas, *Purchas, His Pilgrimes in Five Books* (London, 1625), 1:415.

22. Gaspar Mollien, *Travels in the Interior of Africa to the Sources of the Senegal and Gambia* (1820; repr., London: Frank Cass, 1967), 155.

23. Réné Caillié, *Travels through Central Africa to Timbuctoo* (1830; repr., London: Frank Cass, 1968), 1:294, 417.

24. Barbot, *Barbot on Guinea*, 1:186.

25. Ibid., 1:265, 292.

26. Ibid., 2:455.

27. Mungo Park, *Travels in the Interior Districts of Africa*, ed. Kate Ferguson Marsters (Durham: Duke University Press, 2000), 72–73. According to the editor's note, "Calavances are chick peas, or garbanzo beans; cassavi are cassava plants; pompions are pumpkins. Esculent simply means edibles" (72 n. 3).

28. W. Morgan and Pugh, *West Africa*, 326–27.

29. Ibid., 83, 97.

30. Ibid., 112.

31. Ibid., 105–9; Jack R. Harlan, "The Tropical African Cereals," in *The Archaeology of Africa: Food, Metals and Towns*, ed. Thurstan Shaw et al. (New York: Routledge, 1993), 53–58; Bassey Andah, "Identifying Early Farming Traditions of West Africa," in T. Shaw et al., *Archaeology of Africa*, 248–52.

32. Balandier, *Daily Life*, 94.

33. Hilton, *Kingdom of Kongo*, 5; Thornton, *Kingdom of Kongo*, 36; J. Miller, *Way of Death*, 19; Filippo Pigafetta, *A Report of the Kingdom of Congo and the*

Surrounding Countries; Drawn out of the Writings and Discourses of the Portuguese, Duarte Lopez, trans. Margarite Hutchinson (1881; repr., New York: Negro Universities Press, 1969), 67.

34. Harms, *Games against Nature,* 92–93.

35. Balandier, *Daily Life,* 95–96.

36. Harms, *Games against Nature,* 92–93.

37. W. Morgan and Pugh, *West Africa,* 68–69.

38. Walter Hawthorne, "Nourishing a Stateless Society during the Slave Trade: The Rise of Balanta Paddy-Rice Production in Guinea-Bissau," *Journal of African History* 42 (2001): 1–24.

39. Harlan, "Tropical African Cereals," 56.

40. W. Morgan and Pugh, *West Africa,* 100, 104, 120; Wolf, *Peasants,* 28.

41. W. Morgan and Pugh, *West Africa,* 105; Vansina, *Paths in the Rainforest,* 85.

42. W. Morgan and Pugh, *West Africa,* 104–5; Wilks, *Forests of Gold,* 44–53.

43. Caillié, *Travels through Central Africa,* 1:308, 372, 405, 420.

44. W. Morgan and Pugh, *West Africa,* 116–17; C. A. Folorunso and S. O. Ogundele, "Agriculture and Settlement among the Tiv of Nigeria: Some Ethnoarchaeological Observations," in T. Shaw et al., *Archaeology of Africa,* 276, 281–83.

45. Vansina, *Paths in the Rainforest,* 85.

46. Olaudah Equiano, *Equiano's Travels: His Autobiography, The Interesting Narrative of the Life of Olaudah Equiano or Gustavas Vassa the African,* ed. Paul Edwards (Oxford: Heinemann International, 1967), 7.

47. Skinner, "West African Economic Systems," 92.

48. The analytical tools of tribute-based and kinship-based modes of production are drawn from Wolf, *Europe,* 79–100; de Marees, *Description,* 110–11.

49. Jouke S. Wigboldus, "Trade and Agriculture in Coastal Benin," *A. A. G. Bijdragen* 28 (1986): 327–58.

50. Robert Norris notes the central role of women in agricultural production in Dahomey in his *Memoirs of the Reign of Bassa Ahadee, King of Dahomy, an Inland Country of Guiney. To Which Are Added, The Author's Journey to Abomey, the Capital; And A Short Account of the African Slave Trade* (London, 1789), 141–42.

51. Albert van Dantzig, comp. and trans., *The Dutch and the Guinea Coast, 1674–1742: A Collection of Documents from the General Archives of the Hague* (Accra: Ghana Academy of Arts and Science, 1978), 208.

52. McCann, *Maize and Grace,* 37–38.

53. W. Morgan and Pugh, *West Africa,* 326–27.

54. Ibid., 73; Folorunso and Ogundele, "Agriculture and Settlement," 277–78. It is significant to note that even in the roots-dominant belt agricultural workers also cultivated cereal crops.

55. Vansina, *Paths in the Rainforest,* 94.

56. Vansina, *Children of Woot*, 208–9; Balandier, *Daily Life*, 96–99; Vansina, *How Societies Are Born*, 193–94.

57. Pierre Bourdieu, "The Forms of Capital," in *Handbook of Theory and Research for the Sociology of Education*, ed. John G. Richardson (New York: Greenwood Press, 1986), 243.

58. Ibid., 255 n. 7.

59. Marcus Rediker, *The Slave Ship: A Human History* (New York: Viking Press, 2007); Smallwood, *Saltwater Slavery*.

60. Carney, *Black Rice*, 145–47.

61. William Ed Grimé, *Ethno-Botany of the Black Americans* (Algonac, MI: Reference Publications, 1979), 19–20.

62. Donnan, *Documents Illustrative*, 1:221, 226–34, and passim.

63. Ibid., 2:376.

64. Brown Family Papers, B466, Folder 1, John Carter Brown Library, Providence, RI.

65. Donnan, *Documents Illustrative*, 2:15.

66. Barbot, *Barbot on Guinea*, 2:781.

67. Donnan, *Documents Illustrative*, 2:15, 163, 376.

68. Carney, *Black Rice*, 72, 145–47.

69. Barbot, *Barbot on Guinea*, 2:775.

70. Equiano, *Equiano's Travels*, 26–27.

71. "Voyage to Guinea, Antego, Bay of Campeachy, Cuba Barbadoes, etc." [1712–23], Additional MS 39946, British Library, London. As Equiano also noted, submission to their captors' demands was enforced through sheer terror. Pain continued, "To put a stop to this danger the captain [?] this Strategem, to show them he could prevent their returning to their own country. He ordered the Carpenter to cut off the head of a dead Negro with his ax and fix it on a Pole made fast to the Ship's side and to throw the limbs about the Deck, he threatened the same to all that would not eat their victuals." One hundred twenty of the enslaved died during this voyage. For a larger discussion of this question, see Vincent Brown, *The Reaper's Garden: Death and Power in the World of Atlantic Slavery* (Cambridge, MA: Harvard University Press, 2008).

72. Carney, *Black Rice*, 155–59; Grimé, *Ethno-Botany*, 22–23, 26.

73. Vernon A. Ives, ed., *The Rich Papers: Letters from Bermuda, 1615–1646. Eyewitness Accounts Sent by the Early Colonists to Sir Nathaniel Rich* (Toronto: University of Toronto Press, 1984), 17–19 and passim.

74. Jerome S. Handler, "Amerindians and Their Contributions to Barbadian Life in the Seventeenth Century," *Journal of the Barbados Museum and Historical Society* 35:3 (1977): 197–98.

75. Hilary M. Beckles, *White Servitude and Black Slavery in Barbados* (Knoxville: University of Tennessee Press, 1989), 3.

76. David Watts, *Man's Influence on the Vegetation of Barbados, 1627 to 1800* (Hull: University of Hull Publications, 1966), chs. 3 and 4.

77. Richard Ligon, *A True and Exact History of the Island of Barbadoes* (1673; repr., London: Frank Cass, 1970), 22.

78. De Marees, *Description*, 28; Barbot, *Barbot on Guinea*, vol. 2, 461.

79. Father Andrew White, *Narrative of a Voyage to Maryland*, ed. E. A. Dalrymple (Baltimore: Maryland Historical Society, 1874), 23–24; Puckrein, *Little England*, 3–7, 53; *Colonising Expeditions to the West Indies and Guiana, 1623–1667*, 2nd ser., no. 56 (London: Hakluyt Society, 1924), 30; Blackburn, *Making of New World Slavery*, 230; Richard Dunn, *Sugar and Slaves: The Rise of the Planter Class in the English West Indies, 1624–1713* (Chapel Hill: University of North Carolina Press, 1972), 122–44, 167–78.

80. Antoine Biet, "Father Antoine Biet's Visit to Barbados in 1654," ed. and trans. Jerome Handler, *Journal of the Barbados Museum and Historical Society* 32 (May 1967): 66.

81. Ibid.

82. Felix Christian Spoeri, "A Swiss Medical Doctor's Description of Barbados in 1661: The Account of Felix Christian Spoeri," ed. and trans. Alexander Gunkel and Jerome S. Handler, *Journal of the Barbados Museum and Historical Society* 33 (May 1969): 7. Depending upon the interaction of a number of factors, including access to markets and the availability of land, some plantations imported food while others moved toward self-sufficient food production. In Barbados, plantations devoted most of their labor and arable land to sugarcane production, allowing little room for slaves to cultivate food crops for their own consumption or to market. In contrast, in Jamaica, while sugarcane was also essential, the enslaved African workforce had much greater access to land to grow food provisions. Sidney Mintz, *Caribbean Transformations* (1974; repr., New York: Columbia University Press, 1989), 180–94.

83. Griffith Hughes, *Natural History of Barbados* (London, 1750), 226, 254.

84. George Washington, *The Daily Journal of George Washington in 1751–2: Kept While on a Tour from Virginia to the Island of Barbadoes, with His Invalid Brother, Maj. Lawrence Washington* (Albany, NY: J. Munsell's Sons, 1892), 59.

85. "Journal of a Voyage from New England to New York in 1756 and of a Cruise Round the West Indies in 1756 and 1757," West Indies and Special Collections Library, University of the West Indies, Mona, Jamaica.

86. "A Particular Description of Cat Island Taken by Order of Woodes Rogers Esqr. Late Governr of Ye Bahama Islands in December 1731," Codex Eng 17, John Carter Brown Library, Providence, RI.

87. Edmund Hickeringill, *Jamaica Viewed; With All the Ports, Harbours, and their Several Soundings, Towns, and Settlements Thereunto Belonging* (London, 1661), 23; Richard Blome, *A Description of the Island of Jamaica; With the other*

Isles and Territories in America, to which the English are Related (London: L. Milbourn, 1672), 18.

88. Hans Sloane, *A Voyage to the Islands Madera, Barbados, Nieves, St. Christophers and Jamaica, with the Natural History of the Herbs and Trees, Four-footed Beasts, Fishes, Birds, Insects, Reptiles, Etc.* (London, 1707), 1:xix; Carney, *Black Rice*, 155–59; Vansina, *Paths in the Rainforest*, 85; Chaplin, *Anxious Pursuit*, 156.

89. Additional MS 61602, fols. 35–61, British Library.

90. Sloane, *Voyage to the Islands*, 1:105; David R. Harris, "The Ecology of Swidden Cultivation in the Upper Orinoco Rain Forest, Venezuela," *Geographical Review* 61 (October 1971): 475–95.

91. Sloane, *Voyage to the Islands*, 1:xv.

92. John Oldmixon, *The British Empire in America, Containing the History of the Discovery, Settlement, Progress and Present State of all the British Colonies, On the Continent and Islands of America* (London, 1708), 2:119, 122.

93. Bryan Edwards, *The History, Civil and Commercial, of the British Colonies of the West Indies* (London, 1793), 1:193, 203, 403.

94. "Journal and Account of Greenpark and Springvale Estate, 1790–1815," MS 236, Institute of Jamaica, Kingston, Jamaica.

95. "Journal of Somerset Plantation," MS 229, Institute of Jamaica, Kingston, Jamaica.

96. J. Stewart, *A View of the Present State of the Island of Jamaica* (1823; repr., New York: Negro Universities Press, 1969), 65.

97. Barry Higman, *Jamaica Surveyed: Plantation Maps and Plans of the Eighteenth and Nineteenth Century* (Kingston: University of West Indies Press, 2001), 266.

98. "Overseer's Journal, Somerset Vale, 1776–80," Somerset Vale Records, John Carter Brown Library, Providence, RI.

99. Richard Sheridan, "The Crisis of Slave Subsistence in the British West Indies during and after the American Revolution," *William and Mary Quarterly*, 3rd ser., 33 (October 1976): 615–41.

100. Higman, *Jamaica Surveyed*, 273–76.

101. Weynette Parks Haun, *Surry County, Virginia, Court Records, Deed Book III, 1672–1682* (Durham, NC, 1989), 25, 88, 127.

102. "An Inventory of the Estate of James Stone, 3rd January 1649," York County Records, reel 1, Library of Virginia, Richmond.

103. "An Inventory of the Estate of William Hughes, 20th and 21st January 1661," York County Records (transcript), reel 2a, Library of Virginia, Richmond.

104. Benjamin B. Weisiger, *York County, Virginia Records, 1665–72, Deed Book 4* (Richmond, VA, 1987), 107, 156, 166.

105. Weynette Parks Haun, *Surry County, Virginia, Court Records, Deed Book II, 1664–1671* (Durham, NC, 1987), 130.

106. Haun, *Surry County, Virginia, Court Records, Deed Book III*, 89.

107. Charles City County Records, Orders, August 1692, reel 13, Library of Virginia.

108. E. Morgan, *American Slavery, American Freedom,* 52–54; William E. Doolittle, *Cultivated Landscapes of North America* (New York: Oxford University Press, 2000), ch. 5, quote from 145.

109. Mark Catesby, *Catesby's Birds of Colonial America,* ed. Alan Feduccia (Chapel Hill: University of North Carolina Press, 1985), 151.

110. Marion Tingling, ed., *The Correspondence of the Three William Byrds of Westover, Virginia, 1684–1776* (Charlottesville: University Press of Virginia, 1977), 1:42, 66, 69.

111. William Hugh Grove, "Journal of Travels in England, Flanders, and America, 1698–1732," Special Collections Library, University of Virginia.

112. Frederick Douglass, *Life and Times of Frederick Douglass: His Early Life as a Slave, His Escape from Bondage, and His Complete History* (1881; repr., New York: Gramercy Books, 1993), 2, 4; Sterling Stuckey, *Going through the Storm: The Influence of African American Art in History* (New York: Oxford University Press, 1994), 33–36; Patricia M. Samford, *Subfloor Pits and the Archaeology of Slavery in Colonial Virginia* (Tuscaloosa: University of Alabama Press, 2007), 124–37.

113. South Carolina Historical Society, *Collections,* 5:126, 211, 263, 297, 333–34.

114. Thomas Jefferson, *The Garden and Farm Books of Thomas Jefferson,* ed. Robert C. Baron (Golden, CO: Fulcrum, 1987), 195; Savannah Unit, Georgia Writers' Project, Work Projects Administration, comp., *Drums and Shadows: Survival Studies among the Georgia Coastal Negroes* (1940; repr., Athens: University of Georgia Press, 1986), 71, 178.

115. Catesby, *Catesby's Birds,* 152.

116. Francis D. West, "John Bartram and Slavery," *South Carolina Historical Magazine* 56 (April 1955): 117.

117. Chaplin, *Anxious Pursuit,* 156.

118. Carney, *Black Rice.*

119. P. Wood, *Black Majority,* 35–62; Littlefield, *Rice and Slaves,* 74–114.

120. Peter Manigault to Charles Alexander, June 3, 1768, in "Letterbook of Peter Manigault, October 20, 1763–May 3, 1773," typescript by Maurice A. Crouse, author's files.

121. Henry Laurens to Henry Bright, September 9, 1762, in Henry Laurens, *The Papers of Henry Laurens,* vol. 3, *1759–1763* (Columbia: University of South Carolina Press, 1972), 118; Peter Manigault to Benjamin Stead, March 10, 1771, in "Letterbook of Peter Manigault."

122. Peter Manigault to Sarah Nickleson & Co., July 4, 1765, Peter Manigault to Mr. John Harris Cruger, September 6, 1771, and Peter Manigault to Thomas Harrison, June 10, 1772, all in "Letterbook of Peter Manigault."

123. "A List of Males at Cominge," microfiche, Ball Family Papers, South Carolina Historical Society, Charleston.

124. Wilks, *Forests of Gold*, ch. 2; Gomez, *Exchanging Our Country Marks*, 110; J. Miller, *Way of Death*, 12–14.

125. Catesby, *Catesby's Birds*, 151–53; Janet Schaw, *Journal of a Lady of Quality: Being the Narrative of a Journey from Scotland to the West Indies, North Carolina, and Portugal in the Years 1774 to 1776*, ed. Evangeline Walker Andrews (New Haven: Yale University Press, 1927), 163.

126. "Samuel Mathias Journal, March–July 1781," South Caroliniana Library, Columbia.

CHAPTER 3

1. Jerome Handler, "An African–Type Healer/Diviner and His Grave Goods: A Burial from a Plantation Slave Cemetery in Barbados, West Indies," *International Journal of Historical Archaeology* 1:2 (1997): 106–9, 112–14; Walsh, *From Calabar*, 106–7; Matthew C. Emerson, "African Inspirations in New World Art and Artifact: Decorated Pipes from the Chesapeake," in *"I, Too, Am America": Archaeological Studies of African-American Life*, ed. Theresa A. Singleton (Charlottesville: University Press of Virginia, 1999), 47–82; for an alternative perspective, see L. Daniel Mouer et al., "Colonoware Pottery, Chesapeake Pipes, and 'Uncritical Assumptions,'" in Singleton, *"I, Too, Am America,"* 95–113.

2. Mark D. Groover, "Evidence for Folkways and Cultural Exchange in the 18th Century South Carolina Backcountry," *Historical Archaeology* 28:1 (1994): 52–54.

3. Van Dantzig, *Dutch and the Guinea Coast*, 177–78, 318; Barbot, *Barbot on Guinea*, 2:462, 560.

4. Purchas, *Purchas, His Pilgrimes*, 1:415.

5. Richard Jobson, *The Golden Trade, or A Discovery of the River Gambra, and the Golden Trade of the Aethiopians, Set Down as They were Collected in Travelling Part of the Yeares 1620 and 1621* (1623; repr., London: Penguin Press, 1932), 168, 171.

6. Barbot, *Barbot on Guinea*, 2:547.

7. Equiano, *Equiano's Travels*, 7.

8. Littlefield, *Rice and Slaves*, 76–77; Mungo Park, *Travels in the Interior Districts of Africa: Performed Under the Direction of the Patronage of the African Association in the Years 1795, 1796, and 1797*, 3rd ed. (London: W. Bulmer, 1799), 34.

9. Caillié, *Travels through Central Africa*, 1:433.

10. Jobson, *Golden Trade*, 167; James Anquandah, *Rediscovering Ghana's Past* (London: Longman, 1982), 27–28 and passim; L. B. Crossland, *Pottery from the Begho-B2 Site, Ghana*, African Occasional Papers no. 4 (Calgary: University of Calgary Press, 1989); Marla C. Berns, "Art, History, and Gender: Women and Clay in West Africa," *African Archaeological Review* 11 (1993): 129–48. Though

Berns does not deal explicitly with the manufacture of clay pipes, her emphasis on the role of women in African pottery traditions and art bears upon this consideration of the manufacture of clay pipes.

11. Vansina, "Peoples of the Forest," 107–9.

12. Vansina, *Children of Woot*, 176; Pierre de Maret, "From Potter Groups to Ethnic Groups in Central Africa," in *African Archaeology*, ed. Ann Brower Stahl (Malden, MA: Blackwell, 2005), 425.

13. Ives, *Rich Papers*, 3–5, 46, 303–11.

14. Ibid., 59, 233–34; Rich adds that he was more valuable than other Africans, perhaps underestimating their experience with tobacco.

15. Linda M. Heywood, and John K. Thornton, *Central Africans, Atlantic Creoles and the Foundation of the Americas, 1585–1660* (New York: Cambridge University Press, 2007), 291.

16. Puckrein, *Little England*, 53; Biet, "Father Antoine Biet's Visit," 69.

17. Sloane Manuscripts, fol. 55, British Museum.

18. Handler, "Amerindians and Their Contributions," 198; Puckrein, *Little England*, 31–32, 40–72; *Colonising Expeditions*, 30.

19. Biet, "Father Antoine Biet's Visit," 66.

20. Ligon, *True and Exact History*, 22, 24.

21. Puckrein, *Little England*, 53.

22. Ibid., 59; Sloane Manuscripts, fols. 59–60, British Museum.

23. Eltis, "New Estimates of Exports," 638.

24. G. Hughes, *Natural History of Barbados*, 171.

25. Hickeringill, *Jamaica Viewed*, 338, 368.

26. Sloane, *Voyage to the Islands*, 1:lxiii.

27. Ibid., 1:cxxiv.

28. Handler, "Amerindians and Their Contributions," 207; Sloane, *Voyage to the Islands*, 1:147.

29. Sale of Sothesby and Co., West Indies-Bahamas Folder, Rare Books and Manuscripts Division, New York Public Library.

30. Edwards, *History, Civil and Commercial*, 1:403.

31. Eltis et al., Voyages database.

32. G. Melvin Herndon, *William Tatham and the Culture of Tobacco* (Coral Gables: University of Miami Press, 1969), 107–13; T. H. Breen details the other dimensions of tobacco production in *Tobacco Culture: The Mentality of the Great Tidewater Planters on the Eve of Revolution* (Princeton: Princeton University Press, 1985), 46–53.

33. W. Jeffrey Bolster, *Black Jacks: African American Seamen in the Age of Sail* (Cambridge, MA: Harvard University Press, 1997), 44–67; David S. Cecelski, *The Waterman's Song: Slavery and Freedom in Maritime North Carolina* (Chapel Hill: University of North Carolina Press, 2001), 4–5.

34. Peter H. Wood, "Whetting, Setting, and Laying Timbers: Black Builders in the Early South," *Southern Exposure* 8 (Spring 1980): 3–8; Bolster, *Black Jacks*, 44–67; Cecelski, *Waterman's Song*, 4–5.

35. The extensive literature on cotton production in precolonial West Africa is overviewed in Richard L. Roberts, *Two Worlds of Cotton: Colonialism and the Regional Economy in the French Soudan, 1800–1946* (Stanford: Stanford University Press, 1996), 51–52.

36. Thornton, *Africa and Africans*, 55; Crone, *Voyages of Cadamosto*, 31–32, 48.

37. Duarte Pacheco Pereira, *Esmeraldo de Situ Orbis*, ed. and trans. George T. Kimble (London: Hakluyt Society, 1937), 90–92. On the basis of Pereira's mention of the "Guoguliis" (92), Kimble suggests that he is employing an ethnonym, referring particularly to the Gola. In relation to African ethnicity in general, and the Gola in particular, see Gomez, *Exchanging Our Country Marks*, 88–105.

38. Jobson, *Golden Trade*, 171.

39. Kwabina B. Dickson, *A Historical Geography of Ghana* (New York: Cambridge University Press, 1969), 75–76; David Eltis, *The Rise of African Slavery in the Americas* (New York: Cambridge University Press, 2000), 137–49.

40. John Thornton argues that though West Africa expanded their textile imports from European traders, domestic production still accounted for well over 90 percent of West African textile consumption (*Africa and Africans*, 48–52).

41. Sandra E. Greene, *Gender, Ethnicity, and Social Change on the Upper Slave Coast: A History of the Anlo-Ewe* (Portsmouth, NH: Heinemann, 1996), 20–47.

42. Van Dantzig, *Dutch and the Guinea Coast*, 206. In relation to the kinship mode of production, Eric Wolf has defined kinship "as a way of committing social labor to the transformation of nature through appeals to filiation and marriage, and to consanguinity and affinity." This analytical device is particularly useful when viewing the changes within ethnic groups such as the Anlo-Ewe as they interacted with neighboring states and European traders on the coast. Wolf, *Europe*, 91.

43. K. Y. Daaku, *Gonja*, UNESCO Research Project on Oral Traditions, no. 1 (Legon: Institute of African Studies, University of Ghana, November 1969), interviews of Madam Adjoa Maman, 105–7, and Konde Jima, 102–4.

44. Hugh Clapperton, *Missions to the Niger*, vol. 4, *The Bornu Mission, 1822–25*, pt. 3, ed. E. W. Bovill (Cambridge: Cambridge University Press, 1966), 653, 658. It is worth noting that P. Amaury Talbot observed the same method in southern Nigeria in the early twentieth century. He writes, "The seeding of cotton and the spinning of the thread are always done by women or children in the intervals of farm work; the former by rolling it between a smooth log and an iron rod, and the latter by fastening the lint on to a wooden spindle

whorl—which is then spun round by a jerk and draws out the cotton to the required fineness." Talbot, *Peoples of Southern Nigeria,* 3:939.

45. Testimony of John Barnes, in *Minutes of the Evidence Taken Before a Committee of the House of Commons, Being a Committee of the Whole House, to Whom It Was Referred to Consider the Circumstances of the Slave Trade, Complained of in the Several Petitions Which Were Presented to the House in the Last Session of Parliament, Relative to the State of the African Slave Trade* (London, 1789), 32; Park, *Travels* [1799], 282–83.

46. Caillié, *Travels through Central Africa,* 1:426.

47. Roy Dilley, "Tukulor Weavers and the Organisation of the Craft in Village and Town," *Africa* 56:2 (1986): 123–29. Camara Laye recalls that when his mother took cotton to the weaver she "received back only a piece of cotton cloth half the weight of the original bundle," the other half of the cotton being given by custom as payment. He also noted that after his rite of passage into adulthood the elders of his community strung cotton thread across the rooftops and *Bombax* trees, adding to the mystery of the public ceremony that followed his initiation rites into adulthood. Laye, *Dark Child,* 41, 107–9.

48. Barbot, *Barbot on Guinea,* 1:101.

49. Mungo Park, *Travels* [1799], 35, 203; M. Abitbol, "The End of the Songhay Empire," in Ogot, *General History of Africa,* vol. 5, *Africa from the Sixteenth to the Eighteenth Century,* 302, 319.

50. J. F. Ade Ajayi and Michael Crowder, eds., *Historical Atlas of Africa* (Harlow, Essex: Longman, 1985), maps 32 and 35; Clapperton, *Missions to the Niger,* 4:653, 658.

51. Barth is quoted in Skinner, "West African Economic Systems," 84.

52. De Marees, *Description,* 229–31.

53. Van Dantzig, *Dutch and the Guinea Coast,* 208–9. During the seventeenth century Benin withdrew from participation in the slave trade, but it reentered in the eighteenth century. See Alan Ryder, *Benin and the Europeans, 1485–1897* (London: Longmans, 1969), 45, 159; Barbot observed in Fernando Po that "lamps are orange skins filled with palm oil and with cotton [as a wick]" (*Barbot on Guinea,* 2:724).

54. Equiano, *Equiano's Travels,* 4–10.

55. Adanson, *Voyage to Senegal,* 285.

56. R. B. Handy, "History and General Statistics of Cotton," in *The Cotton Plant: Its History, Botany, Chemistry, Culture, Enemies, and Uses,* ed. U.S. Department of Agriculture, Office of Experiment Stations, under the supervision of A. C. True (Washington, DC: Government Printing Office, 1896), 26–29.

57. White, *Narrative of a Voyage,* 23–24; Puckrein, *Little England,* 3–7, 53; *Colonising Expeditions,* 30; Africans were possibly familiar with the kind of cotton grown in the Americas. As one scholar has suggested, cotton from Africa arrived in the Americas before the Columbian era. Dolores R. T. Piperno, *The*

Origins of Agriculture in the Lowland Neotropics (San Diego: Academic Press, 1998), 149.

58. Fletcher is quoted in Puckrein, *Little England*, 53.

59. Jerome S. Handler and Frederick W. Lange, *Plantation Slavery in Barbados: An Archaeological and Historical Investigation* (Cambridge, MA: Harvard University Press, 1978), 15; White, *Narrative of a Voyage*, 24–25; Ligon, *True and Exact History*, 22–24; Ligon notes that the Hilliard plantation also contained a blacksmith shop, which is of interest, given that some Africans would have brought smithing skills to the island.

60. Heinrich von Uchteritz, "A German Indentured Servant in Barbados in 1652: The Account of Heinrich von Uchteritz," ed. and trans. Alexander Gunkel and Jerome S. Handler, *Journal of the Barbados Museum and Historical Society* 33 (May 1970): 93. See also Spoeri, "Swiss Medical Doctor's Description," 8.

61. Biet, "Father Antoine Biet's Visit," 66; Guyer and Belinga, "Wealth in People," 91–120.

62. John Scott, Sloane Manuscripts 3662, fol. 55, British Library.

63. Eltis, "New Estimates of Exports," 638, 642; "List of such ships and vessells as have imported and exported any commodities to and from this their Majesties Islands of Barbados," Colonial Office Papers 33, vols. 13, 14, and 15, British Public Record Office.

64. Great Britain, Public Record Office, *Calendar of State Papers, Colonial Series, American and West Indies* (London, 1860–1969) (hereafter referred to as *CSP*), *1661–68*, 146–48, 163; W. Hubert Miller, "The Colonization of the Bahamas, 1647–1670," *William and Mary Quarterly*, 3rd ser., 2 (January 1945): 44.

65. South Carolina Historical Society, *Collections*, 5:160–61.

66. *CSP, 1675–76*, 418.

67. Michael Craton and Gail Saunders, *Islanders in the Stream: A History of the Bahamian People*, vol. 1, *From Aboriginal Times to the End of Slavery* (Athens: University of Georgia Press, 1992), 79–89.

68. Blome, *Description of the Island of Jamaica*, 10; Hickeringill, *Jamaica Viewed*, 23; Frank Wesley Pitman, *The Development of the British West Indies, 1700–1763* (1917; repr., Hamden, CT: Archon Books, 1967), 17; Dunn, *Sugar and Slaves*, 170.

69. P. Lea, "A New Mapp of the Island of Jamaica" (1685), Geography and Map Division, Library of Congress.

70. M. Cranfield, "Observations of the Present State of Jamaica, December 14, 1675," in *Appendix to the First Volume of the Journals of the Assembly of Jamaica* (Jamaica, 1811), 42.

71. John Ogilby, *America: Being the Latest and Most Accurate Description of the New World; Containing the Original of the Inhabitants and the Remarkable Voyages Thither* (London, 1671), 338.

72. *CSP, 1681–85*, 283, 286.

73. Donnan, *Documents Illustrative*, 1:380.

74. Jacques-Nicolas Bellin, "Map of Jamaica" (ca. 1757), John Carter Brown Library, Providence, RI.

75. Pitman, *Development of the British West Indies*, 105–7. In the late seventeenth century, thirty thousand pounds weight of cotton was valued at between 150 and 200 pounds sterling. *An Historical Account of the Rise and Growth of the West India Colonies; and of the great Advantages they are to England, in respect trade. Licensed According to Order,* in *The Harleian Miscellany: A Collection of Scarce, Curious, and Entertaining Pamphlets and Tracts* (1690; repr., London: John White and John Murray, 1809), 2:370. In the middle of the eighteenth century, British Caribbean slave societies exported well over a million pounds of cotton annually; see Barbara Gaye Jaquay, "The Caribbean Cotton Production: An Historical Geography of the Region's Mystery Crop" (PhD diss., Texas A&M University, 1997), 75.

76. Edwards, *History, Civil and Commercial*, 2:270–71.

77. Whitemarsh Seabrook, *A Memoir on the Origin, Cultivation and Uses of Cotton, from the Earliest Ages to the Present Time, with Special Reference to the Sea-Island Cotton Plant, Including the Improvements in Its Cultivation, and the Preparation of the Wool, &c. in Georgia and South Carolina* (Charleston, SC: Miller and Browne, 1844), 18.

78. Dunn, *Sugar and Slaves*, 191; John Oldmixon, *The British Empire in America, Containing the History of the Discovery, Settlement, Progress, and State of the British Colonies on the Continent and Islands of America*, 2nd ed. (London, 1741), 2:107; William Hughes, *The American Physitian; or a Treatise of the Roots, Plants, Trees, Shrubs, Fruit, Herbs, ets., Growing in the English Plantations in America* (London, 1672), 71; G. Hughes, *Natural History of Barbados*, 191.

79. Edwards, *History, Civil and Commercial*, 2:272.

80. Hans Sloane is quoted in Carl Bridenbaugh and Roberta Bridenbaugh, *No Peace beyond the Line: The English in the Caribbean, 1624–1690* (New York: Oxford University Press, 1972), 57; Edwards refers to similar gins during the eighteenth century in *History, Civil and Commercial*, 2:272.

81. Grimé, *Ethno-Botany*, 122.

82. Hilary M. Beckles, *Natural Rebels: A Social History of Enslaved Black Women in Barbados* (New Brunswick: Rutgers University Press, 1989), 85–86; David Barry Gaspar, *Bondmen and Rebels: A Study of Master-Slave Relations in Antigua* (Baltimore: Johns Hopkins University Press, 1985), 145–48.

83. Philip Alexander Bruce, *Economic History of Virginia in the Seventeenth Century* (New York: Macmillan, 1896), 1:194, 331; Purchas, *Purchas His Pilgrimes*, 4:1784.

84. Alexander Spotswood, *The Official Letters of Alexander Spotswood, Lieutenant-Governor of the Colony of Virginia, 1710–1722*, ed. R. A. Brock (Richmond: Virginia Historical Society, 1882), 1:72; Bruce, *Economic History of Virginia*, 1:466–67; E. Morgan, *American Slavery, American Freedom*, 359. Bruce argues

that the Virginia soil and climate hindered cotton cultivation, preventing it from growing on a larger scale.

85. P. Morgan, *Slave Counterpoint*, 241; Thomas Jefferson, *Farm Book*, ed. Edwin Morris Betts (Princeton: Princeton University Press, 1953), 29, 40, 248, and *Garden Book, 1766–1824*, ed. Edwin Morris Betts (Philadelphia: American Philosophical Society, 1944), 219. Jefferson, in his *Notes on the State of Virginia*, first published in 1785, wrote, "The climate suits rice well enough wherever the lands do. Tobacco, hemp, flax, and cotton are staple commodities. Indico yields two cuttings." *Notes on the State of Virginia*, ed. William Peden (Chapel Hill: University of North Carolina Press, 1955), 42.

86. William Hugh Grove Diary, July 13, 1732, Special Collections, Alderman Library, University of Virginia; Jefferson, *Farm Book*, 29, 40, 248, and *Garden Book*, 219. In spite of these efforts, Jefferson still had to later buy cloth to distribute to his black labor force, a small token for their unfree labor.

87. Tench Coxe, "The Origin of the Cotton Culture of the United States," *American Farmer* (Baltimore) 2 (May 26, 1820): 67.

88. *CSP, 1661–68*, 157; South Carolina Historical Society, *Collections*, 5:127, 333, 377 n. 1.

89. Peter Purry, "Proposals by Peter Purry of Newfchatel," in *Historical Collections of South Carolina, Embracing Many Rare and Valuable Pamphlets, and Other Documents, Relating to the History of That State, from Its First Discovery to Its Independence, in the Year 1776*, ed. B. R. Carroll (New York: Harper and Brothers, 1836), 2:133.

90. P. Wood, *Black Majority*, 25.

91. *CSP, 1574–1660*, 439; Richard B. Sheridan, *Sugar and Slavery: An Economic History of the British West Indies, 1623–1775* (Baltimore: Johns Hopkins University Press, 1973), 189, 192; Eliza Pinckney, *The Letterbook of Eliza Lucas Pinckney, 1739–1762*, ed. Elise Pinckney with Marvin R. Zahniser (Chapel Hill: University of North Carolina Press, 1972), 8.

92. Harriet Horry Ravenel, *Eliza Pinckney* (New York: Charles Scribner's Sons, 1896), 128.

93. "Extract of a Letter from Dr. Alexander Garden of South Carolina Communicated by Mr. Henry Baker, Charles Town, April 5, 1756," Royal Society, London, Letters and Papers, Decade III, photostat in Manuscript Division, Library of Congress.

94. *South Carolina and American General Gazette*, January 20, 1777, quoted in "Historical Notes," *South Carolina Historical Gazette and Magazine* 8 (October 1907), 220.

95. Laurens, *Papers*, 5:357.

96. Ralph Izard, *Correspondence of Ralph Izard of South Carolina*, vol. 1, *1774–1777* (New York: Charles S. Francis, 1844), 174, 296, 300.

97. Chaplin, *Anxious Pursuit*, 208–26.

CHAPTER 4

1. Virginia Gail Jelatis, "Tangled Up in Blue: Indigo Culture and Economy in South Carolina, 1747–1800" (PhD diss., University of Minnesota, 1999), 160; Jenny Balfour-Paul, *Indigo* (1998; repr., Chicago: Fitzroy Dearborn, 2000), 66; "Letters of Morris and Brailsford to Thomas Jefferson," ed. Richard Walsh, *South Carolina Historical Magazine* 58 (1957): 137; *A Description of South Carolina: Containing Many Curious and Interesting Particulars Relating to the Civil, Natural and Commercial History of that Colony* (London: R. and J. Dodsley, 1761), in Carroll, *Historical Collections of South Carolina*, 2:204.

2. Lewis Cecil Gray, *History of Agriculture in the Southern United States to 1860* (New York: Peter Smith, 1941), 1:290.

3. Chaplin, *Anxious Pursuit*, 192; Elise Pinckney, "Eliza Lucas Pinckney: Biographical Sketch," in Eliza Pinckney, *Letterbook of Eliza Lucas Pinckney*, xvi–xxi.

4. Nell S. Graydon, *Eliza of Wappoo: A Tale of Indigo* (Columbia, SC: R. L. Bryan, 1967); Frances Leigh Williams, *Plantation Patriot: A Biography of Eliza Lucas Pinckney* (New York: Harcourt, Brace and World), 1967); Ravenel, *Eliza Pinckney*; Susan Lee, *Eliza Lucas* (Danbury, CT: Children's Press, 1977).

5. Berlin, *Many Thousands Gone*, 148–49.

6. P. Wood, *Black Majority*, ch. 2; Berlin, *Many Thousands Gone*, ch. 6.

7. Elise Pinckney, "Eliza Lucas Pinckney," xvi–xviii.

8. Ives, *Rich Papers*, 18–19, 55.

9. Beckles, *White Servitude*, 26; Puckrein, *Little England*, 60; Ligon, *True and Exact History*, 24.

10. William Legett, *Ancient and Medieval Dyes* (Brooklyn: Chemical Publishing Co., 1944; Balfour-Paul, *Indigo*, 26–27; Rita Bolland, *Tellem Textiles: Archaeological Finds from Burial Caves in Mali's Bandiagara Cliffs* (Amsterdam: Tropenmuseum / Royal Tropical Institute, 1991).

11. Thomas Phillips, *A Journal of a Voyage Made in the Hannibal of London, Ann. 1693, 1694, from England to Cape Monseradoe, in Africa; And thence Along the Coast of Guiney to Whidaw, the Island of St. Thomas, and So Forward to Barbadoes* (1746), in *A Collection of Voyages and Travels, Some Now First Printed from Original Manuscripts, Others Now First Published in English*, 3rd ed., ed. Answham Churchill (London, 1746), 6:236.

12. Thornton, *Africa and Africans*, 49–50.

13. Carney, *Black Rice*, 15.

14. Nyendael quoted in Talbot, *Peoples of Southern Nigeria*, 3:942; Basil Davidson, *West Africa before the Colonial Era: A History to 1850* (London: Longman, 1998), 121; Van Dantzig, *Dutch and the Guinea Coast*, 208–9.

15. De Marees, *Description*, 11; Olfert Dapper, *Olfert Dapper's Description of Benin* [1668], ed. and trans. Adam Jones (Madison: African Studies Program,

University of Wisconsin-Madison, 1998), 14; Adam Jones, "A Collection of African Art in Seventeenth-Century Germany: Cristoph Weickmann's *Kunst- und Naturkammer,*" *African Arts* 27 (April 1994): 33, 35–36; Richard Blome, *A Geographical Description of the World, Taken from the Works of the Famous Monsieur Sanson, Late Geographer to the Present French King, 1680, in Cosmography and Geography in Two Parts* (London, 1682), 380; Talbot, *Peoples of Southern Nigeria,* 3:941–42; F. R. Irvine, *Text-Book of West African Agriculture: Soils and Crops,* 2nd ed. (London: Oxford University Press, 1953), 155–57.

16. Adanson, *Voyage to Senegal,* 151, 166.

17. Mollien, *Travels in the Interior,* 155, 321; Richard Lander, *The Niger Journal of Richard and John Lander,* ed. Robin Hallett (New York: Praeger, 1965), 125.

18. Carney, *Black Rice,* 27, 53, 74; Irvine, *Text-Book,* 105–10.

19. Adanson, *Voyage to Senegal,* 295.

20. Testimony of William Littleton, in *Minutes of the Evidence,* 212.

21. Van Dantzig, *Dutch and the Guinea Coast,* 206.

22. Testimony of Littleton, in *Minutes of the Evidence,* 212; Claire Polakoff, *Into Indigo: African Textiles and Dyeing Techniques* (Garden City, NJ: Anchor Books, 1980); 25–26; Mungo Park, *Journal of a Mission to the Interior of Africa, in the Year 1805* (London, 1815), 10–11; Adanson, *Voyage to Senegal,* 296; Balfour-Paul, *Indigo,* 119–21; Judith Byfield, "Women, Economy and the State: A Study of the Adire Industry in Abeokuta, 1890–1930" (PhD diss., Columbia University, 1993), 127–30.

23. Park, *Journal of a Mission,* 10–11; Balfour-Paul, *Indigo,* 142; Byfield, "Women, Economy," 124–27.

24. George Roberts, *The Four Years Voyages of Captain George Roberts* (London, 1726), 397.

25. Balfour-Paul, *Indigo,* 44–55; Robert S. Smith, "Indigo Production and Trade in Colonial Guatemala," *Hispanic American Historical Review* 39 (May 1959): 181–211.

26. Puckrein, *Little England*; George Frederick Zook, *The Company of Royal Adventurers Trading into Africa* (New York: Negro University Press, 1969), 72; Donnan, *Documents Illustrative,* 1:74–78. These indigo workers developed the raw material for the West African textile industry. A. Hampete Ba discusses the traditions of textile workers in the West African savannah and Sahel in "Living Tradition," 180–87.

27. Spoeri, "Swiss Medical Doctor's Description," 7–8.

28. In Virginia during the 1620s, indigo production failed because the colonists did not know how to process the crop. Bruce, *Economic History of Virginia,* 1:246.

29. John Scott, Sloane Manuscripts 3662, fol. 62, British Library; Blackburn, *Making of New World Slavery,* 230; Dunn, *Sugar and Slaves,* 122–44, 167–78.

30. Dunn, *Sugar and Slaves*, 167–68; Eltis et al., Voyages database; Eric Williams, *From Columbus to Castro: The History of the Caribbean* (1970; repr., New York: Vintage Books, 1980), 114–15; Eltis, "New Estimates of Exports," 639, 643; Pitman, *Development of the British West Indies*, 234.

31. K. N. Chaudhuri, *The Trading World of Asia and the English East India Company, 1660–1760* (New York: Cambridge University Press, 1978), 334.

32. Eltis, "New Estimates of Exports," 639, 643; Dunn, *Sugar and Slaves*, 169; Sheridan placing the number of indigo works in 1670 at forty-nine, *Sugar and Slavery*, 212; P. Lea, "A New Mapp of the island of Jamaica" (1685), Geography and Map Division, Library of Congress.

33. Edwards, *History, Civil and Commercial*, 2:280; Balfour-Paul, *Indigo*, 91–93; William Sherman, *Forced Native Labor in Sixteenth-Century Central America* (Lincoln: University of Nebraska Press, 1979), 252–54; David H. Rembert Jr., "The Indigo of Commerce in Colonial North America," *Economic Botany* 33:2 (1979): 128–30; Alfred W. Crosby, *The Columbian Exchange: Biological and Cultural Consequences of 1492* (Westport, CT: Greenwood, 1972).

34. Irvine, *Text-Book*, 155; Balfour-Paul, *Indigo*, 91–92, 95; Polakoff, *Into Indigo*, 25, 42.

35. Edwards, *History, Civil and Commercial*, 2:281–83; Oldmixon, *British Empire in America* [1741], 2:400.

36. Colonel Charles Long to Peter Haywood, October 16, 1707, to May 6, 1708, West Indies Folder, West Indies Box, Rare Books and Manuscripts Division, New York Public Library.

37. Balfour-Paul, *Indigo*, 109–10.

38. Oldmixon, *British Empire in America* [1741], 2:400. Another lengthy description of the process of indigo fermentation in Jamaica is in Edwards, *History, Civil and Commercial*, 2:284–86. Some slaves drew upon their knowledge of indigo for domestic consumption. As the natural scientist Hans Sloane remarked, "Those of *Madagascar* beat Leaves to a Lump and make use of it to dye with." Sloane, *Voyage to the Islands*, 2:36.

39. Jean Baptiste du Tertre, *Histoire générale des Antilles habitées par les François* (Paris, 1667–71), vol. 2; Walter Edgar, *South Carolina: A History* (Columbia: University of South Carolina Press, 1998), 144–49.

40. Edwards, *History, Civil and Commercial*, 2:287.

41. Sloane, *Voyage to the Islands*, 2:35–36.

42. P. Wood, *Black Majority*, 21; South Carolina Historical Society, *Collections*, 5:211.

43. South Carolina Historical Society, *Collections*, 5:124–27, 266–67, 297; as noted earlier, he was also advised to draw upon Native American expertise to establish his plantation.

44. Ibid., 5:333–34, 377–78; P. Wood, *Black Majority*, 25, 39.

45. Alexander S. Salley Jr., ed., *Narratives of Early Carolina, 1650–1708* (New York: Charles Scribner's Sons, 1911), 147; *A Letter from South Carolina, Giving an Account of the Soil, Air, Product, Trade, Government, Laws, Religion, People, Military Strength, Etc. of that Province Together with the Manner and Necessary Charges of Settling a Plantation there, and the Annual Profit it Will Produce*, written by a Swiss gentleman, to his friend at Bern (London: A. Baldwin, 1710), 16.

46. South Carolina Historical Society, *Collections*, 5:211; Purry, "Proposals by Mr. Peter Purry," 2:127.

47. Eliza Pinckney, *Letterbook of Eliza Lucas Pinckney*, 8, 16. Though it is not clear what kind of indigo was grown on the Lucas plantations, by the 1750s at least two kinds predominated, *Indigofera tinctoria*, or "French" indigo, and *Indigofera suffruticosa*. Rembert, "Indigo Commerce," 128–33.

48. Elise Pinckney, "Eliza Lucas Pinckney," xvii–xviii.

49. Blackburn, *Making of New World Slavery*, 295; Clarence J. Munford, *The Ordeal of Black Slavery and Slave Trading in the French West Indies, 1625–1715*, vol. 2, *The Middle Passage and the Plantation Economy* (Lewiston, NY: Edwin Mellen Press), 544–45.

50. Ravenel, *Eliza Pinckney*, 105.

51. Elise Pinckney, "Eliza Lucas Pinckney," xv–xvi; Ravenel, *Eliza Pinckney*, 104; "Col. Lucas's List of Negroes at Garden Hill from Murray, May 1745," in Pinckney Family Papers, South Carolina Historical Society, Charleston; for a treatment of Akan names, Florence Dolphyne, *A Comprehensive Course in Twi (Asante) for the Non-Twi Learner* (Accra: Ghana Universities Press, 1996), 14; for Akan day names in Côte D'Ivoire, Richard R. Day and Albert B. Saraka, *An Introduction to Spoken Baoule* (Washington, DC: Center for Applied Linguistics, 1968), cycles 16–18; Sjarief Hale, "Kente Cloth of Ghana," *African Arts* 3:3 (1970): 26–29; Dennis M. Warren, "Bono Royal Regalia," *African Arts* 8 (Winter 1975): 16–21; Anquandah, *Rediscovering Ghana's Past*, 93–94; Ivor Wilks, "The Mossi and Akan States," in Ajayi and Crowder, *History of West Africa*, 1:369; Boahen, "States and Cultures," 5:428.

52. Elise Pinckney, "Eliza Lucas Pinckney," xvii. The figure of indigo exports is from "An Account of Goods Exported from Charles Town of the Produce of South Carolina from the 1st November 1749 to the 1st November 1750," in *Records in the British Public Records Office Relating to South Carolina, B. T.*, 16:366–67.

53. *Description of South Carolina*, 2:204; William Gerard de Brahm, *Philosophico-Historico-Hydrogeography of South Carolina, Georgia, and East Florida*, in *Documents Connected with the History of South Carolina*, ed. Plowden Charles Jennett Weston (London, 1856), 197.

54. *Description of South Carolina*, 2:204.

55. Breen, *Tobacco Culture*; Jelatis, "Tangled Up in Blue"; Chaplin, *Anxious Pursuit*, 190–208.

56. David Coon, "Eliza Lucas Pinckney and the Reintroduction of Indigo Culture in South Carolina," *Journal of Southern History* 42 (February 1976): 71–74; Philip Miller, *The Gardener's Dictionary: Containing the Methods of Cultivating and Improving the Kitchen, Fruit and Flower Garden* (London, 1731); *Gentleman's Magazine,* May 1755, 201–3, and June 1755, 256–59. The constant comparison and anxiety that Carolinians had about their indigo was not unlike that of tobacco planters as discussed in Breen in *Tobacco Culture*.

57. George C. Rogers Jr., *The History of Georgetown County, South Carolina* (Columbia: University of South Carolina Press, 1970), 77, 87, 91–92; Ravenel, *Eliza Pinckney*, 106; Chaplin, *Anxious Pursuit*, 201.

58. Peter Manigault to Daniel Blake, February 6, 1770, in "Peter Manigault Letterbook," 113.

59. I draw the term *symbolic capital* from Pierre Bourdieu, *The Logic of Practice*, trans. Richard Nice (Cambridge: Polity Press, 1990), 112–21. William de Brahm, "A Map of South Carolina and a Part of Georgia (1757)," Geography and Map Division, Library of Congress; James Cook, "A Map of the Province of South Carolina (1773)," Geography and Map Division, Library of Congress; Henry Mouzon Jr., "A Map of the Parish of St. Stephen in Craven County (1773)," Rare Book, Manuscript, and Special Collections Library, Duke University.

60. Henry Laurens, *Papers*, 1:241, 324.

61. Eltis et al., Voyages database; Littlefield, *Rice and Slaves*; Donnan, *Documents Illustrative*, 4:377.

62. *South Carolina Gazette*, October 11, 1760.

63. The method of producing indigo in South Carolina was essentially the same as it was in the Caribbean. Guion Griffis Johnson, *A Social History of the Sea Islands, with Special Reference to St. Helena Island, South Carolina* (Chapel Hill: University of North Carolina Press, 1930), 20–21; Peter Manigault to Benjamin Stead, February 6, 1770, in "Peter Manigault Letterbook"; Jelatis, "Tangled Up in Blue," 150–59; P. Morgan, *Slave Counterpoint*, 159–64.

64. Testimony of Littleton, in *Minutes of the Evidence*, 212; Polakoff, *Into Indigo*, 25–26; Park, *Journal of a Mission*, 10–11; Adanson, *Voyage to Senegal*, 296; Balfour-Paul, *Indigo*, 119–21; Byfield, "Women, Economy," 124–27.

65. P. Morgan, *Slave Counterpoint*, 164.

66. Margaret Washington Creel, *"A Peculiar People": Slave Religion and Community Culture among the Gullahs* (New York: New York University Press, 1988), 321; Julie Dash draws upon these cultural practices in her film *Daughters of the Dust* (1992), as in the prominence of indigo-dyed clothing and the blue-stained hands of Nana Peazant.

67. Balfour-Paul, *Indigo*, 70–76.

CHAPTER 5

1. De Marees, *Description*, 118.
2. Barbot, *Barbot on Guinea*, 2:382, 516.
3. Christopher R. DeCorse, *An Archaeology of Elmina: Africans and Europeans on the Gold Coast, 1400–1900* (Washington, DC: Smithsonian Institution Press, 2001), ch. 4.
4. Ives, *Rich Papers*, 27.
5. Hilary M. Beckles, "Plantation Production and White 'Proto-Slavery': White Indentured Servants and the Colonisation of the English West Indies, 1624–1645," *Americas* 41 (January 1985): 35–37.
6. Beckles, *White Servitude*, 129–30.
7. Dunn, *Sugar and Slaves*, 182, 268; Beckles, *White Servitude*, 138.
8. Ligon, *True and Exact History*, 23; Handler, "Amerindians and Their Contributions," 192–96, 203–7, quote from 207; Oldmixon, *British Empire in America* [1708], quotes from 2:238, 239; Sloane, *Voyage to the Islands*, 2:39–40.
9. Dawson, "Enslaved Swimmers and Divers," 1327–55; Thornton, *Africa and Africans*, 135; de Marees, *Description*, 186.
10. Ligon, *True and Exact History*, 52.
11. Ibid., 35.
12. Trevor Burnard, *Mastery, Tyranny, and Desire: Thomas Thistlewood and His Slaves in the Anglo-Jamaican World* (Chapel Hill: University of North Carolina Press, 2004), 198–200.
13. Blome, *Description of the Island*, 48–49.
14. Dunn, *Sugar and Slaves*, 190–201; Beckles, *White Servitude*, 125–27.
15. "Overseer's Journal, Somerset Vale, 1776–80," Somerset Vale Records, John Carter Brown Library, Providence, RI.
16. "An Account of Duckenfield Hall Estate's Negroes," Codex Eng 183, John Carter Brown Library, Providence, RI.
17. Mathew Gregory Lewis, *Journal of a West India Proprietor, Kept during a Residence in the Island of Jamaica* (1834; repr., New York: Negro Universities Press, 1969), 187.
18. Ligon, *True and Exact History*, 49.
19. Sloane, *Voyage to the Islands*, 1:lii. After slaves from Angola used drums to notify other slaves of the uprising at the Stono River, the 1740 South Carolina slave code banned slaves from possessing "wooden swords, and other mischievous and dangerous weapons, or using or keeping of drums, horns, or other loud instruments, which may call together, or give sign or notice to one another of their wicked designs or purposes." Dena Epstein, *Sinful Tunes and Spirituals: Black Folk Music to the Civil War* (Urbana: University of Illinois Press, 1977), 59.
20. Douglas V. Armstrong, "Archaeology and Ethnohistory of the Caribbean Plantation," in Singleton, "*I, Too, Am America*," 174–78.

21. David Geggus, "Sugar and Coffee Cultivation in Saint Domingue and the Shaping of the Slave Labor Force," in Berlin and Morgan, *Cultivation and Culture,* 86, 88.

22. Thornton, *Africa and Africans,* 135–36; John S. Otto and Nain E. Anderson, "The Origins of Southern Cattle-Grazing: A Problem in West Indian History," *Journal of Caribbean History* 21:2 (1988): 148; P. Wood, *Black Majority,* 28–34.

23. Blome, *Description of the Island,* 10.

24. J. Miller, *Way of Death,* 80; Barbot, *Barbot on Guinea,* 1:103; Donnan, *Documents Illustrative,* 2:193.

25. Oldmixon, *British Empire in America* [1708], 2:103, 104, 321.

26. Blome, *Description of the Island,* 11.

27. Thornton, *Africa and Africans,* 139, 165; Hall, *Slavery and African Ethnicities,* 67–68.

28. Candace Goucher, "African Metallurgy in the Atlantic World," *African Archaeological Review* 11 (1993): 206.

29. Armstrong, "Archaeology and Ethnohistory," 178–80.

30. Oldmixon, *British Empire in America* [1708], 2:120.

31. Edmund Morgan, *Virginians at Home: Family Life in the Eighteenth Century* (Williamsburg, VA: Colonial Williamsburg, Inc., 1952), 53–54.

32. Weynette Parks Haun, *Surry County, Virginia, Court Records, Book V, 1691–1700* (Durham, NC, 1991), 12; Mechal Sobel, *The World They Made Together: Black and White Values in Eighteenth Century Virginia* (Princeton: Princeton University Press, 1987), 44–53.

33. Sobel, *World They Made Together,* 112–26, 132–33.

34. Affidavit by Peter Legrand, Spragins Family Papers, MSS1, sp 716a, 1726–33, Virginia Historical Society, Richmond.

35. Jefferson, *Garden and Farm Books,* 225.

36. John Michael Vlach, *The Afro-American Tradition in the Decorative Arts* (1978; repr., Athens: University of Georgia Press, 1990), 108.

37. Laura Croghan Kamoie, *Neabsco and Occoquan: The Tayloe Family Iron Plantations, 1730–1830* (Charlottesville: University of Virginia Press, 2007), 87.

38. *Made of Iron,* exh. cat. (Houston: University of St. Thomas Art Department, 1966), 106.

39. James A. McMillin, *The Final Victims: Foreign Slave Trade to North America, 1783–1810* (Columbia: University of South Carolina Press, 2004), 32; Ira Berlin, *Many Thousands Gone,* 308–09; Eltis et al., Voyages database.

40. Barbot, *Barbot on Guinea,* 2:519; de Marees, *Description,* 122–25.

41. John R. Commons et al., eds., *A Documentary History of American Industrial Society,* vol. 1, *Plantation and Frontier,* ed. Ulrich Bonnell Phillips (New York: Russell and Russell, 1958), 205–6; de Marees, *Description,* 121; Sylvia Frey, *Water from the Rock: Black Resistance in a Revolutionary Age* (Princeton: Princeton University Press, 1991), 281.

42. Henry Box Brown, *Narrative of Henry Box Brown: Who Escaped from Slavery Enclosed in a Box 3 Feet Long and 2 Feet Wide,* Afro-American History Series, no. 205 (1849; repr., Philadelphia: Historic Publications, 1969), 25.

43. Guion Griffis Johnson, *Ante-Bellum North Carolina: A Social History* (Chapel Hill: University of North Carolina Press, 1937), 556.

44. De Marees, *Description,* 121.

45. West, "John Bartram and Slavery," 118–19.

46. P. Wood, *Black Majority,* 123; John Michael Vlach, *Afro-American Tradition,* 97–107; Charles Ball, *Fifty Years in Chains; Or, The Life of an American Slave* (New York: H. Dayton, 1859), 211; Lewis, *Journal,* 50, 67.

47. Ball, *Fifty Years in Chains,* 17, 203–18; Judith Carney makes a similar argument about the ways that slaves used their knowledge of rice cultivation to extract the task system from their owners in *Black Rice,* 98–101.

48. Release from Mortgage, George Lucas to Charles Alexander, Miscellaneous Records, vol. GG (1746–49), South Carolina Department of Archives and History, Columbia.

49. Bill of Sale, Charles Alexander to Charles Pinckney, Miscellaneous Records, vol. HH (1749–51), South Carolina Department of Archives and History, Columbia.

50. "A List of all ye Negroes at Warrhall," Taylor Family Papers, South Caroliniana Library, Columbia.

51. *City Gazette,* March 29, 1788.

52. Bill of Sale, January 1, 1803, vol. NNN, and Bill of Sale, August 16, 1809, vol. AAAA, both in Miscellaneous Records, South Carolina Department of Archives and History, Columbia.

53. Bills of Sale, January 14 and July 9, 1789, Miscellaneous Records, vol. QQ, South Carolina Department of Archives and History, Columbia.

54. Ferguson, *Uncommon Ground;* Vlach, *Afro-American Tradition.*

55. George Rawick, ed., *The American Slave: A Composite Autobiography,* vol. 2, *South Carolina Narratives, Parts 1 and 2* (Westport, CT: Greenwood, 1972), pt. 1, p. 198.

56. John Michael Vlach, *Charleston Blacksmith: The Work of Philip Simmons* (Athens: University of Georgia Press, 1981).

57. G. P. Collins, "Discovery of Lake Scuppernong (Phelps), North Carolina," *Publications of the Southern History Association* 6 (1902): 24; Robert Hunter Jr., *Quebec to Carolina in 1785–1786: Being the Travel Diary and Observations of Robert Hunter, Jr., a Young Merchant of London,* ed. Louis B. Wright and Marion Tingling (San Marino, CA: Huntington Library, 1943), 265; William S. Tarlton, "Somerset Place and Its Restoration," report prepared for the Department of Conservation and Development Division of State Parks, Raleigh, NC, August 1, 1954, 6; "Survey Made by Richard Slaughter to Explore the Lands of Messrs. Collins, Allen and Dickinson, July 27, 1787," Josiah Collins Papers, Josiah Collins

Elder Box, Collins, Allen and Dickinson Folder, North Carolina State Archives, Raleigh; Wayne K. Durrill, "Slavery, Kinship, and Dominance: The Black Community at Somerset Place Plantation, 1786–1860," *Slavery and Abolition* 13 (August 1992): 3; Dorothy Spruill Redford, *Somerset Homecoming: Recovering a Lost Heritage* (New York: Doubleday, 1988), 103–7.

58. Collins, "Discovery of Lake Scuppernong," 23; "An Act Enabling Certain Persons to Perfect a Canal Between Scuppernong River and the Lake Near Its Head," in *The State Records of North Carolina* (New York: AMS Press, 1968–78), 24:861–62; Edmund Ruffin, *Agricultural, Geological, and Descriptive Sketches of Lower North Carolina and the Adjacent Lands* (Raleigh, NC: Institution for the Deaf and Dumb and the Blind, 1861), 234.

59. Durrill, "Slavery, Kinship," 6–7; Tarlton, "Somerset Place," 7.

60. Carney, *Black Rice*, 63–68.

61. Edmund Ruffin, *Farmers' Register*, no. 12 (1839): 729; Tarlton, "Somerset Place," 7–11.

62. Frederick Douglass, *My Bondage and My Freedom* (1855; repr., New York: Dover Publications, 1969), 69–70.

63. Samuel Gourdin Gaillard, "Recollections of Samuel Gourdin Gaillard," *South Carolina Historical and Genealogical Magazine* 57 (July 1956): 120–23. African work practices on the plantation probably paralleled religious worship, which was prominent. Gaillard describes worship thus: "The 'Fireside' or day nursery was quite a large building, and had one very large room that was maintained as a chapel, holding benches to see the congregation. The 'preaching' was really an exhortation and reading from the Bible, after which the seats were removed and the floor cleared for the 'Shouting.' This—the shouting— must have come with the slaves from Africa. It was weird in the extreme. It began by someone—a woman—starting a low moaning hymn, gradually joined in by the entire congregation. As the singing increased in crescendo, one by one of the congregation slipped out into the center of the floor and began to 'shout'—(that is whirl around and sing and clap hands, and go round and round in circles). After a time as this went on, the enthusiasm became a frenzy and only the ablebodied men and women remained—the weak dropping out one by one, returning to the 'side lines' to clap and urge the 'shouters' on" (123).

64. William J. Faulkner, *The Days When the Animals Talked: Black American Folktales and How They Came to Be* (Trenton, NJ: Africa World Press, 1993), 21, 102–9; for example, in West Central Africa, agriculturalists who grew manioc could leave the crop in the ground for storage. Marvin P. Miracle, *Agriculture in the Congo Basin: Tradition and Change in African Rural Economies* (Madison: University of Wisconsin Press, 1967), 193; Samford, *Subfloor Pits*.

65. Rawick, *American Slave*, vol. 12, *Georgia Narratives, Parts 1 and 2*, pt. 1, pp. 4, 22, and vol. 17, *Florida Narratives*, 335–36.

66. Charles L. Perdue Jr., Thomas E. Barden, and Robert K. Phillips, eds., *Weevils in the Wheat: Interviews with Virginia Ex-Slaves* (Charlottesville: University Press of Virginia, 1976), 13.

67. Louis Hughes, *The Autobiography of Louis Hughes: Thirty Years a Slave; From Bondage to Freedom; The Institution of Slavery as Seen on the Plantation in the Home of the Planter* (Montgomery, AL: New South Books, 2002), 34–36.

68. Solomon Northrup, *Twelve Years a Slave: Narrative of Solomon Northrup, a Citizen of New York, Kidnapped in Washington City in 1841 and Rescued in 1853, from a Cotton Plantation Near the Red River, in Louisiana*, ed. Sue Eakin and Joseph Logsdon (1853; repr., Baton Rouge: Louisiana State University Press, 1968), 127–31, 159–63.

69. Adam Rothman, *Slave Country: American Expansion and the Origins of the Deep South* (Cambridge, MA: Harvard University Press, 2005), 75, 84–91; Berlin, *Many Thousands Gone*, 314; Walter Johnson, *Soul by Soul: Life inside the Antebellum Slave Market* (Cambridge, MA: Harvard University Press, 1999); McMillin, *Final Victims*, 18–48.

70. Northrup, *Twelve Years a Slave*, 141–43.

71. Rawick, *American Slave*, vol. 17, *Florida Narratives*, 336. For a fuller discussion of slave accounts of being tricked aboard slave ships with red cloth, see Gomez, *Exchanging Our Country Marks*, 199–210. Others in Africa heard stories about people being enticed by ship captains and were much more cautious in their dealings with European merchants. Otto Friedrich Von Der Groeben of Brandenburg stated that when he attempted to trade on the West African coast, a group of African traders "did come aboard, and they promised to come with ivory the following day. Their fear derived from the fact that French ships often arrive, pretending to trade, and then, when they have attracted ten or twenty Negroes into the ship, the Blacks are caught, taken to the West Indies and sold as slaves." Adam Jones, ed., *Brandenburg Sources for West African History, 1680–1700* (Stuttgart: Franz Steiner, 1985), 29.

72. Rawick, *American Slave*, vol. 12, *Georgia Narratives, Parts 1 and 2*, pt. 1, p. 75.

73. Ibid., pt. 1, p. 94.

74. George Rawick, *The American Slave: A Composite Autobiography. Supplement, Series 1*, vol. 4, *Georgia Narratives, Part 2*, 632.

75. Rawick, *American Slave*, vol. 3, *South Carolina Narratives, Parts 3 and 4*, pt. 4, pp. 222–23.

76. Rawick, *American Slave*, vol. 17, *Florida Narratives*, 59.

77. Toni Morrison, *Beloved* (New York: Plume, 1987), 60.

78. "Account Book, 1806, of John Tayloe," Tayloe Family Papers, MSS1 T218 g7 Tayloe, Virginia Historical Society, Richmond.

79. Rawick, *American Slave*, vol. 12, *Georgia Narratives, Parts 1 and 2*, pt. 1, p. 3.

80. Ibid., pt. 1, p. 22.

81. Perdue, Barden, and Phillips, *Weevils in the Wheat*, 6, 8.

82. Rawick, *American Slave*, vol. 12, *Georgia Narratives, Parts 1 and 2*, pt. 1, p. 93.

83. Rawick, *American Slave*, vol. 17, *Florida Narratives*, 230.

84. Savannah Unit, Georgia Writers' Project, *Drums and Shadows*, 188.

85. Perdue, Barden, and Phillips, *Weevils in the Wheat*, 17.

86. Savannah Unit, Georgia Writers' Project, *Drums and Shadows*, 66, 101, 179; Vlach, *Afro-American Tradition*, 44–55; P. Wood, "Whetting, Setting," 3–8.

87. Delany, *Condition, Elevation, Emigration*, 64.

88. Leon Litwack, *Been in the Storm So Long: The Aftermath of Slavery* (New York: Alfred A. Knopf, 1979), 425.

CHAPTER 6

1. Hilda Vitzthum, *Torn Out by the Roots: The Recollections of a Former Communist*, ed. and trans. Paul Schach (Lincoln: University of Nebraska Press, 1993), 129. Vitzthum was brought to my attention in an insightful essay by Peter H. Wood, "Slave Labor Camps in Early America: Overcoming Denial and Discovering the Gulag," in *Inequality in Early America*, ed. Carla Gardina Pestana and Sharon V. Salinger (Hanover, NH: University Press of New England), 222–38.

2. Vitzthum, *Torn Out by the Roots*, 3–4, quotation from 185.

3. Wolf, *Europe*, 390.

4. My use of the term *mnemonic devices* derives, in part, from Africanist literature on memory and history. Mary Nooter Roberts and Allen F. Roberts, *Memory: Luba Art and the Making of History* (New York: Museum for African Art, 1996); Joseph C. Miller, "History and Africa/Africa and History," *American Historical Review* 104 (February 1999): 10.

5. Savannah Unit, Georgia Writers' Project, *Drums and Shadows*, 17.

6. Edward C. L. Adams, *Tales of the Congaree*, ed. Robert G. O'Meally (Chapel Hill: University of North Carolina Press, 1987), 48–49.

7. Frederick Douglass, *Narrative of the Life of Frederick Douglass* (1845; repr., Cambridge, MA: Harvard University Press, 1988), 47.

8. Rawick, *American Slave, Supplement, Series 1*, vol. 4, *Georgia Narratives, Part 2*, 355.

9. Alan Lomax, *The Folk Songs of North America in the English Language* (Garden City, NY: Doubleday, 1960), 514.

10. Perdue, Barden, and Phillips, *Weevils in the Wheat*, 309.

11. Rawick, *American Slave*, vol. 12, *Georgia Narratives, Parts 1 and 2*, pt. 2, p. 222.

12. H. Brown, *Narrative of Henry Box Brown*, 19.

13. Ibid., 54.

14. Northrup, *Twelve Years a Slave*, 86.

15. Rawick, *American Slave*, vol. 12, *Georgia Narratives, Parts 1 and 2*, pt. 2, p. 322.

16. William Wells Brown, *Narrative of William Wells Brown, A Fugitive Slave*, in *Puttin on Ole Massa: The Slave Narratives of Henry Bibb, William Wells Brown, and Solomon Northrup*, ed. Gilbert Osofsky (New York: Harper and Row, 1969), 190.

17. Faulkner, *Days When the Animals Talked*, 30.

18. W. Johnson, *Soul by Soul*, 1–18.

19. H. Brown, *Narrative of Henry Box Brown*, 15.

20. Ibid., p. 56; W. Brown, *Narrative of William Wells Brown*, 210.

21. Adams, *Tales of the Congaree*, 5.

22. Duarte Lopez, *A Report of the Kingdom of Congo* (1597; repr., New York: Da Capo Press, 1970), 54.

23. Savannah Unit, Georgia Writers' Project, *Drums and Shadows*, 4, 68; Perdue, Barden, and Phillips, *Weevils in the Wheat*, 51, 189; Rawick, *American Slave*, vol. 12, *Georgia Narratives, Parts 1 and 2*, pt. 1, p. 18.

24. William Dusinberre, *Them Dark Days: Slavery in the American Rice Swamps* (Athens: University of Georgia Press, 2000), 235–45.

25. Adams, *Tales of the Congaree*, 5.

26. Gomez, *Exchanging Our Country Marks*, 119–20.

27. Northrup, *Twelve Years a Slave*, 74.

28. H. Brown, *Narrative of Henry Box Brown*, 19–20.

29. William Wells Brown, *My Southern Home: Or, The South and Its People* (1880; repr., Upper Saddle River, NJ: Gregg Press, 1968), 154–55.

30. Sterling A. Brown, Arthur P. Davis, and Ulysses Lee, eds., *Negro Caravan: Writings by American Negroes* (1941; repr., Salem, NH: Ayer, 1991), 449.

31. W. Brown, *My Southern Home*, 66.

32. Douglass, *My Bondage and My Freedom*, 252–53.

33. Faulkner, *Days When the Animals Talked*, 18.

34. Ibid., 17.

35. Ira Berlin, Marc Favreau, and Stephen F. Miller, eds., *Remembering Slavery: African Americans Talk about Their Personal Experiences of Slavery and Freedom* (New York: New Press, 1998), tape 1; Mia Bay, *The White Image in the Black Mind: African American Ideas about White People* (New York: Oxford University Press, 2000), 127–49. This sentiment has resonances into the age of Jim Crow, when Fannie Lou Hamer lived on a plantation that provided better accommodations for the owner's dog than for Hamer and her family.

36. Henry Bibb, *Narrative of the Life and Adventures of Henry Bibb, an American Slave. Written by Himself with an Introduction by Lucius C. Matlock*, ed. Charles J. Heglar (1849; repr., Madison: University of Wisconsin Press, 2001), 66.

37. Harriet Jacobs, *Incidents in the Life of a Slave Girl, Written by Herself*, enl. ed., ed. Jean Fagan Yellin (1861; repr., Cambridge, MA: Harvard University Press, 2000), 76.

38. H. Brown, *Narrative of Henry Box Brown*, 29, 56.

39. Faulkner, *Days When the Animals Talked*, 116.

40. Bibb, *Narrative*, 131.

41. Gavin Wright, *Slavery and American Economic Development* (Baton Rouge: Louisiana State University Press, 2006).

42. Perdue, Barden, and Phillips, *Weevils in the Wheat*, 4.

43. Jacobs, *Incidents in the Life*, 19.

44. Ibid., 112–13.

45. Douglass, *My Bondage and My Freedom*, 283.

46. Emmanuel Akyeampong and Pashington Obeng, "Spirituality, Gender, and Power in Asante History," *International Journal of African Historical Studies* 28:3 (1995): 481–508.

47. Nat Turner, *The Confessions of Nat Turner, Leader of the Late Insurrection of Southampton, Virginia, as Fully and Voluntarily Made to Thos C. Gray, in the Prison Where He Was Confined—and Acknowledged by Him to Be Such, When Read before the Court of Southampton, Convened at Jerusalem, November 5, 1831, for His Trial* (1861; repr., Miami, FL: Mnemosyne, 1969), 4–5.

48. Herbert Aptheker, ed., *A Documentary History of the Negro People of the United States*, vol. 1, *From the Colonial Times through the Civil War* (1951; repr., New York: Citadel Press, 1990), 71.

49. Turner, *Confessions of Nat Turner*, 5–6.

50. Perdue, Barden, and Phillips, *Weevils in the Wheat*, 310.

51. Northrup, *Twelve Years a Slave*, 35, 99.

52. S. Brown, Davis, and Lee, *Negro Caravan*, 430.

53. Savannah Unit, Georgia Writers' Project, *Drums and Shadows*, 150–51.

54. Sarah H. Bradford, *Harriet Tubman: The Moses of Her People* (1869; repr., Gloucester, MA: Peter Smith, 1981), 114.

55. Bibb, *Narrative*, 124.

56. Faulkner, *Days When the Animals Talked*, 60–65.

57. Sidney Bechet, *Treat It Gentle* (1960; repr., New York: Da Capo Press, 1978), 7.

58. Zora Neale Hurston, *The Sanctified Church* (New York: Marlowe, 1981), 85.

59. Northrup, *Twelve Years a Slave*, 104–5.

60. Perdue, Barden, and Phillips, *Weevils in the Wheat*, 63, 66–67, and 286; for an in-depth study of the place of forests in the lives of Africans in the Low-country, see Stuckey, *Slave Culture*, 6–8, and Ras Michael Brown, "Walk in the Feenda: West Central Africans and the Forest in the South Carolina-Georgia Lowcountry," in *Central Africans and Cultural Transformations in the American*

Diaspora, ed. Linda Heywood (New York: Cambridge University Press, 2002), 289–318.

   61. John Thornton, *Africa and Africans*, 274–79.

   62. Perdue, Barden, and Phillips, *Weevils in the Wheat*, 42, 57, 78, 152–54.

   63. Wyatt MacGaffey, *Religion and Society in Central Africa: The BaKongo of Lower Zaire* (Chicago: University of Chicago Press, 1986), 109–11.

   64. Douglass, *My Bondage and My Freedom*, 234.

   65. Ibid., 234–46.

   66. W. Brown, *My Southern Home*, 70–75.

   67. Wyatt MacGaffey, "The Cultural Traditions of Forest West Africa," in *Insight and Artistry in African Divination*, ed. John Pemberton III (Washington, DC: Smithsonian Institution Press, 2000), 17–18.

   68. Rawick, *American Slave*, vol. 2, *South Carolina Narratives, Parts 1 and 2*, pt. 2, pp. 15–16; Jacobs, *Incidents in the Life*, 90–91.

   69. Stuckey, *Slave Culture*, ch. 1.

   70. Savannah Unit, Georgia Writers' Project, *Drums and Shadows*, 195, 171–72.

   71. Perdue, Barden, and Phillips, *Weevils in the Wheat*, 39.

   72. S. Brown, Davis, and Lee, *Negro Caravan*, 465.

   73. Faulkner, *Days When the Animals Talked*, 4–5.

   74. Bechet, *Treat It Gentle*, 30.

   75. Perdue, Barden, and Phillips, *Weevils in the Wheat*, 267.

   76. Ibid., 39.

   77. Northrup, *Twelve Years a Slave*, 108.

   78. Perdue, Barden, and Phillips, *Weevils in the Wheat*, 6.

   79. L. Hughes, *Autobiography of Louis Hughes*, 56.

   80. Jacobs, *Incidents in the Life*, 83.

   81. Savannah Unit, Georgia Writers' Project, *Drums and Shadows*, 176.

   82. Perdue, Barden, and Phillips, *Weevils in the Wheat*, 173–78.

   83. Rawick, *American Slave*, vol. 12, *Georgia Narratives, Parts 1 and 2*, pt. 2, p. 166.

   84. Perdue, Barden, and Phillips, *Weevils in the Wheat*, 83; Rastus Jones, interviewed in Rawick, *American Slave*, vol. 4, *Texas Narratives, Parts 1 and 2*, pt. 2, p. 356.

   85. Rawick, *American Slave*, vol. 4, *Texas Narratives, Parts 1 and 2*, pt. 2, p. 21.

   86. Perdue, Barden, and Phillips, *Weevils in the Wheat*, 115.

   87. Vlach, *Afro-American Tradition*, 45–48.

   88. Rawick, *American Slave, Supplement, Series 1*, vol. 3, *Georgia Narratives, Part 1*, 135.

   89. Rawick, *American Slave*, vol. 3, *South Carolina Narratives, Parts 3 and 4*, pt. 4, p. 268.

90. Faulkner, *Days When the Animals Talked*, 56.

91. Bradford, *Harriet Tubman*, 30.

92. Bibb, *Narrative*, 66, 169–70.

93. Rawick, *American Slave*, vol. 4, *Texas Narratives, Parts 1 and 2*, pt. 2, p. 5.

94. Rawick, *American Slave*, vol. 12, *Georgia Narratives, Parts 1 and 2*, pt. 1, p. 310.

95. Rawick, *American Slave*, vol. 4, *Texas Narratives, Parts 1 and 2*, pt. 2, pp. 215–16.

96. Rawick, *American Slave*, vol. 19, *God Struck Me Dead*, 112, 125.

97. Ibid., 5, 49, 55.

98. Ibid., 32, 147–48, 163.

99. Rawick, *American Slave, Supplement, Series 1*, vol. 3, *Georgia Narratives, Part 1*, 322–23.

100. Faulkner, *Days When the Animals Talked*, 53–58.

Bibliography

MANUSCRIPTS

British Library, London
    Additional Manuscripts
    Sloane Manuscripts
British Public Records Office
    Colonial Office Papers 33, vols. 13, 14, and 15
Duke University, Rare Book, Manuscript, and Special Collections Library
    Henry Mouzon Jr., "A Map of the Parish of St. Stephen in Craven County
        [1773]"
Institute of Jamaica, Kingston, Jamaica
    "Journal and Account of Greenpark and Springvale Estate, 1790–1815"
    "Journal of Somerset Plantation"
John Carter Brown Library, Providence, Rhode Island
    Jacques Nicolas Bellin Map
    Somerset Vale Records
    Brown Family Papers
    Codex Eng 17
    Codex Eng 183
Library of Congress
    Geography and Map Division
    Royal Society, London, Letters and Papers
Library of Virginia
    York County Records, reels 1 and 2a
    Charles City County Records, reel 3
New York Public Library, Rare Books and Manuscripts Division
    West Indies Papers
North Carolina State Archives, Raleigh, North Carolina
    Josiah Collins Papers
South Carolina Department of Archives and History
    Miscellaneous Records, vols. GG, HH, QQ, NNN, and AAAA
South Carolina Historical Society, Charleston, South Carolina
    Ball Family Papers [microfiche]

Records in the British Public Records Office Relating to South Carolina, B. T.,
    vol. 16
"Peter Manigault Letterbook" (typescript in possession of the author)
Pinckney Family Papers
Thomas J. Tobias Papers
South Caroliniana Library, Columbia, South Carolina
    Samuel Mathias Journal
    Taylor Family Papers
University of Ghana, Balme Library Special Collections
    Furley Collections
University of the West Indies, West Indies and Special Collections Library, Mona,
    Jamaica
    "Journal of a Voyage from New England to New York in 1756 and of a Cruise
        Round the West Indies in 1756 and 1757"
University of Virginia, Special Collections Library
    William Hugh Grove Diary
Virginia Historical Society
    Spragins Family Papers
    Tayloe Family Papers

PRINTED PRIMARY SOURCES

"An Act Enabling Certain Persons to Perfect a Canal between Scuppernong River
    and the Lake Near Its Head." In *The State Records of North Carolina,* 24:861–
    62. New York: AMS Press, 1968–78.
Adams, Edward C. L. *Tales of the Congaree.* Ed. Robert G. O'Meally. Chapel Hill:
    University of North Carolina Press, 1987.
Adanson, Michel. *A Voyage to Senegal, the Isle of Goree, and the River Gambia.*
    London: J. Nourse and W. Johnston, 1759.
Aptheker, Herbert, ed. *A Documentary History of the Negro People of the United
    States.* Vol. 1. *From the Colonial Times through the Civil War.* 1951. Reprint,
    New York: Citadel Press, 1990.
Ball, Charles. *Fifty Years in Chains; Or, The Life of an American Slave.* New York:
    H. Dayton, 1859.
Barbot, Jean. *Barbot on Guinea: The Writings of Jean Barbot on West Africa,
    1768–1712.* Ed. P. E. H. Hair, Adam Jones, and Robin Law. London: Hakluyt
    Society, 1992.
——. *A Description of the Coasts of North and South-Guinea.* London, 1732.
Bechet, Sidney. *Treat It Gentle.* 1960. Reprint, New York: Da Capo Press, 1978.
Berlin, Ira, Marc Favreau, and Stephen F. Miller, eds. *Remembering Slavery: Afri-
    can Americans Talk about Their Personal Experiences of Slavery and Freedom.*
    Tape 1. New York: New Press, 1998.

Bibb, Henry. *Narrative of the Life and Adventures of Henry Bibb, an American Slave. Written by Himself with an Introduction by Lucius C. Matlock.* Ed. Charles J. Heglar. 1849. Reprint, Madison: University of Wisconsin Press, 2001.

Biet, Antoine. "Father Antoine Biet's Visit to Barbados in 1654." Ed. and trans. Jerome Handler. *Journal of the Barbados Museum and Historical Society* 32 (May 1967): 56–76.

Blome, Richard. *A Description of the Island of Jamaica; With the other Isles and Territories in America, to which the English are Related.* London: L. Milbourn, 1672.

———. *A Geographical Description of the World, Taken from the Works of the Famous Monsieur Sanson, Late Geographer to the Present French King, 1680, in Cosmography and Geography in Two Parts.* London, 1682.

Bosman, William. *A New and Accurate Description of the Coast of Guinea.* Ed. John Ralph Willis, J. D. Fage, and R. E. Bradbury. 1705. Reprint, London: Cass, 1967.

Bradford, Sarah H. *Harriet Tubman: The Moses of Her People.* 1869. Reprint, Gloucester, MA: Peter Smith, 1981.

Brown, Henry Box. *Narrative of Henry Box Brown: Who Escaped from Slavery Enclosed in a Box 3 Feet Long and 2 Feet Wide.* Afro-American History Series, no. 205. 1849. Reprint, Philadelphia: Historic Publications, 1969.

Brown, Sterling A., Arthur P. Davis, and Ulysses Lee, eds. *Negro Caravan.* 1941. Reprint, Salem, NH: Ayer, 1991.

Brown, William Wells. *My Southern Home: Or, The South and Its People.* 1880. Reprint, Upper Saddle River, NJ: Gregg Press, 1968.

———. *Narrative of William Wells Brown, a Fugitive Slave.* In *Puttin on Ole Massa: The Slave Narratives of Henry Bibb, William Wells Brown, and Solomon Northrup,* ed. Gilbert Osofsky. New York: Harper and Row, 1969.

Caillié, Réné. *Travels through Central Africa to Timbuctoo.* 1830. Reprint, London: Frank Cass, 1968.

Carroll, B. R., ed. *Historical Collections of South Carolina; Embracing Many Rare and Valuable Pamphlets, and Other Documents, Relating to the History of That State, from Its First Discovery to Its Independence, in the Year 1777.* 2 vols. New York: Harper and Brothers, 1836.

Catesby, Mark. *Catesby's Birds of Colonial America.* Ed. Alan Feduccia. Chapel Hill: University of North Carolina Press, 1985.

City Gazette (South Carolina).

Clapperton, Hugh. *Missions to the Niger.* Vol. 4. *The Bornu Mission, 1822–25.* Ed. E. W. Bovill. Cambridge: Cambridge University Press, 1966.

Colonising Expeditions to the West Indies and Guiana, 1623–1667. 2nd ser., no. 56. London: Hakluyt Society, 1924.

Commons, John R., et al., eds. *A Documentary History of American Industrial Society.* Vol. 1. *Plantation and Frontier.* Ed. Ulrich Bonnell Phillips. New York: Russell and Russell, 1958.

Coxe, Tench. "The Origin of the Cotton Culture of the United States." *American Farmer* (Baltimore) 2 (May 26, 1820): 67.

Cranfield, M. "Observations of the Present State of Jamaica, December 14, 1675." *Appendix to the First Volume of the Journals of the Assembly of Jamaica* (Jamaica, 1811): 42.

Crone, G. R., ed. *The Voyages of Cadamosto and Other Documents on Western Africa*. 2nd ser., no. 80. London: Hakluyt Society, 1937.

Crouse, Maurice A., ed. "The Letterbook of Peter Manigault, 1763–1773." *South Carolina Historical Magazine* 70 (July 1969): 177–95.

Daaku, K. Y. *Gonja*. UNESCO Research Project on Oral Traditions, no. 1. Legon: Institute of African Studies, University of Ghana, November 1969.

Dapper, Olfert. *Olfert Dapper's Description of Benin* [1668]. Ed. and trans. Adam Jones. Madison: African Studies Program, University of Wisconsin-Madison, 1998.

De Brahm, William Gerard. *Philosophico-Historico-Hydrogeography of South Carolina, Georgia, and East Florida*. In *Documents Connected with the History of South Carolina*, ed. Plowden Charles Jennett Weston. London, 1856.

De Marees, Pieter. *Description and Historical Account of the Gold Kingdom of Guinea (1602)*. Ed. and trans. Albert Van Dantzig and Adam Jones. New York: Oxford University Press, 1987.

Delany, Martin. *The Condition, Elevation, Emigration, and Destiny of the Colored People of the United States*. 1852. Reprint, Baltimore: Black Classics Press, 1993.

Denham, Major F. R. S., Captain Clapperton, and the Late Doctor Oudney. *Narrative of Travels and Discoveries in Northern and Central Africa in the Years 1822, 1823, and 1824*. Vol. 2. 1826. Reprint, London: Darf, 1985.

A Description of South Carolina: Containing Many Curious and Interesting Particulars Relating to the Civil, Natural and Commercial History of that Colony (London: R. and J. Dodsley, 1761). In *Historical Collections of South Carolina, Embracing Many Rare and Valuable Pamphlets, and Other Documents, Relating to the History of That State, From Its First Discovery to Its Independence, in the Year 1776*, ed. B. R. Carroll, vol. 2. New York: Harper and Brothers, 1836.

Donnan, Elizabeth, ed. *Documents Illustrative of the Slave Trade to America*. 4 vols. 1930–35. Reprint, New York: Octagon Books, 1965.

Douglass, Frederick. *Life and Times of Frederick Douglass: His Early Life as a Slave, His Escape from Bondage, and His Complete History*. 1881. Reprint, New York: Gramercy Books, 1993.

———. *My Bondage and My Freedom*. 1855. Reprint, New York: Dover Publications, 1969.

———. *Narrative of the Life of Frederick Douglass*. 1845. Reprint, Cambridge, MA: Harvard University Press, 1988.

Du Tertre, Jean Baptiste. *Histoire générale des Antilles habitées par les François*. Vol. 2. Paris, 1667–71.

Edwards, Bryan. *The History, Civil and Commercial, of the British Colonies of the West Indies.* 2 vols. London, 1793.

Eltis, David, et al. Voyages: The Trans-Atlantic Slave Trade Database. www.slave-voyages.org/tast/database/index.faces.

Equiano, Olaudah. *Equiano's Travels: His Autobiography, The Interesting Narrative of the Life of Olaudah Equiano or Gustavas Vassa the African.* Ed. Paul Edwards. Oxford: Heinemann International, 1967.

Fage, J. D. "The Effect of the Export Slave Trade on African Populations." In *The Population Factor in African Studies.*, ed. R. P. Moss and R. J. A. R. Rathbone, 15–23. London: University of London Press, 1975.

Faulkner, William J. *The Days When the Animals Talked: Black American Folktales and How They Came to Be.* Trenton, NJ: Africa World Press, 1993.

Finch, William. "Observations of William Finch, Merchant, Taken out of his large Journall" (August 1607). In *Purchas, His Pilgrimes in Five Books*, ed. Samuel Purchas, vol. 1. London, 1625.

Freeman, Richard Austin. *Travels and Life in Ashanti and Jaman.* 1898. Reprint, London: Frank Cass, 1967.

Gaillard, Samuel Gourdin. "Recollections of Samuel Gourdin Gaillard." *South Carolina Historical and Genealogical Magazine* 57 (July 1956): 119–34.

Gentleman's Magazine, May 1755, 201–3, and June 1755, 256–59.

Great Britain. Public Record Office. *Calendar of State Papers, Colonial Series, American and West Indies.* London, 1860–1969.

The Harleian Miscellany: A Collection of Scarce, Curious, and Entertaining Pamphlets and Tracts. Vol. 2. 1690. Reprint, London: John White and John Murray, 1809.

Haun, Weynette Parks. *Surry County, Virginia, Court Records, Deed Book II, 1664–1671.* Durham, NC, 1987.

———. *Surry County, Virginia, Court Records, Deed Book III, 1672–1682.* Durham, NC, 1989.

———. *Surry County, Virginia, Court Records, Book V, 1691–1700.* Durham, NC, 1991.

Hickeringill, Edmund. *Jamaica Viewed; With All the Ports, Harbours, and their Several Soundings, Towns, and Settlements Thereunto Belonging.* London, 1661.

An Historical Account of the Rise and Growth of the West India Colonies; and of the great Advantages they are to England, in respect to trade. Licensed According to Order. In *The Harleian Miscellany: A Collection of Scarce, Curious, and Entertaining Pamphlets and Tracts,* vol. 2. 1690. Reprint, London: John White and John Murray, 1809.

"Historical Notes." *South Carolina Historical Gazette and Magazine* 8 (October 1907).

Hughes, Griffith. *Natural History of Barbados.* London, 1750.

Hughes, Louis. *The Autobiography of Louis Hughes: Thirty Years a Slave; From Bondage to Freedom; The Institution of Slavery as Seen on the Plantation in the Home of the Planter*. 1897. Reprint, Montgomery, AL: New South Books, 2002.

Hughes, William. *The American Physitian; or a Treatise of the Roots, Plants, Trees, Shrubs, Fruit, Herbs, ets., Growing in the English Plantations in America*. London, 1672.

Hunter, Robert. *Quebec to Carolina in 1785–1786: Being the Travel Diary and Observations of Robert Hunter, Jr., a Young Merchant of London*. Ed. Louis B. Wright and Marion Tingling. San Marino, CA: Huntington Library, 1943.

Hurston, Zora Neale. *The Sanctified Church*. New York: Marlowe, 1981.

Ives, Vernon A., ed. *The Rich Papers: Letters from Bermuda, 1615–1646. Eyewitness Accounts Sent by the Early Colonists to Sir Nathaniel Rich*. Toronto: University of Toronto Press, 1984.

Izard, Ralph. *Correspondence of Ralph Izard of South Carolina*. Ed. Anne Izard Deas. Vol. 1. New York: Charles S. Francis, 1844.

Jacobs, Harriet. *Incidents in the Life of a Slave Girl, Written by Herself*. Enl. ed. Ed. Jean Fagan Yellin. 1861. Reprint, Cambridge, MA: Harvard University Press, 2000.

Jefferson, Thomas. *Farm Book*. Ed. Edwin Morris Betts. Princeton, NJ: Princeton University Press, 1953.

———. *The Garden and Farm Books of Thomas Jefferson*. Ed. Robert C. Baron. Golden, CO: Fulcrum, 1987.

———. *Garden Book, 1766–1824*. Ed. Edwin Morris Betts. Philadelphia: American Philosophical Society, 1944.

———. *Notes on the State of Virginia*. Ed. William Peden. Chapel Hill: University of North Carolina Press, 1964.

Jobson, Richard. *The Golden Trade, or A Discovery of the River Gambra, and the Golden Trade of the Aethiopians, Set Down as They were Collected in Travelling Part of the Yeares 1620 and 1621*. 1623. Reprint, London: Penguin Press, 1932.

Jones, Adam, ed. *Brandenburg Sources for West African History, 1680–1700*. Stuttgart: Franz Steiner, 1985.

Lander, Richard. *The Niger Journal of Richard and John Lander*. Ed. Robin Hallett. New York: Praeger, 1965.

Laurens, Henry. *The Papers of Henry Laurens*. Ed. Philip M. Hamer. Columbia: University of South Carolina Press, 1968–.

Laye, Camara. *The Dark Child: The Autobiography of an African Boy*. New York: Farrar, Straus and Giroux, 1954.

A Letter from South Carolina, Giving an Account of the Soil, Air, Product, Trade, Government, Laws, Religion, People, Military Strength, Etc. of that Province Together with the Manner and Necessary Charges of Settling a Plantation there, and the Annual Profit it Will Produce. Written by a Swiss gentleman, to his friend at Bern. London: A. Baldwin, 1710.

Lewis, Mathew Gregory. *Journal of a West India Proprietor, Kept during a Residence in the Island of Jamaica*. 1834. Reprint, New York: Negro Universities Press, 1969.

Ligon, Richard. *A True and Exact History of the Island of Barbadoes*. 1673. Reprint, London: Frank Cass, 1970.

Lomax, Alan. *The Folk Songs of North America in the English Language*. Garden City, NY: Doubleday, 1960.

Lopez, Duarte. *A Report of the Kingdom of Congo*. 1597. Reprint, New York: Da Capo Press, 1970.

Miller, Philip. *The Gardener's Dictionary: Containing the Methods of Cultivating and Improving the Kitchen, Fruit and Flower Garden*. London, 1731.

Minutes of the Evidence Taken Before a Committee of the House of Commons, Being a Committee of the Whole House, to Whom It Was Referred to Consider the Circumstances of the Slave Trade, Complained of in the Several Petitions which were presented to the House in the Last Session of Parliament, Relative to the State of the African Slave Trade. London, 1789.

Mollien, Gaspar. *Travels in the Interior of Africa to the Sources of the Senegal and Gambia*. 1820. Reprint, London: Frank Cass, 1967.

Norris, Robert. *Memoirs of the Reign of Bassa Ahadee, King of Dahomy, an Inland Country of Guiney. To Which Are Added, The Author's Journey to Abomey, the Capital; And A Short Account of the African Slave Trade*. London, 1789.

Northrup, Solomon. *Twelve Years a Slave: Narrative of Solomon Northrup, a Citizen of New York, Kidnapped in Washington City in 1841 and Rescued in 1853, from a Cotton Plantation Near the Red River, in Louisiana*. Ed. Sue Eakin and Joseph Logsdon. 1853. Reprint, Baton Rouge: Louisiana State University Press, 1968.

Ogilby, John. *America: Being the Latest and Most Accurate Description of the New World; Containing the Original of the Inhabitants and the Remarkable Voyages Thither*. London, 1671.

Oldmixon, John. *The British Empire in America, Containing the History of the Discovery, Settlement, Progress and Present State of all the British Colonies On the Continent and Islands of America*. Vol. 2. London, 1708.

———. *The British Empire in America, Containing the History of the Discovery, Settlement, Progress, and State of the British Colonies on the Continent and Islands of America*. 2nd ed. Vol. 2. London, 1741.

Park, Mungo. *Journal of a Mission to the Interior of Africa in the Year 1805*. London, 1815.

———. *Travels in the Interior Districts of Africa*. Ed. Kate Ferguson Marsters. Durham: Duke University Press, 2000.

———. *Travels in the Interior Districts of Africa: Performed Under the Direction of the Patronage of the African Association in the Years 1795, 1796, and 1797*. 3rd ed. London: W. Bulmer, 1799.

Perdue, Charles, L., Jr., Thomas E. Barden, and Robert K. Phillips, eds. *Weevils in the Wheat: Interviews with Virginia Ex-Slaves*. Charlottesville: University Press of Virginia, 1976.

Pereira, Duarte Pacheco. *Esmeraldo de Situ Orbis*. Ed. and trans. George T. Kimble. London: Hakluyt Society, 1937.

A Perfect Description of Virginia; Being a Full and True Relation of the Present State of the Plantation, their Health, Peace, and Plenty, the Number of People, with the Abundance of Cattell, Fowl, Fish, etc. London, 1649.

Phillips, Thomas. *A Journal of a Voyage Made in the Hannibal of London, Ann. 1693, 1694, from England to Cape Monseradoe, in Africa; And thence Along the Coast of Guiney to Whidaw, the Island of St. Thomas, and So Forward to Barbadoes* (1746). In *A Collection of Voyages and Travels, Some Now First Printed from Original Manuscripts, Others Now First Published in English*, 3rd ed., ed. Answham Churchill, vol. 6. London, 1746.

Pigafetta, Filippo. *A Report of the Kingdom of Congo and the Surrounding Countries; Drawn out of the Writings and Discourses of the Portuguese, Duarte Lopez*. Trans. Margarite Hutchinson. 1881. Reprint, New York: Negro Universities Press, 1969.

Pinckney, Eliza. *The Letterbook of Eliza Lucas Pinckney, 1739–1762*. Ed. Elise Pinckney with Marvin R. Zahniser. Chapel Hill: University of North Carolina Press, 1972.

Purchas, Samuel. *Purchas, His Pilgrimes in Five Books*. London, 1625.

Purry, Peter. "Proposals by Peter Purry of Newfchatel." In *Historical Collections of South Carolina; Embracing Many Rare and Valuable Pamphlets, and Other Documents, Relating to the History of That State, from Its First Discovery to Its Independence, in the Year 1776*, ed. B. R. Carroll, vol. 2. New York: Harper and Brothers, 1836.

Rawick, George, ed. *The American Slave: A Composite Autobiography*. Westport, CT: Greenwood, 1972–77.

———, ed. *The American Slave: A Composite Autobiography. Supplement, Series 1*. Westport, CT: Greenwood, 1977.

———, ed. *The American Slave: A Composite Autobiography. Supplement, Series 2*. Westport, CT: Greenwood, 1979.

Roberts, George. *The Four Years Voyages of Captain George Roberts*. London, 1726.

Ruffin, Edmund. *Agricultural, Geological, and Descriptive Sketches of Lower North Carolina and the Adjacent Lands*. Raleigh, NC: Institution for the Deaf and Dumb and the Blind, 1861.

———. *Farmers' Register*, nos. 3–12 (1839).

Salley, Alexander S., Jr., ed. *Narratives of Early Carolina, 1650–1708*. New York: Charles Scribner's Sons, 1911.

Saunders, William L., ed. *State Records of North Carolina.* Vol. 24. New York: AMS Press, 1968–78.

Savannah Unit, Georgia Writers' Project, Work Projects Administration, comp. *Drums and Shadows: Survival Studies among the Georgia Coastal Negroes.* 1940. Reprint, Athens: University of Georgia Press, 1986.

Schaw, Janet. *Journal of a Lady of Quality: Being the Narrative of a Journey from Scotland to the West Indies, North Carolina, and Portugal in the Years 1774 to 1776.* Ed. Evangeline Walker Andrews. New Haven: Yale University Press, 1927.

Seabrook, Whitemarsh. *A Memoir on the Origin, Cultivation and Uses of Cotton, from the Earliest Ages to the Present Time, with Special Reference to the Sea-Island Cotton Plant, Including the Improvements in Its Cultivation, and the Preparation of the Wool, &c. in Georgia and South Carolina.* Charleston, SC: Miller and Browne, 1844.

Sloane, Hans. *A Voyage to the Islands Madera, Barbados, Nieves, St. Christophers and Jamaica, with the Natural History of the Herbs and Trees, Four-footed Beasts, Fishes, Birds, Insects, Reptiles, Etc.* 2 vols. London, 1707.

South Carolina Historical Society. *Collections of the South Carolina Historical Society.* Vol. 5. Charleston: South Carolina Historical Society, 1897.

Spoeri, Felix Christian. "A Swiss Medical Doctor's Description of Barbados in 1661: The Account of Felix Christian Spoeri." Ed. and trans. Alexander Gunkel and Jerome S. Handler. *Journal of the Barbados Museum and Historical Society* 33 (May 1969): 3–13.

Spotswood, Alexander. *The Official Letters of Alexander Spotswood, Lieutenant-Governor of the Colony of Virginia, 1710–1722.* Ed. R. A. Brock. Vol. 1. Richmond: Virginia Historical Society, 1882.

Stewart, J. *A View of the Present State of the Island of Jamaica.* 1823. New York: Negro Universities Press, 1969.

Talbot, P. Amory. *The Peoples of Southern Nigeria: A Sketch of Their History, Ethnology and Languages, with an Abstract of the 1921 Census.* Vol. 3. *Ethnology.* London: Oxford University Press, 1926.

Tingling, Marion, ed. *The Correspondence of the Three William Byrds of Westover, Virginia, 1684–1776.* 2 vols. Charlottesville: University Press of Virginia, 1977.

Turner, Nat. *The Confessions of Nat Turner, Leader of the Late Insurrection of Southampton, Virginia, as Fully and Voluntarily Made to Thos C. Gray, in the Prison Where He Was Confined—and Acknowledged by Him to Be Such, When Read before the Court of Southampton, Convened at Jerusalem, November 5, 1831, for His Trial.* 1861. Reprint, Miami, FL: Mnemosyne, 1969.

Uchteritz, Heinrich von. "A German Indentured Servant in Barbados in 1652: The Account of Heinrich von Uchteritz." Ed. and trans. Alexander Gunkel and Jerome S. Handler. *Journal of the Barbados Museum and Historical Society* 33 (May 1970): 91–100.

U.S. Department of Commerce. *Historical Statistics of the United States.* Part 2. *Colonial Times to 1970.* Washington, DC: U.S. Department of Commerce, 1975.

Van Dantzig, Albert, comp. and trans. *The Dutch and the Guinea Coast, 1674–1742: A Collection of Documents from the General Archives of the Hague.* Accra: Ghana Academy of Arts and Science, 1978.

Van Den Broecke, Pieter. *Journal of Voyages to Cape Verde, Guinea, and Angola (1605–1612).* Ed. and trans. J. D. La Fleur. London: Hakluyt Society, 2000.

"A View of the Condition of Jamaica, The 1st of October, 1664." *Appendix to the First Volume of the Journals of the Assembly of Jamaica* (Jamaica, 1811), 21.

Villault, Nicolas. *A Relation of the Coasts of Africk called Guinee; With a Description of the Countreys, Manners and Customs of the Inhabitants; of the Productions of the Earth, and the Merchandise and Commodities it Affords; with Some Historical Observations upon the Coasts.* London: John Starkey, 1670.

Vitzthum, Hilda. *Torn Out by the Roots: The Recollections of a Former Communist.* Ed. and trans. Paul Schach. Lincoln: University of Nebraska Press, 1993.

Walsh, Richard, ed. "Letters of Morris and Brailsford to Thomas Jefferson." *South Carolina Historical Magazine* 58 (1957): 129–44.

Washington, George. *The Daily Journal of George Washington in 1751–2: Kept While on a Tour from Virginia to the Island of Barbadoes, with His Invalid Brother, Maj. Lawrence Washington.* Albany, NY: J. Munsell's Sons, 1892.

Weisiger, Benjamin B. *York County, Virginia Records, 1665–72, Deed Book 4.* Richmond, 1987.

West, Frances. "John Bartram and Slavery." *South Carolina Historical Magazine* 56 (April 1955): 115–19.

White, Father Andrew. *Narrative of a Voyage to Maryland.* Ed. E. A. Dalrymple. Baltimore: Maryland Historical Society, 1874.

SECONDARY SOURCES

Abitbol, M. "The End of the Songhay Empire." In *General History of Africa,* vol. 5, *Africa from the Sixteenth to the Eighteenth Century,* ed. B. A. Ogot, 300–326. Berkeley: University of California Press, 1992.

Addo-Fenning, R. "The Gyadam Episode, 1824–70: An Aspect of Akyem Abuakwa History." *Universitas: An Interfaculty Journal* (University of Ghana), n.s., 6 (May 1997): 179–94.

Ajayi, J. F. Ade, and Michael Crowder, eds. *Historical Atlas of Africa.* Harlow, Essex: Longman, 1985.

Akyeampong, Emmanuel, and Pashington Obeng. "Spirituality, Gender, and Power in Asante History." *International Journal of African Historical Studies* 28:3 (1995): 481–508.

Andah, Bassey W. "Identifying Early Farming Traditions of West Africa." In *The Archaeology of Africa: Food, Metals and Towns,* ed. Thurstan Shaw, Paul Sinclair, Bassey Andah, and Alex Okpoko, 240–54. New York: Routledge, 1993.

Anderson, David M., and Richard Rathbone, eds. *Africa's Urban Past.* Portsmouth, NH: Heinemann, 2000.

Anquandah, James A. *Rediscovering Ghana's Past.* London: Longman, 1982.

Armstrong, Douglas V. "Archaeology and Ethnohistory of the Caribbean Plantation." In *"I, Too, Am America": Archaeological Studies of African-American Life,* ed. Theresa A. Singleton, 173–92. Charlottesville: University Press of Virginia, 1999.

Ba, A. Hampete. "The Living Tradition." In *General History of Africa,* vol. 1, *Methodology and Prehistory,* ed. J. Ki-Zerbo, 166–205. Berkeley: University of California Press, 1981.

Bailey, Ronald. "The Slave(ry) Trade and the Development of Capitalism in the United States: The Textile Industry in New England." *Social Science History* 14 (Autumn 1990): 373–414.

Balandier, Georges. *Daily Life in the Kingdom of Kongo: From the Sixteenth to the Eighteenth Century.* Trans. Helen Weaver. London: Allen and Unwin, 1968.

Balfour-Paul, Jenny. *Indigo.* 1998. Reprint, Chicago: Fitzroy Dearborn, 2000.

Bay, Mia. *The White Image in the Black Mind: African American Ideas about White People.* New York: Oxford University Press, 2000.

Beckles, Hilary M. *Natural Rebels: A Social History of Enslaved Black Women in Barbados.* New Brunswick: Rutgers University Press, 1989.

———. "Plantation Production and White 'Proto-Slavery': White Indentured Servants and the Colonisation of the English West Indies, 1624–1645." *Americas* 41 (January 1985): 21–45.

———. *White Servitude and Black Slavery in Barbados.* Knoxville: University of Tennessee Press, 1989.

Berlin, Ira. *Many Thousands Gone: The First Two Centuries of Slavery in North America.* Cambridge, MA: Harvard University Press, 1998.

Berlin, Ira, and Philip Morgan, eds. *Cultivation and Culture: Labor and the Shaping of Slave Life in America.* Charlottesville: University Press of Virginia, 1993.

Berns, Marla C. "Art, History, and Gender: Women and Clay in West Africa." *African Archaeological Review* 11 (1993): 129–48.

Birmingham, David. "Early African Trade in Angola and Its Hinterland." In *Precolonial African Trade,* ed. Richard Gray and David Birmingham, 163–73. New York: Oxford University Press, 1970.

———. "Society and Economy before A.D. 1400." In *History of Central Africa,* ed. David Birmingham and Phyllis M. Martin, 1:1–29. New York: Longman, 1983.

Birmingham, David, and Phyllis M. Martin, eds. *History of Central Africa.* Vol. 1. New York: Longman, 1983.

Blackburn, Robin. *The Making of New World Slavery: From the Baroque to the Modern, 1492–1800*. New York: Verso Press, 1997.

Boahen, A. A. "The States and Cultures of the Lower Guinea Coast." In *General History of Africa*, vol. 5, *Africa from the Sixteenth to the Eighteenth Centuries*, ed. B. A. Ogot, 399–433. Berkeley: University of California Press, 1992.

Bolland, Rita. *Tellem Textiles: Archaeological Finds from Burial Caves in Mali's Bandiagara Cliffs*. Amsterdam: Tropenmuseum / Royal Tropical Institute, 1991.

Bolster, W. Jeffrey. *Black Jacks: African American Seamen in the Age of Sail*. Cambridge, MA: Harvard University Press, 1997.

Bourdieu, Pierre. "The Forms of Capital." In *The Handbook of Theory and Research for the Sociology of Education*, ed. John G. Richardson, 241–58. New York: Greenwood Press, 1986.

———. *The Logic of Practice*. Trans. Richard Nice. Cambridge: Polity Press, 1990.

Braudel, Fernand. *Afterthoughts on Material Civilization and Capitalism*. Trans. Patricia M. Ranum. Baltimore: Johns Hopkins University Press, 1977.

———. *Civilization and Capitalism, 15th–18th Century*. Vol. 1. *The Structures of Everyday Life*. Trans. Sian Reynolds. New York: Harper and Row, 1981.

Breen, T. H. *Tobacco Culture: The Mentality of the Great Tidewater Planters on the Eve of Revolution*. Princeton: Princeton University Press, 1985.

Bridenbaugh, Carl, and Roberta Bridenbaugh. *No Peace beyond the Line: The English in the Caribbean, 1624–1690*. New York: Oxford University Press, 1972.

Brown, Ras Michael. "Walk in the Feenda: West Central Africans and the Forest in the South Carolina-Georgia Lowcountry." In *Central Africans and Cultural Transformations in the American Diaspora*, ed. Linda Heywood, 298–318. New York: Cambridge University Press, 2002.

Brown, Vincent. *The Reaper's Garden: Death and Power in the World of Atlantic Slavery*. Cambridge, MA: Harvard University Press, 2008.

Bruce, Philip Alexander. *Economic History of Virginia in the Seventeenth Century*. 2 vols. New York: Macmillan, 1896.

Burnard, Trevor. "European Migration to Jamaica, 1655–1780." *William and Mary Quarterly*, 3rd ser., 53 (October 1996): 769–96.

———. *Mastery, Tyranny, and Desire: Thomas Thistlewood and His Slaves in the Anglo-Jamaican World*. Chapel Hill: University of North Carolina Press, 2004.

Byfield, Judith. "Women, Economy and the State: A Study of the Adire Industry in Abeokuta, 1890–1930." PhD diss., Columbia University, 1993.

Carney, Judith. *Black Rice: The African Origins of Rice Cultivation in the Americas*. Cambridge, MA: Harvard University Press, 2001.

Cecelski, David S. *The Waterman's Song: Slavery and Freedom in Maritime North Carolina*. Chapel Hill: University of North Carolina Press, 2001.

Chaplin, Joyce E. *An Anxious Pursuit: Agricultural Innovation and Modernity in the Lower South, 1730–1815*. Chapel Hill: University of North Carolina Press, 1993.

Chaudhuri, K. N. *The Trading World of Asia and the English East India Company, 1660–1760.* New York: Cambridge University Press, 1978.

Clark, J. Desmond, and Steven A. Brandt, eds. *From Hunters to Farmers: The Causes and Consequences of Food Production in Africa.* Berkeley: University of California Press, 1984.

Collins, G. P. "Discovery of Lake Scuppernong (Phelps), North Carolina." *Publications of the Southern History Association* 6 (1902): 24–25.

Connah, Graham. "African City Walls: A Neglected Source?" In *Africa's Urban Past*, ed. David M. Anderson and Richard Rathbone, 36–51. Portsmouth, NH: Heinemann, 2000.

———. *African Civilizations: An Archaeological Perspective.* New York: Cambridge University Press, 2001.

———. *The Archeology of Benin: Excavations and Other Researches in and around Benin City, Nigeria.* Oxford: Clarendon Press, 1975.

Coon, David. "Eliza Lucas Pinckney and the Reintroduction of Indigo Culture in South Carolina." *Journal of Southern History* 42 (February 1976): 61–76.

Craton, Michael. *Searching for the Invisible Man: Slaves and Plantation Life in Jamaica.* Cambridge, MA: Harvard University Press, 1978.

Craton, Michael, and Gail Saunders. *Islanders in the Stream: A History of the Bahamian People.* Vol. 1. *From Aboriginal Times to the End of Slavery.* Athens: University of Georgia Press, 1992.

Creel, Margaret Washington. *"A Peculiar People": Slave Religion and Community Culture Among the Gullahs.* New York: New York University Press, 1988.

Crosby, Alfred W. *The Columbian Exchange: Biological and Cultural Consequences of 1492.* Westport, CT: Greenwood, 1972.

Crossland, L. B. *Pottery from the Begho-B2 Site, Ghana.* African Occasional Papers no. 4. Calgary: University of Calgary Press, 1989.

Davidson, Basil. *West Africa before the Colonial Era: A History to 1850.* London: Longman, 1998.

Dawson, Kevin. "Enslaved Swimmers and Divers in the Atlantic World." *Journal of American History* 92 (March 2006): 1327–55.

Day, Richard R., and Albert B. Saraka. *An Introduction to Spoken Baoule.* Washington, DC: Center for Applied Linguistics, 1968.

De Barros, Philip. "Bassar: A Quantified, Chronologically Controlled, Regional Approach to a Traditional Iron Production Centre in West Africa." *Africa* 56:2 (1986): 148–74.

De Maret, Pierre. "From Potter Groups to Ethnic Groups in Central Africa." In *African Archaeology*, ed. Ann Brower Stahl, 420–40. Malden, MA: Blackwell, 2005.

DeCorse, Christopher R. *An Archaeology of Elmina: Africans and Europeans on the Gold Coast, 1400–1900.* Washington, DC: Smithsonian Institution Press, 2001.

Diarra, S. "Historical Geography: Physical Aspects." In *General History of Africa,* vol. 1, *Methodology and Prehistory,* ed. J. Ki-Zerbo, 316–22. Berkeley: University of California Press, 1981.

Dickson, Kwabina. *A Historical Geography of Ghana.* New York: Cambridge University Press, 1969.

Dilley, Roy. "Tukulor Weavers and the Organisation of the Craft in Village and Town." *Africa* 56:2 (1986): 123–47.

Dolphyne, Florence. *A Comprehensive Course in Twi (Asante) for the Non-Twi Learner.* Accra: Ghana Universities Press, 1996.

Doolittle, William E. *Cultivated Landscapes of North America.* New York: Oxford University Press, 2000.

Du Bois, W. E. B. *Black Reconstruction: An Essay toward a History of the Part Black Folk Played in the Attempt to Reconstruct Democracy in America, 1860–1880.* 1935. Reprint, Millwood, NY: Kraus-Thomson, 1976.

——. *The Souls of Black Folk.* 1903. Reprint, Greenwich, CT: Fawcett Publications, 1961.

Dunn, Richard. *Sugar and Slaves: The Rise of the Planter Class in the English West Indies, 1624–1713.* Chapel Hill: University of North Carolina Press, 1972.

Durrill, Wayne K. "Slavery, Kinship, and Dominance: The Black Community at Somerset Place Plantation, 1786–1860." *Slavery and Abolition* 13 (August 1992): 1–19.

Dusinberre, William. *Them Dark Days: Slavery in the American Rice Swamps.* Athens: University of Georgia Press, 2000.

Edgar, Walter. *South Carolina: A History.* Columbia: University of South Carolina Press, 1998.

Ehret, C. "Historical/Linguistic Evidence for Early African Food Production." In *From Hunters to Farmers: The Causes and Consequences of Food Production in Africa,* ed. J. Desmond Clark and Steven A. Brandt, 26–36. Berkeley: University of California Press, 1984.

Eltis, David. "Free and Coerced Transatlantic Migrations: Some Comparisons." *American Historical Review* 88 (April 1983): 251–80.

——. "New Estimates of Exports from Barbados and Jamaica, 1665–1701." *William and Mary Quarterly,* 3rd ser., 52 (October 1995): 631–48.

——. *The Rise of African Slavery in the Americas.* New York: Cambridge University Press, 2000.

Eltis, David, Philip Morgan, and David Richardson. "Agency and Diaspora in Atlantic History: Reassessing the African Contributions to Rice Cultivation in the Americas." *American Historical Review* 112 (December 2007): 1329–58.

Emerson, Matthew C. "African Inspirations in New World Art and Artifact: Decorated Pipes from the Chesapeake." In *"I, Too, Am America": Archaeological Studies of African-American Life,* ed. Theresa A. Singleton, 47–82. Charlottesville: University Press of Virginia, 1999.

Epstein, Dena. *Sinful Tunes and Spirituals: Black Folk Music to the Civil War*. Urbana: University of Illinois Press, 1977.

Fage, J. D. "The Effect of the Export Slave Trade on African Populations." In *The Population Factor in African Studies*, ed. R. P. Moss and R. J. A. R. Rathbone, 15–23. London: University of London Press, 1975.

Ferguson, Leland. *Uncommon Ground: Archeology and Early Afro-American Life*. Washington, DC: Smithsonian Institution Press, 1992.

Fogleman, Aaron S. "From Slaves, Convicts, and Servants to Free Passengers: The Transformation of Immigration in the Era of the American Revolution." *American Historical Review* 85 (June 1998): 43–76.

Folorunso, C. A., and S. O. Ogundele. "Agriculture and Settlement among the Tiv of Nigeria: Some Ethnoarchaeological Observations." In *The Archaeology of Africa: Food, Metals and Towns*, ed. Thurstan Shaw, Paul Sinclair, Bassey Andah, and Alex Okpoko, 274–88. New York: Routledge, 1993.

Frey, Sylvia. *Water from the Rock: Black Resistance in a Revolutionary Age*. Princeton: Princeton University Press, 1991.

Fynn, J. K. *Asante and Its Neighbours, 1700–1807*. Evanston: Northwestern University Press, 1971.

Garlake, Peter. *The Kingdoms of Africa*. Oxford: Elsevier-Phaidon, 1978.

Garrard, Timothy F. *Akan Weights and the Gold Trade*. New York: Longman, 1980.

Gaspar, David Barry. *Bondmen and Rebels: A Study of Master-Slave Relations in Antigua*. Baltimore: Johns Hopkins University Press, 1985.

Geggus, David. "Sugar and Coffee Cultivation in Saint Domingue and the Shaping of the Slave Labor Force." In *Cultivation and Culture: Labor and the Shaping of Slave Life in America*, ed. Ira Berlin and Philip Morgan, 73–98. Charlottesville: University Press of Virginia, 1993.

Giblin, James. "Trypanosomiasis Control in African History: An Evaded Issue?" *Journal of African History* 31:1 (1990): 54–80.

Gomez, Michael. *Exchanging Our Country Marks: The Transformation of African Identities in the Colonial and Antebellum South*. Chapel Hill: University of North Carolina Press, 1998.

Goucher, Candace. "African Metallurgy in the Atlantic World." *African Archaeological Review* 11 (1993): 197–215.

Goucher, Candace L., and Eugenia W. Herbert. "The Blooms of Banjeli: Technology and Gender in West African Iron Making." In *The Culture and Technology of African Iron Production*, ed. Peter R. Schmidt, 40–57. Gainesville: University Press of Florida, 1996.

Gray, Lewis Cecil. *History of Agriculture in the Southern United States to 1860*. 2 vols. New York: Peter Smith, 1941.

Graydon, Nell S. *Eliza of Wappoo: A Tale of Indigo*. Columbia, SC: R. L. Bryan, 1967.

Greene, Jack. "The American Revolution." *American Historical Review* 105 (February 2000): 93–102.

Greene, Sandra E. *Gender, Ethnicity, and Social Change on the Upper Slave Coast: A History of the Anlo-Ewe.* Portsmouth, NH: Heinemann, 1996.

Grimé, William Ed. *Ethno-Botany of the Black Americans.* Algonac, MI: Reference Publications, 1979.

Groover, Mark D. "Evidence for Folkways and Cultural Exchange in the 18th Century South Carolina Backcountry." *Historical Archaeology* 28:1 (1994): 41–64.

Guyer, Jane I., and Samuel M. Eno Belinga. "Wealth in People as Wealth in Knowledge: Accumulation and Composition in Equatorial Africa." *Journal of African History* 36 (1995): 91–120.

Hale, Sjarief. "Kente Cloth of Ghana." *African Arts* 3:3 (1970): 26–29.

Hall, Gwendolyn Midlo. *Africans in Colonial Louisiana: The Development of Afro-Creole Culture in the Eighteenth Century.* Baton Rouge: Louisiana State University Press, 1992.

———. *Slavery and African Ethnicities in the Americas: Restoring the Links.* Chapel Hill: University of North Carolina Press, 2005.

Handler, Jerome S. "An African-Type Healer/Diviner and His Grave Goods: A Burial from a Plantation Slave Cemetery in Barbados, West Indies." *International Journal of Historical Archaeology* 1:2 (1997): 191–230.

———. "Amerindians and Their Contributions to Barbadian Life in the Seventeenth Century." *Journal of the Barbados Museum and Historical Society* 35:3 (1977): 189–210.

Handler, Jerome S., and Frederick W. Lange. *Plantation Slavery in Barbados: An Archaeological and Historical Investigation.* Cambridge, MA: Harvard University Press, 1978.

Handy, R. B. "History and General Statistics of Cotton." In *The Cotton Plant: Its History, Botany, Chemistry, Culture, Enemies, and Uses,* ed. U.S. Department of Agriculture, Office of Experiment Stations, under the supervision of A. C. True, 17–66. Washington, DC: Government Printing Office, 1896.

Harding, Rachel. *A Refuge in Thunder: Candomble and Alternative Spaces of Blackness.* Bloomington: Indiana University Press, 2000.

Harlan, Jack R. "The Origins of Indigenous African Agriculture." In *The Cambridge History of Africa,* ed. J. D. Fage and Roland Oliver, vol. 1, *From Earliest Times to c. 500 B.C.,* ed. J. Desmond Clark, 625–57. New York: Cambridge University Press, 1982.

———. "The Tropical African Cereals." In *The Archaeology of Africa: Food, Metals and Towns,* ed. Thurstan Shaw, Paul Sinclair, Bassey Andah, and Alex Okpoko, 53–60. New York: Routledge, 1993.

Harlow, Vincent T. *A History of Barbados, 1625–1685.* 1926. Reprint, New York: Negro Universities Press, 1969.

Harms, Robert W. *The Diligent: A Voyage through the Worlds of the Slave Trade.* New York: Basic Books, 2002.

———. *Games against Nature: An Eco-Cultural History of the Nunu of Equatorial Africa.* New York: Cambridge University Press, 1987.

———. *River of Wealth, River of Sorrow: The Central Zaire Basin in the Era of the Slave and Ivory Trade, 1500–1891.* New Haven: Yale University Press, 1981.

Harris, David R. "The Ecology of Swidden Cultivation in the Upper Orinoco Rain Forest, Venezuela." *Geographical Review* 61 (October 1971): 475–95.

———. "Traditional Systems of Plant Food Production and the Origins of Agriculture in West Africa." In *Origins of African Plant Domestication,* ed. Jack R. Harlan, Jan M. J. de Wet, and Ann B. L. Stemler, 311–56. The Hague: Mouton, 1976.

Hatfield, April. *Atlantic Virginia: Intercolonial Relations in the Seventeenth Century.* Philadelphia: University of Pennsylvania Press, 2004.

Hawthorne, Walter. "Nourishing a Stateless Society during the Slave Trade: The Rise of Balanta Paddy-Rice Production in Guinea-Bissau." *Journal of African History* 42 (2001): 1–24.

Herbert, Eugenia. *The Red Gold of Africa: Copper in Precolonial History and Culture.* Madison: University of Wisconsin Press, 1984.

Herndon, G. Melvin. *William Tatham and the Culture of Tobacco.* Coral Gables, FL: University of Miami Press, 1969.

Herskovits, Melville. *The Myth of the Negro Past.* 1941. Reprint, Boston: Beacon Press, 1990.

Heywood, Linda M., and John K. Thornton. *Central Africans, Atlantic Creoles and the Foundation of the Americas, 1585–1660.* New York: Cambridge University Press, 2007.

Higman, Barry. *Jamaica Surveyed: Plantation Maps and Plans of the Eighteenth and Nineteenth Century.* Kingston: University of West Indies Press, 2001.

Hilton, Anne. *Kingdom of Kongo.* New York: Oxford University Press, 1985.

Hogendorn, Jan, and Marion Johnson. *The Shell Money of the Slave Trade.* Cambridge: Cambridge University Press, 1986.

Hull, Richard. *African Cities and Towns before the European Conquest.* New York: W. W. Norton, 1976.

Hutcheson, Harold. *Tench Coxe: A Study in American Economic Development.* New York: Da Capo Press, 1969.

Insoll, Timothy. "Iron-Age Gao: An Archaeological Contribution." *Journal of African History* 38:1 (1997): 1–30.

Irvine, F. R. *The Fish and Fisheries of the Gold Coast.* London: Crown Agents for the Colonies, 1947.

———. *A Text-Book of West African Agriculture: Soils and Crops.* 2nd ed. London: Oxford University Press, 1953.

Jaquay, Barbara Gaye. "The Caribbean Cotton Production: An Historical Geography of the Region's Mystery Crop." PhD diss., Texas A&M University, 1997.

Jelatis, Virginia Gail. "Tangled Up in Blue: Indigo Culture and Economy in South Carolina, 1747–1800." PhD diss., University of Minnesota, 1999.

Johnson, Guion Griffis. *Ante-Bellum North Carolina: A Social History.* Chapel Hill: University of North Carolina Press, 1937.

———. *A Social History of the Sea Islands, with Special Reference to St. Helena Island, South Carolina.* Chapel Hill: University of North Carolina Press, 1930.

Johnson, Walter. *Soul by Soul: Life inside the Antebellum Slave Market.* Cambridge, MA: Harvard University Press, 1999.

Jones, Adam. "A Collection of African Art in Seventeenth-Century Germany: Cristoph Weickmann's *Kunst- und Naturkammer." African Arts* 27 (April 1994): 28–43, 92–94.

Jones, William O. *Manioc in Africa.* Stanford: Stanford University Press, 1959.

Kamoie, Laura Croghan. *Neabsco and Occoquan: The Tayloe Family Iron Plantations, 1730–1830.* Charlottesville: University of Virginia Press, 2007.

Kea, Ray. *Settlements, Trade, and Polities in the Seventeenth-Century Gold Coast.* Baltimore: Johns Hopkins University Press, 1982.

Kelley, David H. "An Essay on Pre-Columbian Contacts between the Americas and Other Areas, with Special Reference to the Work of Ivan Van Sertima." In *Race, Discourse, and the Origin of the Americas: A New World View,* ed. Vera Lawrence Hyatt and Rex Nettleford, 103–22. Washington, DC: Smithsonian Institution Press, 1995.

Ki-Zerbo, J., ed. *General History of Africa.* Vol. 1. *Methodology and Prehistory.* Berkeley: University of California Press, 1981.

Lawrence, A. W. *Fortified Trade-Posts: The English in West Africa, 1645–1822.* London: Jonathan Cape, 1963.

Lee, Susan. *Eliza Lucas.* Danbury, CT: Children's Press, 1977.

Legett, William. *Ancient and Medieval Dyes.* Brooklyn: Chemical Publishing Co., 1944.

Littlefield, Daniel C. *Rice and Slaves: Ethnicity and the Slave Trade in Colonial South Carolina.* 1981. Reprint, Urbana: University of Illinois Press, 1991.

Litwack, Leon. *Been in the Storm So Long: The Aftermath of Slavery.* New York: Alfred A. Knopf, 1979.

Lokko, Sophia D. "Hunger Hooting Festival in Ghana." *Drama Review* 25 (Winter 1981): 43–50.

Lovejoy, Paul E. *Caravans of Kola: The Hausa Kola Trade, 1700–1900.* Zaria, Nigeria: Ahmadu Bello University, 1980.

———. "The Internal Trade of West Africa to 1800." In *History of West Africa,* 3rd ed., ed. J. F. E. Ajayi and Michael Crowder, 1:648–90. London: Longman, 1985.

Mabogunje, Akin L. "Historical Geography: Economic Aspects." In *General History of Africa,* vol. 1, *Methodology and Prehistory,* ed. J. Ki-Zerbo, 333–47. Berkeley: University of California Press, 1981.

———. *Urbanization in Nigeria.* New York: Africana, 1968.

Mabogunje, Akin L., and Paul Richards. "Land and People: Models of Spatial and Ecological Processes in West African History." In *History of West Africa,* 3rd ed., ed. J. F. A. Ajayi and Michael Crowder, 1:5–47. New York: Longman, 1985.

MacGaffey, Wyatt. "The Cultural Traditions of Forest West Africa." In *Insight and Artistry in African Divination,* ed. John Pemberton III. Washington, DC: Smithsonian Institution Press, 2000.

———. *Religion and Society in Central Africa: The BaKongo of Lower Zaire.* Chicago: University of Chicago Press, 1986.

Made of Iron. Exh. cat. Houston, TX: University of St. Thomas Art Department, 1966.

Marcuse, Herbert. *One-Dimensional Man: Studies in the Ideology of Advanced Industrial Society.* Boston: Beacon Press, 1964.

McCann, James D. *Maize and Grace: Africa's Encounter with a New World Crop.* Cambridge, MA: Harvard University Press, 2005.

McColley, Robert. *Slavery in Jeffersonian Virginia.* 2nd ed. Urbana: University of Illinois Press, 1973.

McFeely, William S. *Frederick Douglass.* New York: W. W. Norton, 1991.

McMillin, James A. *The Final Victims: Foreign Slave Trade to North America, 1783–1810.* Columbia: University of South Carolina Press, 2004.

Menard, Russell R. "The Maryland Slave Population, 1658 to 1730: A Demographic Profile of Blacks in Four Counties." *William and Mary Quarterly,* 3rd ser., 32 (January 1975): 29–54.

Miller, Joseph C. "History and Africa/Africa and History." *American Historical Review* 104 (February 1999): 1–32.

———. "The Paradoxes of Impoverishment in the Atlantic Zone." In *History of Central Africa,* ed. David Birmingham and Phyllis M. Martin, 1:118–59. New York: Longman, 1983.

———. "The Significance of Drought, Disease and Famine in the Agriculturally Marginal Zones of West-Central Africa." *Journal of African History* 23:1 (1982): 17–61.

———. *Way of Death: Merchant Capitalism and the Angolan Slave Trade, 1730–1830.* Madison: University of Wisconsin Press, 1988.

Miller, W. Hubert. "The Colonization of the Bahamas, 1647–1670." *William and Mary Quarterly,* 3rd ser., 2 (January 1945): 33–46.

Mintz, Sidney. *Caribbean Transformations.* 1974. Reprint, New York: Columbia University Press, 1989.

Miracle, Marvin P. *Agriculture in the Congo Basin: Tradition and Change in African Rural Economies.* Madison: University of Wisconsin Press, 1967.

———. *Maize in Tropical Africa.* Madison: University of Wisconsin Press, 1966.

Molen, Patricia A. "Population and Social Patterns in Barbados in the Early Eighteenth Century." *William and Mary Quarterly,* 3rd ser., 28 (April 1971): 287–300.

Morgan, Edmund S. *American Slavery, American Freedom: The Ordeal of Colonial Virginia*. New York: W. W. Norton, 1975.

———. *Virginians at Home: Family Life in the Eighteenth Century*. Williamsburg, VA: Colonial Williamsburg, Inc., 1952.

Morgan, Jennifer. *Laboring Women: Reproduction and Gender in New World Slavery*. Philadelphia: University of Pennsylvania Press, 2004.

Morgan, Philip D. *Slave Counterpoint: Black Culture in the Eighteenth-Century Chesapeake and Lowcountry*. Chapel Hill: University of North Carolina Press, 1998.

Morgan, W. B., and J. C. Pugh. *West Africa*. London: Methuen, 1969.

Morrison, Toni. *Beloved*. New York: Plume, 1987.

Mouer, L. Daniel, et al. "Colonoware Pottery, Chesapeake Pipes, and 'Uncritical Assumptions.'" In *"I, Too, Am America": Archaeological Studies of African-American Life*, ed. Theresa A. Singleton, 95–113. Charlottesville: University Press of Virginia, 1999.

Munford, Clarence J. *The Ordeal of Black Slavery and Slave Trading in the French West Indies, 1625–1715*. Vol. 2. *The Middle Passage and the Plantation Economy*. Lewiston, NY: Edwin Mellen Press, 1991.

Nunoo, Richard B. "Canoe Decoration in Ghana." *African Arts* 7 (Spring 1974): 32–36.

Ogot, B. A., ed. *General History of Africa*. Vol. 5. *Africa from the Sixteenth to the Eighteenth Centuries*. Berkeley: University of California Press, 1992.

Otto, John S., and Nain E. Anderson. "The Origins of Southern Cattle-Grazing: A Problem in West Indian History." *Journal of Caribbean History* 21:2 (1988): 138–53.

Parent, Anthony S. *Foul Means: The Formation of a Slave Society in Virginia, 1660–1740*. Chapel Hill: University of North Carolina Press, 2003.

Pinckney, Elise. "Eliza Lucas Pinckney: Biographical Sketch." In *The Letterbook of Eliza Lucas Pinckney, 1739–1762*, ed. Elise Pinckney with Marvin Zahniser. Chapel Hill: University of North Carolina Press, 1972.

Piperno, Dolores R. T. *The Origins of Agriculture in the Lowland Neotropics*. San Diego: Academic Press, 1998.

Pitman, Frank Wesley. *The Development of the British West Indies, 1700–1763*. 1917. Reprint, Hamden, CT: Archon Books, 1967.

Polakoff, Claire. *Into Indigo: African Textiles and Dyeing Techniques*. Garden City, NJ: Anchor Books, 1980.

Pole, Leonard M. *Iron-Smelting in Ghana*. National Museum of Ghana Occasional Papers, no. 6. Accra: Ghana Museums and Monuments Board.

Posnansky, Merrick. "Early Agricultural Societies in Ghana." In *From Hunters to Farmers: The Causes and Consequences of Food Production in Africa*, ed. J. Desmond Clark and Steven A. Brandt, 147–51. Berkeley: University of California Press, 1984.

Puckrein, Gary A. *Little England: Plantation Society and Anglo-Barbadian Politics, 1627–1700*. New York: New York University Press, 1984.

Ravenel, Harriot Horry. *Eliza Pinckney*. New York: Charles Scribner's Sons, 1896.

Redford, Dorothy Spruill. *Somerset Homecoming: Recovering a Lost Heritage*. New York: Doubleday, 1988.

Rediker, Marcus. *The Slave Ship: A Human History*. New York: Viking Press, 2007.

Rembert, David H., Jr. "The Indigo of Commerce in Colonial North America." *Economic Botany* 33:2 (1979): 128–30.

Richards, Paul. *Indigenous Agricultural Revolution: Ecology and Food Production in Africa*. Boulder, CO: Westview Press, 1985.

Roberts, Mary Nooter, and Allen F. Roberts. *Memory: Luba Art and the Making of History*. New York: Museum for African Art, 1996.

Roberts, Richard L. *Two Worlds of Cotton: Colonialism and the Regional Economy in the French Soudan, 1800–1946* . Stanford: Stanford University Press, 1996.

Robinson, Cedric. *Black Marxism: The Making of the Black Radical Tradition*. 1983. Reprint, Chapel Hill: The University of North Carolina Press, 2000.

Rogers, George C., Jr. *The History of Georgetown County, South Carolina*. Columbia: University of South Carolina Press, 1970.

Rolph-Trouillot, Michel. *Silencing the Past: Power and the Production of History*. Boston: Beacon Press, 1995.

Rothman, Adam. *Slave Country: American Expansion and the Origins of the Deep South*. Cambridge, MA: Harvard University Press, 2005.

Ryder, Alan. *Benin and the Europeans, 1485–1897*. London: Longmans, 1969.

Samford, Patricia M. *Subfloor Pits and the Archaeology of Slavery in Colonial Virginia*. Tuscaloosa: University of Alabama Press, 2007.

Shaw, C. T. "The Prehistory of West Africa." In *General History of Africa*, vol. 1, *Methodology and African Prehistory*, ed. J. Ki-Zerbo, 611–33. Berkeley: University of California Press, 1981.

Shaw, Thurstan, Paul Sinclair, Bassey Andah, and Alex Okpoko, eds. *The Archaeology of Africa: Food, Metals and Towns*. New York: Routledge, 1993.

Sheridan, Richard B. "The Crisis of Slave Subsistence in the British West Indies during and after the American Revolution." *William and Mary Quarterly*, 3rd ser., 33 (October 1976): 615–41.

———. *Sugar and Slavery: An Economic History of the British West Indies, 1623–1775*. Baltimore: Johns Hopkins University Press, 1973.

Sherman, William. *Forced Native Labor in Sixteenth-Century Central America*. Lincoln: University of Nebraska Press, 1979.

Singleton, Theresa A., ed. *"I, Too, Am America": Archaeological Studies of African-American Life*. Charlottesville: University Press of Virginia, 1999.

Skinner, Elliott P. "West African Economic Systems." In *Economic Transition in Africa*, ed. Melville Herskovits and Mitchell Harwitz, 77–97. Evanston: Northwestern University Press, 1964.

Smallwood, Stephanie. *Saltwater Slavery: A Middle Passage from Africa to American Diaspora*. Cambridge, MA: Harvard University Press, 2007.

Smith, Robert S. "Indigo Production and Trade in Colonial Guatemala." *Hispanic American Historical Review* 39 (May 1959): 181–211.

Sobel, Mechal. *The World They Made Together: Black and White Values in Eighteenth Century Virginia*. Princeton: Princeton University Press, 1987.

Stahl, Ann Brower. "A History and Critique of Investigations into Early African Agriculture." In *From Hunters to Farmers: The Causes and Consequences of Food Production in Africa*, ed. J. Desmond Clark and Steven A. Brandt, 9–21. Berkeley: University of California Press, 1984.

———. "Intensification in the West African Late Stone Age: A View from Central Ghana." In *The Archaeology of Africa: Food, Metals and Towns*, ed. Thurstan Shaw, Paul Sinclair, Bassey Andah, and Alex Okpoko, 261–73. New York: Routledge, 1993.

Stahl, Ann, and Maria Das Dores Cruz. "Men and Women in a Market Economy: Gender and Craft Production in West Central Africa ca. 1775–1995." In *Gender in African Prehistory*, ed. Susan Kent, 39–67. Walnut Creek, CA: AltaMira Press, 1998.

Stuckey, Sterling. *Going through the Storm: The Influence of African American Art in History*. New York: Oxford University Press, 1994.

———. *Slave Culture: Nationalist Theory and the Foundations of Black America*. New York: Oxford University Press, 1987.

Sweet, James. *Recreating Africa: Culture, Kinship, and Religion in the African Portuguese World, 1441–1730*. Chapel Hill: University of North Carolina Press, 2003.

Tadman, Michael. "The Demographic Costs of Sugar: Debates on Slave Societies and Natural Increase in the Americas." *American Historical Review* 105 (October 2000): 1534–75.

Tamari, Tal. "The Development of Caste Systems in West Africa." *Journal of African History* 32:2 (1991): 221–50.

Tarlton, William S. "Somerset Place and Its Restoration." Report prepared for the Department of Conservation and Development Division of State Parks, Raleigh, North Carolina, August 1, 1954.

Thompson, Robert Ferris. "African Influence on the Art of the United States." In *Black Studies in the University*, ed. Armstead Robinson, Craig C. Foster, and Donald H. Ogilvie, 122–70. New Haven: Yale University Press, 1969.

———. *Flash of the Spirit: African and Afro-American Art and Philosophy*. New York: Random House, 1983.

Thornton, John K. *Africa and Africans in the Making of the Atlantic World, 1400–1800*. 2nd ed. New York: Cambridge University Press, 1998.

———. *The Kingdom of Kongo: Civil War and Transition, 1641–1718*. Madison: University of Wisconsin Press, 1983.

———. "Mbanza Kongo/Sao Salvador: Kongo's Holy City." In *Africa's Urban Past*, ed. David M. Anderson and Richard Rathbone, 67–84. Portsmouth, NH: Heinemann, 2000.

Vansina, Jan. *The Children of Woot: A History of the Kuba Peoples*. Madison: University of Wisconsin Press, 1978.

———. *How Societies Are Born: Governance in West Central Africa before 1600*. Charlottesville: University of Virginia Press, 2004.

———. *Paths in the Rainforest: Toward a History of Political Tradition in Equatorial Africa*. Madison: University of Wisconsin Press, 1990.

———. "Peoples of the Forest." In *History of Central Africa*, ed. David Birmingham and Phyllis M. Martin, 1:75–117. New York: Longman, 1983.

Vlach, John Michael. *The Afro-American Tradition in the Decorative Arts*. 1978. Reprint, Athens: University of Georgia Press, 1990.

———. *Charleston Blacksmith: The Work of Philip Simmons*. Athens: University of Georgia Press, 1981.

Walsh, Lorena S. *From Calabar to Carter's Grove: The History of a Virginia Slave Community*. Charlottesville: University Press of Virginia, 1997.

Warnier, Jean-Pierre, and Ian Fowler. "A Ruhr in Central Africa." *Africa: Journal of the International African Institute* 49:4 (1979): 329–51.

Warren, Dennis M. "Bono Royal Regalia." *African Arts* 8 (Winter 1975): 16–21.

Watts, David. *Man's Influence on the Vegetation of Barbados, 1627 to 1800*. Hull: University of Hull Publications, 1966.

Wigboldus, Jouke S. "Trade and Agriculture in Coastal Benin." *A. A. G. Bijdragen* 28 (1986): 299–383.

Wilks, Ivor. *Asante in the Nineteenth Century: The Structure and Evolution of a Political Order*. London: Cambridge University Press, 1975.

———. *Forests of Gold: Essays on the Akan and the Kingdom of Asante*. Athens: Ohio University Press, 1993.

———. "The Mossi and Akan States, 1400 to 1800." In *History of West Africa*, 3rd ed., ed. J. F. A. Ajayi and Michael Crowder, 1:344–86. London: Longman, 1985.

Williams, Eric. *Capitalism and Slavery*. Chapel Hill: University of North Carolina Press, 1944.

———. *From Columbus to Castro: The History of the Caribbean*. 1970. Reprint, New York: Vintage Books, 1980.

Williams, Frances Leigh. *Plantation Patriot: A Biography of Eliza Lucas Pinckney*. New York: Harcourt, Brace and World, 1967.

Williamson, Kay. "Linguistic Evidence for the Use of Some Tree and Tuber Food Plants in Southern Nigeria." In *The Archaeology of Africa: Food, Metals and Towns*, ed. Thurstan Shaw, Paul Sinclair, Bassey Andah, and Alex Okpoko, 139–53. New York: Routledge, 1993.

Wolf, Eric R. *Europe and the People without History*. Berkeley: University of California Press, 1982.

——. *Peasants*. Englewood Cliffs, NJ: Prentice Hall, 1966.

Wood, Betty. *The Origins of American Slavery: Freedom and Bondage in the American Colonies*. New York: Hill and Wang, 1997.

Wood, Gordon. *The Radicalism of the American Revolution*. New York: Alfred A. Knopf, 1992.

Wood, Peter H. *Black Majority: Negroes in Colonial South Carolina from 1670 through the Stono Rebellion*. New York: Alfred A. Knopf, 1974.

——. "'It Was a Negro Taught Them': A New Look at African Labor in Early South Carolina." *Journal of Asian and African Studies* 9:3–4 (1974): 160–79.

——. "Slave Labor Camps in Early America: Overcoming Denial and Discovering the Gulag." In *Inequality in Early America*, ed. Carla Gardina Pestana and Sharon V. Salinger, 222–38. Hanover, NH: University Press of New England.

——. "Whetting, Setting, and Laying Timbers: Black Builders in the Early South." *Southern Exposure* 8 (Spring 1980): 3–8.

Woodson, Carter G., and W. E. B. Du Bois. *The African Background Outlined; or, Handbook for the Study of the Negro*. 1936. Reprint, New York: Negro Universities Press, 1968.

Wright, Gavin. *Slavery and American Economic Development*. Baton Rouge: Louisiana State University Press, 2006.

Zahan, Dominique. "Some Reflections on African Spirituality." In *African Spirituality: Forms, Meanings, and Expressions*, ed. Jacob K. Olupona, 3–25. New York: Crossroad, 2000.

Zook, George Frederick. *The Company of Royal Adventurers Trading into Africa*. New York: Negro University Press, 1969.

Index

Adanson, Michel, 27, 91, 92

Afonso I, King, 23

African agricultural ceremonies, 47, 48; Homowo Festival, 39

African currencies, 17, 18–20, 26, 75

African environment: climate zones, 35–36; constraints on agriculture, 10, 34–37; Harmattan season, 35

African ethnic groups: Akan, 13, 57–58, 63, 83, 101–2, 118–19, 121; Balanta, 44, 46; clusters in American colonies, 4; Fon-Ewe, 47; Ga, 39; Gola, 72; Gullah, 108; Ibo, 115, 121, 127; scholarship on, 9–10; 172n. 37; Wangara, 15, 17; Yoruba, 24

African guilds, 23, 75

African modes of production: kinship-based, 34, 46–47, 73, 172n. 40; market-based, 46, 48; patronage networks, 29, 74; tribute-based in Africa, 34, 46–48, 73

African population, 20–21

African states: Akwamu, 73; Akwapem, 101–2; Asante, 25–26, 73, 101–2, 141; Banda chieftaincy, 25; Bondu, 41; Bono, 101–2; Borno, 15; Dagomba, 25; Futa Toro, 41, 91; Gonja, 25, 73; Kanem, 15; Songhay Empire, 14–15

African towns: Ardra, 90; Begho, 21–22; Benguela, 19–20; Benin, 21, 75, 90; Calabar, 50–51; Cape Coast, 15, 21, 26, 66; development in West Africa, 20–22; development in West Central Africa, 21–22; Elmina, 26–27, 112; Gao, 15, 21; Ibadan, 21; Jenne, 15, 21, 91; Kano, 21–23, 75; Katsina, 21; Keta, 73, 92; Kommenda, 26; Kong, 41; Kormantin, 26; Koumbi-Saleh, 21; Luanda, 20; Luango, 20, 22; Mbanza Kongo (Sao Salvador), 20–23, 30; Mouri, 26; Niani, 21; Old Oyo, 21; Salaga, 145; Sansanding, 99; Sego, 75; Sokoto, 21, 24; Timbuktu, 15, 21, 75; town walls, 22–23; Whydah, 47, 90

Agricultural practices: African crop zones, 40–45; crop mixtures in Africa, 7, 9–10, 34–35, 39–43, 45, 47, 91, 112; crop mixtures in the Caribbean, 55–58; crop mixtures in South Carolina, 61–63; crop mixtures in Virginia, 60–61; crop rotations in Africa, 42–45, 56, 84; crop rotations in the Caribbean, 57–58; English colonial practices, 52, 53, 61, 63; fertilization methods in Africa, 35, 43, 45–47; fertilization methods in Jamaica, 56; inventive self-reliance, 39; irrigation, 6, 62, 91, 122–23; Native American fertilization methods, 56, 70; Native American practices, 52, 56, 60–61, 70; origins in Africa, 9; rotational bush fallow, 45; shifting cultivation, 44;

About the Author

FREDERICK C. KNIGHT is an associate professor in the history department at Colorado State University.